Public Reaction to Nuclear Power

Are There Critical Masses?

AAAS Selected Symposia Series

Published by Westview Press, Inc.
5500 Central Avenue, Boulder, Colorado

for the

American Association for the Advancement of Science
1776 Massachusetts Ave., N.W., Washington, D.C.

Public Reaction to Nuclear Power

Are There Critical Masses?

Edited by William R. Freudenburg and Eugene A. Rosa

AAAS Selected Symposium **93**

AAAS Selected Symposia Series

This book is based on a symposium that was held at the 1982 AAAS Annual Meeting in Washington, D.C., January 3-8. The symposium was sponsored by the Rural Sociological Society, the American Sociological Association, and AAAS Section K (Social, Political and Economic Sciences); it was cosponsored by the International Association for Impact Assessment and AAAS Section T (Information, Computing and Communication).

Published in 1984 in the United States of America by Westview Press, Inc., 5500 Central Avenue, Boulder, Colorado 80301; Frederick A. Praeger, Publisher

Library of Congress Catalog Card Number: 84-50899
ISBN: 0-86531-708-9

Printed and bound in the United States of America

10 9 8 7 6 5 4 3 2 1

About the Book

Nuclear power has generated more than just electricity. It has also generated the most sustained controversy of all available energy sources. Public support for the technology, once taken for granted, is now less assured. In fact, public opposition is now often named as one of the reasons the U.S. nuclear power industry is in such serious trouble. No new reactors have been ordered since 1978, and a recent Supreme Court decision may make it even more difficult for utilities to build nuclear plants in the near future.

Although the importance of public reactions is often noted in the nuclear debate, systematic data on actual public attitudes are often missing. Marches and demonstrations make headlines, but the size and noise of the protests may not provide a very accurate indication of the broader public's reactions to nuclear power. Just how widespread is the actual opposition--are there in fact critical masses?

This book demonstrates that it is possible to address the question on the basis of the evidence. The book's authors include some of the persons actually engaged in the nuclear power debate, ranging from one of the best-known critics to one of the highest-ranking officials of the nuclear power industry. The majority of the chapters are by social scientists who have done extensive research on nuclear power attitudes, and on the factors that lie behind them. The result is a readable, state-of-the-art overview of public attitudes toward nuclear power, of the ways in which the attitudes are interpreted by major actors in the ongoing debate, and of the implications that public reactions will have for the future of the nuclear option in the United States.

About the Series

The *AAAS Selected Symposia Series* was begun in 1977 to provide a means for more permanently recording and more widely disseminating some of the valuable material which is discussed at the AAAS Annual National Meetings. The volumes in this *Series* are based on symposia held at the Meetings which address topics of current and continuing significance, both within and among the sciences, and in the areas in which science and technology have an impact on public policy. The *Series* format is designed to provide for rapid dissemination of information, so the papers are reproduced directly from camera-ready copy. The papers are organized and edited by the symposium arrangers who then become the editors of the various volumes. Most papers published in this *Series* are original contributions which have not been previously published, although in some cases additional papers from other sources have been added by an editor to provide a more comprehensive view of a particular topic. Symposia may be reports of new research or reviews of established work, particularly work of an interdisciplinary nature, since the AAAS Annual Meetings typically embrace the full range of the sciences and their societal implications.

WILLIAM D. CAREY
Executive Officer
American Association for the Advancement of Science

Contents

About the Editors and Authors

William R. Freudenburg, associate professor of rural sociology at Washington State University, Pullman, has specialized in social impact assessment and studies of the policy-making process, especially societal decision making on controversial issues. He has written more than two dozen scholarly papers on the social impacts of coal, oil shale, nuclear energy and other types of energy development and is a coeditor of *Paradoxes of Western Energy Development* (with C. M. McKell et al., AAAS Selected Symposium 94, Westview, 1984).

Eugene A. Rosa is associate professor of sociology and coordinator of the Public Opinion Laboratory at Washington State University, Pullman. For the past decade he has been involved in energy policy studies and has published widely on the topics of cross-national comparisons of energy consumption, development of conservation and solar penetration models, and monitoring of public opinion on energy policy issues and human factors in nuclear safeguards.

Barry Commoner, a biologist by training, is director of the Center for the Biology of Natural Systems and professor of earth and environmental studies at Queens College, City University of New York. A long-time environmental activist, he is currently doing research on environmental carcinogenesis and on the origins and significance of the environmental and energy crises, especially in relation to transformations of production technology and their economic consequences. Among his publications are *The Closing Circle* and *The Politics of Energy* (published by Knopf, 1971 and 1979, respectively).

W. Kenneth Davis, a chemical engineer by training, is currently a consultant for the Bechtel Power Corporation in San Francisco, California. A former Deputy Secretary of the Department of Energy and corporate vice president of the Bechtel Group, Inc., he has administered nuclear power plant, advanced reactor and nuclear fuel cycle projects. He has served as vice president of the National Academy of Engineering, on the Governing Board of the National Research Council and as chairman of the Atomic Industrial Forum.

Don A. Dillman, professor in the Departments of Sociology and Rural Sociology at Washington State University, Pullman, has conducted extensive research on residential preferences, quality-of-life issues and survey methods. His books include *Mail and Telephone Surveys: The Total Design Method* (Wiley, 1978) and *Rural Society in the U.S.: Issues for the 1980s* (Westview, 1982).

Barbara Farhar-Pilgrim, a consulting sociologist, was a senior social scientist at the Solar Energy Research Institute in Golden, Colorado, where she initiated the National Study of the Residential Solar Consumer to explore the attitudes, knowledge and practices of consumers with regard to energy usage. Her book, *America's Solar Potential: A National Consumer Study* (with C. Unseld, Praeger, 1982), presents the results of this study. A specialist in interactions between technology and society, she has done research on decision processes, the social aspects of energy, social impact assessments, weather modification and the diffusion of innovations.

Baruch Fischhoff is research associate at Decision Research, a branch of Perceptronics, Inc., in Eugene, Oregon; visiting associate professor of psychology at the University of Oregon at Eugene; and visiting scientist at the Medical Research Council/Applied Psychology Unit in Cambridge, England. A specialist in risk perception, judgment and decision making, he is the author of numerous book chapters and articles, as well as the book *Acceptable Risk* (with S. Lichtenstein et al., Cambridge University Press, 1981).

Cynthia B. Flynn, president of Social Impact Research, Inc., in Seattle, Washington, has been involved in socioeconomic impact assessment, planning and mitigation; public participation programs; and survey and evaluation research. A sociologist by training, she has published on the social and economic effects of nuclear generating stations and of the accident at Three Mile Island.

Sarah Lichtenstein is a research associate at Decision Research, a branch of Perceptronics, Inc., in Eugene, Oregon, and adjunct professor of psychology at the University of Oregon, Eugene. Her research interests are behavioral decision theory, decision aids and risk assessment. She is a coauthor of *Acceptable Risk* (with B. Fischhoff et al., Cambridge University Press, 1981).

Cora Bagley Marrett is professor of sociology at the University of Wisconsin, Madison. A specialist in the behavior of formal organizations, she was a fellow of the National Academy of Sciences and a member of the President's Commission on the Accident at Three Mile Island.

Allan Mazur, professor of sociology at Syracuse University, has specialized in biosociology and the sociology of science and technology. Originally trained as an engineer, he now studies the sociological aspects of technological controversies. He is the author of *The Dynamics of Technical Controversy* (Communications Press, 1981).

Barbara Desow Melber is a research scientist at the Social Change Study Center at Battelle Memorial Institute in Seattle, Washington. A specialist in public opinion and public participation as related to energy policy, she is coauthor of *Nuclear Power and the Public* (with S. M. Nealey et al., Lexington, in press).

Robert Cameron Mitchell, senior fellow at Resources for the Future in Washington, D.C., has specialized in environmental sociology. His research includes studies of the response of the public to the accident at Three Mile Island and public attitudes toward the siting of potentially hazardous facilities.

Stanley M. Nealey is director of research at Battelle Human Affairs Research Centers in Seattle and affiliate associate professor of psychology at the University of Washington, Seattle. Originally trained in industrial, organizational and social psychology, he has recently conducted studies of the attitudes of the public toward nuclear power and nuclear waste disposal.

Marvin E. Olsen, professor of sociology at Washington State University, Pullman, is interested in social change and political and environmental sociology. He has written numerous technical reports and journal articles on energy policy and energy conservation strategies and programs. Among his publications are *Handbook of Applied Sociology: Frontiers of Contemporary Research* (edited with M. Micklin, Praeger, 1981) and *Participatory Pluralism: Political Participation and Influence in the U.S. and Sweden* (Nelson-Hall, 1982).

William L. Rankin is research scientist at Battelle Human Affairs Research Centers in Seattle, Washington. A social psychologist with a specialty in human information processing, he has been doing research on beliefs and attitudes of the public toward nuclear power for five years and has written numerous publications on value measurement techniques, behavior change following value change, media coverage of energy technologies and attitudes of the public toward nuclear power and nuclear waste management.

Paul Slovic is a research associate at Decision Research, a branch of Perceptronics, Inc., Eugene, Oregon, and adjunct professor of psychology at the University of Oregon, Eugene. His specialties include judgment, decision making and risk assessment, and he has written or edited numerous publications on these topics, most recently *Judgment Under Uncertainty: Heuristics and Biases* (co-edited by D. Kahneman and A. Tversky, Cambridge University Press, 1982). He is currently president of the Society for Risk Analysis.

Robert A. Szalay, a mechanical engineer by training, is vice president of the Atomic Industrial Forum, Inc., in Bethesda, Maryland. Currently in charge of the Forum's program activities on nuclear power plant technical and regulatory issues, he has also managed AIF's licensing and safety projects and its activities in response to the accident at Three Mile Island.

Dorothy S. Zinberg, a sociologist, is lecturer in public policy and director of seminars and special projects at the Center for Science and International Affairs at the Kennedy School of Government at Harvard University. Originally trained as a biochemist, she is now conducting an international study of the social dimensions of the energy transition and a study of the links between the peace movement and the defense community in Western Europe and the United States. Her book, *Uncertain Power: The Struggle for a National Energy Policy,* is scheduled for publication this year.

Introduction

Eugene A. Rosa, William R. Freudenburg

1. Nuclear Power at the Crossroads

INTRODUCTION

> It is important to keep in mind that the energy problem does not arise from an overall physical scarcity of resources . . . . Energy policy involves very large social and political components that are much less well understood than the technical factors . . . there will remain an irreducible element of conflicting values and political interests that cannot be resolved except in the political arena.
>
> Harvey Brooks and Edward L. Ginston, Co-chairs, Committee on Nuclear and Alternative Energy Systems, National Academy of Sciences

Nuclear energy, once destined to be a star performer in America's production of energy, struggles along with an uncertain role. It has for several years. Fission energy's performance has been far below expectations, receiving decidedly mixed reviews to date; its presumed rise to stardom is now in serious doubt.

The stalled career of nuclear power contrasts sharply with the promise the technology enjoyed during the 1960s and early 1970s. Throughout those years, the prospects for nuclear energy were proclaimed in a series of rosy and unchallenged projections. The technology, it seemed, had everything going for it. By 1972, just before the oil embargo,

Pp. 3-37 in William R. Freudenburg and Eugene A. Rosa (eds., 1984) *Public Reactions to Nuclear Power: Are There Critical Masses?*

nuclear energy was projected to provide well over half of the nation's electrical generating capacity--almost a third of total energy consumption--by the year 2000 (U.S Atomic Energy Commission, 1972).

Since then, however, events have been uncooperative. Nuclear power in the United States has run headlong into a series of unexpected setbacks; it now provides only about 13% of the nation's electricity, or about 4% of total energy consumption--less end-use energy, by some calculations, than is provided by firewood.

For the past decade projections of nuclear power growth have been revised downward, repeatedly and dramatically. Reactor orders actually peaked in 1972-73; they have been declining ever since. Scores of orders have been cancelled, and many of the remaining orders have been deferred for years--some of them indefinitely. Not a single new nuclear power plant has been ordered since 1978 (Roberts et al., 1982). Nuclear energy has evidently arrived not at stardom, but at a stalemate.

Where did things go wrong? The goal of this volume is to illuminate one of the most important parts of the answer, and one of the most neglected: the social and political acceptability of nuclear technology.

There is now widespread recognition that social and political factors, while potentially decisive to the future of nuclear power, are some of the least-understood features of the nuclear debate. Our meager understanding of the public acceptance factor can be traced to its serious neglect during the days of unbridled optimism for nuclear technology. In the words of Alvin Weinberg, a pioneer in reactor development and a leading nuclear statesman,

> The public perception and acceptance of nuclear energy appears to be the question we missed rather badly in the very early days. This issue has emerged as the most critical question concerning the future of nuclear energy (Weinberg, 1976:19).

Until recently, discussions about U.S. nuclear power have focused almost exclusively on questions of technological feasibility and economic advantage. But after an early history of apparent disinterest, the broader public began to raise other questions--expressing concerns about the equity of risk exposure, doubting the benefits of nuclear growth, and showing a growing mistrust of the concentration of technological decision making in centralized bureaucracies. The appearance of these unanticipated issues--all at the core involving questions of human values--changed the focus of the nuclear debate. Indeed, it has now become conventional wisdom in the energy policy establishment that social, political and human value questions are at the core of the nuclear stalemate--and that the entire future of nuclear power may hinge on their resolution. Under the circumstances, the issue of public acceptance would seem to deserve particularly detailed and systematic study.

While there has been a growing awareness of the importance of social and political factors, however, government and industry efforts to analyze them have been surprisingly limited. Even today, the funding for research on social science aspects of nuclear power remains remarkably small in comparison with the funding for research on the "technical" issues. Despite this fact, a number of social scientists have devoted considerable effort to relevant research. In the process, they have accumulated an important array of findings and insights. But while the researchers themselves are generally quite familiar with the work that has been done, most other persons are not; much of it has been of a fugitive or "underground" nature, scattered among technical reports and prepared for a variety of specialized audiences.

Our aim with this volume is to bring that fugitive literature together in a single location--drawing attention to the larger body of work in the process--and to make the results available to a broader public. In our effort to provide a fair and balanced summary, we have included the views of both supporters and opponents of nuclear power, but the majority of the chapters are by known neutrals--researchers who have a greater commitment to accuracy than to any particular outcome of the continuing controversy. The resultant collection summarizes both the scientific research and the views of key participants in the ongoing debate; it should provide readers with an understanding of the public acceptance theme that will go well beyond the conventional wisdom.

This book does not attempt to deal with every conceivable aspect of the nuclear power debate; indeed, no single volume could do so. Our intention instead is to provide a reasonably detailed account of existing research on key questions, thus helping to fill a serious gap in current understanding of the issues. In our view, this is an essential first step toward resolving the nuclear stalemate--but it is also more. It is also essential to the development of a broader consensus over national energy policy.

After more than a decade of frustration, the nation has yet to arrive at energy policy consensus; one key reason has been the controversy over the nuclear option. A prolonging of the nuclear stalemate would be likely to mean a further postponing of collective agreement over the nation's energy direction. Chances of making progress toward that goal, on the other hand, would be considerably improved with an end to the stalemate. And an end to the stalemate, as noted above, will depend in part on the social and political acceptance of nuclear technology.

The question of public acceptance actually includes a broad class of considerations; they range from very general ones, such as the overall direction of national energy policy, to highly specific decisions over the locations for nuclear power plants and waste repositories. Some of those concerns have been investigated extensively, and others have attracted moderate levels of examination. Still others, however, are barely understood, while the remaining concerns--often incipient ones--have yet to be investigated at all.

The individual chapters in this volume focus on the concerns that have attracted more systematic investigation. In the process they address many (but not all) of the key issues involved in the public acceptability of nuclear power. As a result of their broad coverage, the chapters provide what may be the most comprehensive treatment of the social acceptance theme that is presently available in any single source.

We fully realize that many of our readers will not be social scientists, and that many will not be familiar with the history and technical details of nuclear power development. Rather than trying to discourage such readers, we have tried to accommodate them. We believe that books do not need to be unreadable just because they contain accurate information.

This volume brings together a group of authors who are exceptionally knowledgeable about nuclear power and the public; as noted above, it is intended to make the expertise of the insiders available to a larger portion of that public. Thus the authors have been selected partly on the basis of their expertise and importance in the nuclear power debate, and partly on the basis of their ability to discuss complex issues without miring the reader in jargon. Each chapter is intended to provide readers with an overview of the key issue at hand; at the same time, each author has also been asked to provide references and other documentation that will allow readers to find the more detailed or less accessible sources. Finally, as a way of providing a context for the chapters that follow, the next section of the present chapter will provide a brief overview of the history of nuclear power development in the United States.

SETTING THE STAGE

On December 8, 1953, President Eisenhower presented his "Atoms for Peace" proposal to the United Nations, signaling the beginning of the federal government's commitment to the development of commercial nuclear technology. Earlier that year, Congress had already approved funding for a demonstration power plant that would be constructed in cooperation with private industry--the beginning of what would become a long-sustained cooperative arrangement between government and industry. The plant, located near Shippingport, Pennsylvania, went into operation in 1957, marking the beginning of nuclear-generated electricity for public use.

The Atomic Energy Act of 1954 (P.L. 83-703, 42 U.S.C. 2011 *et seq.*), which was passed on the heels of the Eisenhower speech, expressed a fundamental national commitment to nuclear development:

> Atomic energy is capable of application for peaceful as well as military purposes. It is therefore declared to be the policy of the United States that
>
> a. the development, use and control of atomic energy shall be directed so as to make the

maximum contribution to the general welfare, subject at all times to the paramount objective of making the maximum contribution to the common defense and security; and

b. the development, use and control of atomic energy shall be directed so as to promote world peace, improve general welfare, increase the standard of living and strengthen free competition in private enterprise.

These developments under the Eisenhower Administration set the stage for the commercial development of nuclear power, but only two small pilot plants were in operation by the time President Eisenhower left office.

Further research and development took place under the supportive administration of President Kennedy; roughly a dozen plants had been ordered, and almost half that number had gone into operation, as of late 1963. Even so, nuclear power provided less than 1% of the U.S. electrical generation capacity at that time.

The decade of exhilarating progress for nuclear power took place under the next two administrations--those of Presidents Johnson and Nixon. It was in December of 1963--ten years to the month after Eisenhower's speech at the United Nations--that a New Jersey utility made history with the announcement of the nation's first nuclear reactor to be ordered on a strictly commercial basis. The Oyster Creek plant was expected to produce electricity more cheaply than would its closest competitor, the coal-fired plant. In a remarkably short span of a single decade, nuclear power had evidently grown from a policy vision to a commercial reality.[1]

In an even shorter time, a wave of other reactor orders followed. It was a virtual tidal wave. In the two years of 1966-67, U.S. utilities placed orders for 49 plants, representing more than 40,000 megawatts of capacity--fifty times as much capacity as the five pioneer nuclear reactors that had been operating by 1962 (*Electric Power Monthly*, 1982; Pelham, 1981).

By the time Richard Nixon took office in 1969 the starring role of nuclear power seemed assured. Massive federal support for nuclear energy research and development--and related regulations--had also become a part of national energy policy life. President Nixon's 1971 message to Congress on national energy policy, the first such message ever delivered by a president, also left little doubt about the continued national commitment to the rapid expansion of nuclear power.

At the end of 1972 the AEC's projections called for nuclear energy to provide a full 60% of the nation's electricity needs by the year 2000. These projections represented an almost unbounded optimism about a nuclear future; at least in retrospect, the optimistic outlook seems particularly striking in comparison with the actual generating capacity at that time. In 1972 nuclear energy provided only 3% of the nation's electricity, a figure that translates into a meager 0.8% of total energy production. The projected generating capacity for the year 2000 would have been over 85 times as great as the actual 1972 figure. To reach the projected capacity, the industry would have needed to maintain an astounding growth rate of 17% per year--a doubling of total capacity every four and a half years through the end of the century. Even so, it appeared at the time that the industry had grown out of its infancy; reactor orders were mounting, and public support was strong. By all signs, the technology had come of age.

The rapid growth in utility acceptance derived from nuclear power's one clear advantage over alternative means of generating electricity--it was cheaper, or at least it was widely seen as such. For proponents of the technology, this economic superiority was never in doubt, although "too cheap to meter," the rallying phrase of nuclear enthusiasts, was not so much a literal assertion as a symbol of the technology's economic promise. With the rapidly escalating prices of fossil fuels that were becoming harder to find, the economic advantage of nuclear power seemed all but assured.

But while reactor orders had been rising to their high water mark in the late 1960s, the promise of cheap nuclear electricity could only remain a promise. Without actual operating experience, cost estimates could be nothing more than that--the industry's best guesses about what the costs would eventually be. Actual operating experience and recorded costs would have to wait. And they would have to wait for a full decade, at least. At the time, it took approximately eight years to bring a new plant on line, and additional time was needed to accumulate "real" costs. Indeed, because of this time lag, utilities remained dubious about nuclear energy's highly publicized potential for economic superiority--at least until the years immediately preceding the key reactor orders.

It was not until the decade of the 1970s that actual costs would be available. As they slowly became available, they proved to be embarrassing. Actual costs, it turned out, were substantially higher than anyone had dared to imagine. As the 1970s progressed, it became increasingly apparent that there were often large discrepancies between projected and actual costs.

In spite of the darkening economic picture, however, the nuclear industry remained steadfast in its optimism. Even if the early operating experience of nuclear plants fell short of expectations, the argument went, better days were ahead. First, the industry could look forward to the benefits of "learning effects"--the growing advantage of profiting from early mistakes--as it gained additional operating experience. Second, because typical plant size was increasing, the industry could also look forward to ever-improving economies of scale. This seemed virtually certain for nuclear power, because in comparison with fossil fuel plants, its facilities tend to be larger and more capital intensive (Bupp and Derian, 1981; see also the discussion by Commoner, 1984, in Chapter 11 of this volume).

Industry optimism was becoming more difficult to maintain in the light of nuclear power's awkward economic performance, but it received a boost from other events in the economy. The real dollar price of fossil fuels, which had been declining during most of the 1950s and 1960s, began to inch upward in 1970. With increasing prices for the fossil fuels that were competing with nuclear power, the economic position of fission technology seemed more secure--secure enough, in fact, that a second wave of reactor orders began in the early 1970s: 76 new orders were placed between 1972 and 1974. Even so, the economic advantages of nuclear power remained marginal.

Then, with a stroke of OPEC's pen, the marginality all but disappeared. The 1973-74 oil embargo, coupled as it was with a quadrupling of the price of oil from OPEC (the Organization of Petroleum Exporting Countries), appeared to settle the matter once and for all. The industry could again argue with confidence that nuclear power was the answer for cheap electricity.

Moreover, the embargo also renewed the importance of the industry as an aspect of national security. For many observers, nuclear energy was no longer merely one energy supply option; it became the *only* option that promised to release the nation from the stranglehold of foreign oil. The Nixon Administration's "Project Independence"--designed to achieve just such an outcome--called for substantial growth in the nation's nuclear power capacity. Despite a continued commitment to nuclear power, however, the Report from the Project Independence Nuclear Energy Task Force foreshadowed the problems that were to follow, warning of a "moderate to high risk" that even "the *lower* projections considered reasonable by the Task Force will not be met unless immediate attention is given to existing problems and recent trends are quickly reversed" (U.S. Federal Energy Administration, 1974: 2.0.5, emphasis added).

In fact, as Figure 1 shows, 1974 was a very different sort of turning point for the nuclear power industry than it had been expected to be. The worldwide recession of 1974-75, which emerged abruptly and without warning, placed a difficult obstacle in the path of nuclear power growth. With the recession came an unexpected downturn in demand for electricity--the sole civilian use for nuclear energy.

The drop in demand was not only unexpected; it was virtually unprecedented. Traditionally, growth in electricity demand had been one of the most well-behaved of all social and economic trends in the U.S., assured and predictable. It was soon to become anything but reliable, and energy planners were to find themselves working in an environment of demand and price confusion. Costs for nuclear-generated electricity became difficult--perhaps impossible--to calculate accurately in advance. At the same time, however, actual operating cost figures were becoming more widely available--and the presumed economy of the fission reactor faced a reassessment. If nuclear power did enjoy a cost advantage, it was apparently difficult to find. At least according to critics, it still is (see, e.g., Komanoff, 1981). In fact, the question of cost differences between coal and nuclear power is still an open one; Chapters 10 to 12 of this volume--those by

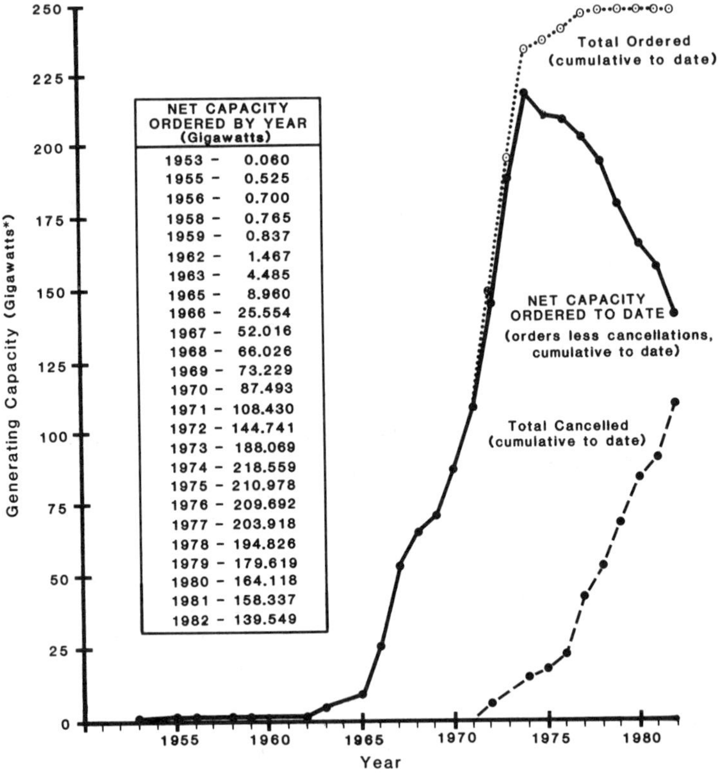

Figure 1. US Nuclear Generating Capacity (cumulative total, to date, as of year indicated)

*A gigawatt is equal to a thousand megawatts, or one billion watts. It is approximately equal to the amount of electricity produced by one large nuclear power plant.

Data Source: Electric Power Monthly, 1982;
US Department of Energy, 1983.

Davis (1984) and Szalay (1984), on the one side, and by Commoner (1984) on the other--summarize the present-day arguments on the issue.

What is not in doubt is that new trends were already in motion; as Figure 1 shows, they have yet to reverse themselves. Instead of pouring in at a continually increasing rate, the industry's new orders soon came to a halt--only to be replaced by a growing wave of cancellations.

Not a single reactor order had been cancelled until 1972, but from 1974 through the end of the decade, reactors were cancelled at an average rate of more than ten per year (Roberts et al., 1982). The subtitle of a regular Department of Energy publication on nuclear power--"Significant Milestones"--took on ever-increasing irony; cancellations, rather than orders, soon provided the milestones of note. By 1980 over a third of all ordered generating capacity had been cancelled. By 1982 the figure passed 40%; other 1982 milestones included 100,000 megawatts of cancelled generating capacity and the 100th cancelled reactor out of the 251 ever ordered (*Electric Power Monthly,* 1982; Roberts et al., 1982; U.S. Department of Energy, 1983). As of 1980, moreover, the cancellations even began to include plants on which actual construction had taken place. Construction had begun on a *majority* of the plants cancelled in 1981-82; by 1982 the cancellations included plants that had abandonment costs of over a billion dollars apiece and that were up to 29% complete by the time they were cancelled (U.S. Energy Information Administration, 1983).

It is important to note that these data represent all the plants on order, and that several dozen reactors are still under construction today; since the new reactors are far larger than the early plants now scheduled for retirement, the nation's total nuclear generating capacity is likely to continue growing somewhat despite the cancellations. As the bold middle line of Figure 1 emphasizes, however--and whether we speak in terms of the number of plants ordered or in terms of their generating capacities--cancellations have exceeded orders every single year since 1974.

Soon after 1974 a parallel trend was to become unmistakable in the once-rosy projections for future nuclear power generation. Expectations were consistently--and markedly--

TABLE 1
PROJECTIONS OF U.S. NUCLEAR POWER CAPACITY

Year and Source of Forecast[b]	Projected Capacity in Gigawatts[a]			
	By End of 1980	By End of 1985	By End of 1990	By End of 2000
1972 U.S. Atomic Energy Commission	132	280	508	1200
1974 Atomic Energy Commission	107	255	487	1145
1975 U.S. Energy Research and Development Administration	---	185	---	720
1975 Dupree and Corsentino (U.S. Department of Interior)	75	200	---	900
1977 Congressional Research Service	81	131	175	433[c]
1980 U.S. Energy Information Administration	---	98	128	180
1981 U.S. Department of Energy	---	96	128	175
1982 U.S. Energy Information Administration	---	90	121	165
1983 U.S. Energy Information Administration	---	80	114	130

[a]A gigawatt is equal to a thousand megawatts, or one billion watts. It is approximately the output of one large nuclear power plant.

[b]Where sources included more than one projection for a given year, the midpoint or "most likely" figures were selected for presentation here.

[c]The original document did not project beyond 1990. The capacity figure for 2000 was extrapolated from the 1990 estimate using the average annual growth rate for the period 1977 to 1990.

Sources: Listed under year of forecast.

revised downward. Table 1 lists the relevant information, and Figure 2 gives a graphic portrayal of the cascading expectations. The 1972 forecast for nuclear electric capacity, 1200 gigawatts by the year 2000, was the subject of deep and successive cuts. The 1983 projection, made just 11 years later, called for nuclear power to provide 130 gigawatts by the same date--a mere 11% of the original estimate.

The decline was probably due in part to the recession and the slowdown in electricity demand growth, but if economics and electricity demand had been the only factors involved, we would expect to see a similar pattern in the projections for nuclear power's closest competitor, the coal-fired power plant. Such was not the case. Even though neither technology enjoyed a clear cost advantage over the other, the coal projections followed a very different pattern. As can be seen from Table 2, the coal projections remained quite stable over the same time period, with none of them being as much as 25% higher or lower than the 11-year average.[2]

The dramatic difference in trends is shown in Figure 2. Expectations for nuclear power followed a consistently downward trend, with the latest figure being 89% below the first one. Yet the coal projections, if anything, showed an *upward* trend, with the mean or average of the last three projections being more than 13% higher than the average of the first three. The net result was the reemergence of coal as the dominant fuel for generating electricity despite the apparent lack of difference in costs. In 1972-73, nuclear power was expected to provide about three times as much of the nation's electricity by the year 2000 as would coal; within a single decade, the expectations were almost exactly the reverse, with the projections for coal being three times as high as those for nuclear power. Clearly, unexpected factors were at work, for the years after the OPEC oil embargo did not turn out to be good ones for the nuclear industry.

The first decade of nuclear power, 1953-63, had been characterized by high expectations and great promise. The decade from 1964-73 was one of virtual euphoria. Over the course of the third decade of nuclear power development, however, the tidal wave of planned capacity growth turned into a trickle. Today, at the beginning of the industry's fourth decade, nuclear power evidently stands at a crossroads.

TABLE 2
PROJECTIONS OF U.S. COAL-FIRED ELECTRICITY GENERATION[a]

Year and Source of Forecast	Projected Fuel Use and Generating Capacity: Quadrillion BTUs[b] (Quads) of Coal Burned to Produce Electricity		Approximate Equivalents in Gigawatts of Generating Capacity[c]	
	By End of 1985	By End of 2000	By End of 1985	By End of 2000
1971 U.S. Federal Power Commission	13.9	20.6[d]	278	412[d]
1972 U.S. Department of Interior	---	20.3	---	406
1972 Dupree and West (U.S. Department of Interior)	14.2	17.5	284	350
1975 Dupree and Corsentino (U.S. Department of Interior)	15.7	20.7	314	414
1977 U.S. Department of Energy	---	---[e]	---	369[e]
1979 U.S. Energy Information Administration	15.4	25.8	292	516
1979 U.S. Department of Energy	14.8	22.6	296	452
1980 U.S. Energy Information Administration	15.6	21.4	312	428
1981 U.S. Department of Energy	14.3	22.0	286	440
1982 U.S. Energy Information Administration	14.5[f]	22.9	290	458

[a]Where sources provided more than one projection for a given year, the midpoint or "most likely" projections were selected for this table.

[b]A British Thermal Unit (BTU) is the amount of heat energy required to raise the temperature of one pound of water by one degree Farenheit. A quad (or quadrillion BTUs--a "1" followed by 15 zeroes) is about the amount of energy produced by burning 125,000 tons of coal every day for a year. Total U.S. energy consumption in 1980 was about 76 quads.

[c]Except as noted below, all figures on coal generating capacity are based on the documents' quads-of-consumption figures, and have been converted to gigawatts at the rate of .05 quads per gigawatt of capacity. Higher or lower estimates would change the overall magnitude of the figures in this table, but not their relative rankings. The .05 quad figure was computed on the assumption that coal-fired plants would operate at about 55% of their capacity, and that electricity would be generated at an average rate of 10,400 BTU per kilowatt-hour (kwh). There are 8760 (365 x 24) hours per year; at 55% of capacity, a plant would produce .55 x 8760 = 4818 kwh per year for each kilowatt of capacity. Multiplying this figure by 10,400 (BTU/kwh) and then by 1,000,000 (kilowatts per gigawatt) gives 50.107 trillion (or roughly .05 quadrillion) BTUs per gigawatt of capacity.

[d]This document did not project beyond 1990. The figure for 2000 is a straight-line extrapolation from the projections for 1980 and 1990.

[e]This document provides only a capacity projection.

[f]This figure is equivalent to an average heat value of 21.4 million BTU/ton for the midpoint projection of 678.8 million short tons of coal consumption.

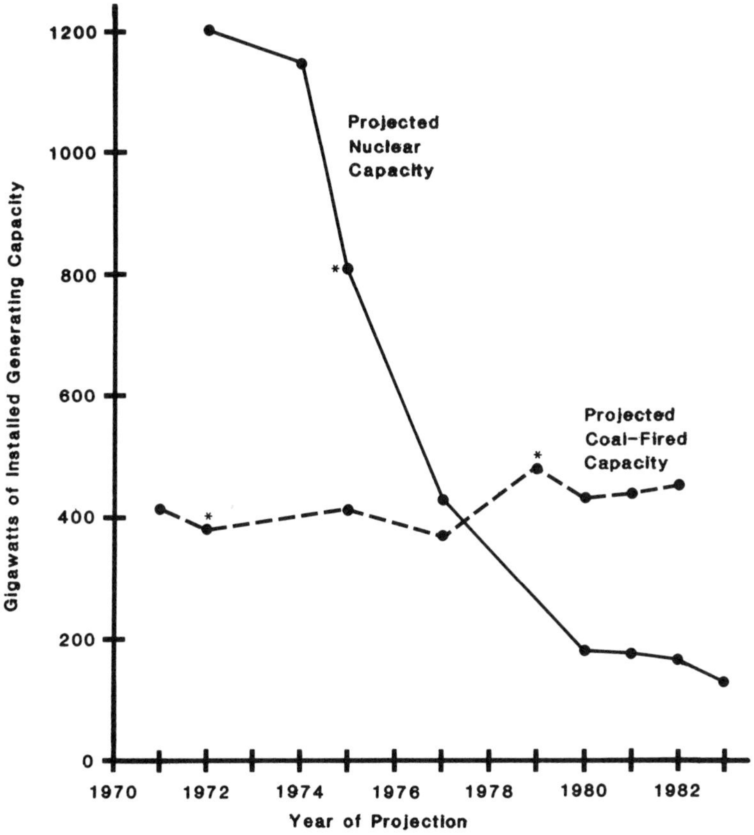

Figure 2. Projected Nuclear and Coal-Fired Generating Capacity, Year 2000, By Year Projection Was Made

* average of two projections made in year indicated

FROM PASSIVE AUDIENCE TO ACTIVE CRITICS

Up to this point, our synopsis has essentially ignored the role played by the general public--as have most such discussions. If we are to come to a thorough understanding of nuclear stalemate, however, and of the directions that are likely to be taken in the future, we must also consider some of the broader social issues that are inherent in the developing nuclear plot.

The most quoted statement in the history of commercial nuclear power in the United States, there is little doubt, was provided by Alvin Weinberg:

> We nuclear people have made a Faustian bargain with society. On the one hand, we offer--in the catalytic burner--an inexhaustible source of energy. But the price that we demand of society for this magical energy source is both vigilance and a longevity of our social institutions that we are quite unaccustomed to (1972:33).

In the early days of the commercialization of nuclear power, both parties seemed to have struck a long-term bargain. The industry could look forward to the challenge of making an extremely complex technology practical. And the American public, voracious consumers of electricity, could look forward to a continuation of inexpensive kilowatt hours. Within this favorable climate, as a rule, the actual construction of nuclear generating facilities got underway quickly and the work proceeded along smoothly. Sustained public challenge to development of nuclear power was virtually nonexistent until the very late 1960s; by all signs, Americans were acquiescing to the imperatives of technological progress, as they had almost always done in the past.

In a historical sense, moreover, the success of nuclear energy seemed almost predestined. The nation's growth--from youthful agrarianism, through an adolescence of industrialization, to the maturity of technological preeminence--had been propelled by fundamental shifts in fuel sources. The successive shifts involved the substitution of relatively cheap, abundant and efficient fuels for those that were scarce, expensive and less efficient. In the eyes of some knowledgeable observers, these substitutions helped account for the nation's rapid rise to industrial leadership (see, e.g., Cook, 1976). Wood fuels had dominated the nation's energy supply during the preindustrial era, later to be succeeded by coal, and then by oil. Nuclear power seemed to be the natural successor as the dominant energy source. After all, it was the nation's state-of-the-art technology, capable of converting tiny bits of raw fuel into vast quantities of "clean, cheap electric energy."

In addition, while the 30-year effort to develop nuclear power as a cheap and dependable energy source has been filled with uncertainties, the supporting role of the federal government has never been in doubt. Debates have raged over differing approaches to development--questions about whether nuclear power ought to be a "public" or a "private" enterprise, for example--but the desirability of nuclear power development has been a matter of steady consensus. In spite of changes in administrations, and regardless of the political party controlling the Congress, support for nuclear energy has been a consistent feature of national energy policy for the last three decades.

Under all presidential administrations, nuclear energy has enjoyed massive federal funding. As of 1978, the federal government had spent more than 20 billion dollars on nuclear energy (Cone et al., 1980), one of the largest single industrial subsidies in U.S. history. Aside from the fact that the $20 billion estimate is expressed in 1978 dollars--the 1982 equivalent would be closer to $30 billion, and a later study came up with an estimate of about $38 billion in 1979 dollars (U.S. Energy Information Administration, 1981)--the figure is undoubtedly on the conservative side. It excludes not only some basic research performed for military nuclear purposes, for example, but also the indirect subsidies provided through support of electric power development and through federal limits on the liabilities that utilities can incur through nuclear accidents. The initial figure also excludes the expenditures that occurred after the Three Mile Island accident in 1979, and even the later estimate excludes most of them.

Every single President since the dawn of the nuclear age--including Presidents Truman, Eisenhower, Kennedy, Johnson, Nixon, Ford and Carter, as well as President

Reagan--has been a strong supporter of nuclear power development. Although Presidents Ford and Carter showed a greater commitment to conservation than had previous presidents, both of them--particularly Carter, a former nuclear engineer--continued to place a high priority on the streamlining of nuclear power plant licensing. While Ronald Reagan is widely perceived to be the most ardent supporter of nuclear power among recent presidents, it appears that the main difference between his administration and previous ones is in the Reagan cutbacks for alternative sources of energy supply, such as solar power and energy conservation.

Despite the frequent assertion by proponents that the federal government has impeded nuclear power, in other words, it is clear that the government has generally been quite sympathetic to the nuclear power industry. To the extent to which the government can be seen as representing the broader public, it would appear that nuclear power has been playing to a very appreciative audience.

If we consider that audience directly, however, a far more complicated picture emerges. Particularly by the time the 1960s came to a close, proposed power plants had begun to attract the concern of local citizen groups. Backed by a rising national concern with environmental issues, and given additional leverage through environmental legislation (such as the National Environmental Protection Act of 1969, P.L. 91-190, 42 U.S.C. 4321 *et seq.*), local protesters started to focus on the environmental hazards posed by nuclear reactors.

Thermal pollution to lakes and rivers--caused by non-radioactive waste heat through the normal operation of a nuclear plant--was the object of the most serious concern at the time. Local opposition to power plants led to the cancellation of plans to build three plants: Bell Station on Cayuga Lake in upstate New York, Ravenswood Plant in New York City, and the Bodega Bay Plant near San Francisco (Nelkin, 1971). The political and judicial efforts of local opposition groups culminated in the lawsuit filed by opponents to the Calvert Cliffs facility, planned for construction on the Chesapeake Bay by the Baltimore Gas and Electric Company. In a landmark decision, the U.S. Court of Appeals in Washington, D.C. ruled in 1971 that environmental law required the Atomic Energy Commission to consider the broader environmental effects as well as the potential radiological dangers of nuclear power plants (*Calvert Cliffs' Coordinating Committee v. U.S. Atomic Energy Commission*, 499 S.2d 1109 [D.C. Cir. 1971]).

These early efforts to intervene in the licensing of nuclear plants did not represent a challenge to nuclear power generally. Rather the focus was on local issues, especially on the siting of specific plants--the harbinger of growing distaste for having a nuclear plant in one's "back yard." At the same time, however, additional concerns were being expressed about possible cancers and genetic damage from the routine emissions of radiation at normally operating nuclear plants. Added to these concerns were continuing questions about the activities of the Atomic Energy Commission, the sole agency responsible for nuclear power; the AEC was the object of sharp criticism because of the fine line separating its dual roles of promoting and regulating nuclear technology. Although some of these problems have since been resolved--and although others have fallen away from public concern--they were the early warning signs of things to come.

Things to come would include serious concern with reactor safety. In July of 1971, the Union of Concerned Scientists, an expert group of M.I.T. scientists who devoted part of their time to social and environmental issues, released a report examining the emergency core cooling system of nuclear reactors. The system's crucial purpose is to prevent a reactor core meltdown by flooding the reactor with water in the event of serious overheating; the report charged that AEC safety regulations were seriously flawed, and that nuclear power therefore posed greater threats to public health than the government and the industry had led citizens to believe. Release of the report attracted widespread media attention. Combined with vigorous protest by national environmental groups, it was instrumental in prompting the Joint Committee on Atomic Energy--a legislative oversight body--to hold a series of generic hearings on reactor safety.

Meanwhile, with the issue of reactor safety in the air and rapidly becoming a public issue, the AEC commissioned a comprehensive study of the risks of a catastrophic nuclear accident. Directed by M.I.T. professor Norman Rasmussen, the study led to a final report--The Reactor Safety Study, WASH-1400--which supported the arguments that had been maintained all along by the nuclear industry and the AEC (U.S. Atomic Energy Commission, 1975). The risk of a citizen being killed by a serious reactor mishap was infinitesimal, the report concluded--roughly equal to the probability that he or she would be killed by a falling meteorite. Although the methodology and credibility of the report would later attract fire (see Shapley, 1977; see also Chapter 5 of this volume, by Slovic et al., 1984) the Rasmussen report provided important reassurance of the nuclear industry's safety record, and encouraged the industry's continued expansion.

Continued expansion, however, was threatened on other fronts. By 1975 a new issue had solidified to further complicate nuclear growth. From the days when nuclear power was first promoted by the federal government, there was every expectation that spent fuel from reactors would be reprocessed. The reprocessed fuel would then be used over again in reactor operation, thereby making greater use of the same original materials and lowering the fuel costs of nuclear power. As another fuel-saving measure, commercial nuclear power in the United States was also expected to turn increasingly to fuel generated in breeder reactors--reactors that put out more fuel than is used up in the production of electricity.

Both reprocessing and breeder technology, however, produce significant quantities of plutonium--and plutonium can be used to produce nuclear weapons. The issue of safeguarding bomb-grade nuclear materials thus soon joined the growing list of concerns over peaceful use of the atom.

Fears were also expressed over proliferation--the threat that other countries would acquire nuclear weapons, particularly in cases where those countries were provided with nuclear reactors. These fears had been reinforced in 1974 when India exploded a nuclear device with materials obtained from a Canadian-supplied commercial reactor. Proliferation worries were exacerbated by concerns about safeguards to keep hazardous nuclear materials away from terrorists and saboteurs. Small quantities of plutonium could be used for malevolent purposes--including the poisoning of air or drinking water in heavily populated areas, as well as the fashioning of bombs--and domestic as well as foreign terrorists were seen as envisioning distinctly unpeaceful uses for "the peaceful atom."

Increasing quantities of plutonium in the nuclear fuel cycle also compounded an existing problem. Plutonium is tenaciously radioactive: a given quantity of this substance will still have half as much radioactivity in 24,000 years as it does today. Naturally occurring or "background" levels of radioactivity are inherent aspects of life on earth, and properly operating nuclear power plants put out virtually no radiation, but human exposure to higher levels of radioactivity can result in genetic damage, cancer, or--if the dosage is high enough--death. Thus especially the high-level radioactive wastes must be isolated from human populations, and some of the wastes must be disposed of in a way that keeps them isolated for literally thousands of years. Although the problem of nuclear waste disposal had long been known to energy experts and officials, the public had generally remained unaware or unconcerned about it. With increasing uneasiness about the rising quantities of nuclear materials, however, the need for safe and acceptable waste disposal became still another issue to be added to the growing list of public concerns.

By the mid-1970s the potential hazards of nuclear power had received sufficient attention that the issues found their way into voting booths. In June of 1976 voters in California encountered Proposition 15, a public initiative for a moratorium on nuclear development. The measure would have prohibited the construction of new nuclear plants unless three conditions were met: removal of the federal government's limitation on damage liability in the event of an accident, tighter safety standards that required two-thirds approval by the state legislature, and a waste management program that required similar legislative approval. It was defeated by a margin of nearly two to one.

Seven states--Washington, Oregon, Arizona, Colorado, Montana, Missouri and Ohio--followed with similar moratorium initiatives on the November ballots. All of these were also defeated, often by large majorities.

The election outcomes were, of course, a source of considerable relief for the federal government and the nuclear industry. Here at last direct political action confirmed what proponents of nuclear power had said all along: public fears of nuclear power had been stirred up by the actions of a small group of organized agitators and exaggerated by the media. As a result, the public had become terribly misinformed. But once the "true" facts became known, the public would show overwhelming support for fission technology. The referenda defeats, it seemed, bore all this out. Perhaps the question of the broader public's stance on nuclear power had at last been settled, once and for all.

But other developments warned proponents to treat the victories cautiously. By the time the state referenda went to a vote, there were signs of rising influence from the "soft technology" or alternative energy movement (Schumacher, 1973; Lovins, 1976). The movement broadened the nuclear controversy considerably. Now the debate over nuclear power became not simply a matter of distaste for the technology itself, but part of a much larger controversy that questioned the entire large-scale, centralized energy supply system of the United States. That system was described as being an energy-wasting, dehumanizing technocratic structure that needed to be rebuilt from the ground up. Replacing it, the argument went, should be an entirely new system based on energy conservation, self-sufficiency and smaller-scale, more efficient technologies.

Whatever initial effect the alternative energy movement might have had on public mistrust of nuclear power, it was soon overshadowed by a far more dramatic influence: the accident at Three Mile Island near Harrisburg, Pennsylvania, in March of 1979. A loss of reactor coolant, something that nuclear experts considered to be so unlikely as to be almost impossible, proved to be quite possible indeed. It took several weeks to cool the reactor to a safe level. In the meantime, daily in the press and night after night on nationwide television, the American public was reminded of some of its worst fears about nuclear energy.

No other single event, it is now clear, has led to a greater decline in support for peaceful use of the atom. Public confidence in the nation's nuclear program was shaken to the core. Shaken, too, was the future of nuclear power. The accident cast a deep shadow over what had already become a cloudy future.

Indeed, by the early 1980s, the nuclear industry's 1976 election victories had all but vanished from memory. Three states--California, Connecticut and Maine--passed legislation prohibiting further power plant construction until the government could demonstrate the safe and permanent disposal of nuclear wastes. Five new initiatives restricting the development of nuclear power had made the ballot in 1980, and they were successful in three of the five states--Montana, Oregon and Washington.

While the legal status of several state measures is still in doubt, and while others have been overturned in the courts, the U.S. Supreme Court unanimously upheld the constitutionality of the California statute on April 20, 1983. The short-term implications of the decision may have been relatively minor, despite the argument in a U.S. Justice Department brief that "the result would be the virtual elimination of nuclear power as a potential energy source" (Wermiel, 1982: 13); the California law applied only to new facilities, and as noted above, new orders have been in extremely short supply since the early 1970s. The longer-term implications could prove more difficult, however, particularly if the nuclear power industry were to show signs of renewed vitality or if the federal government were to encounter difficulties in its efforts to develop radioactive waste storage facilities, since the decision may have opened the way for other states to adopt similar laws.

Meanwhile the nuclear power industry continued to experience difficulties in living down the legacy of Three Mile Island. On January 25, 1982, a stuck valve at the Ginna nuclear plant near Rochester, New York, set in motion the potential for another serious mishap. The situation was declared a "site emergency," but the plant operators successfully brought the system under control some 33 hours after the accident began. About a year later, on February 22, 1983, the Salem-1 reactor in southern New Jersey failed to shut down when it was ordered to do so by the plant's electronic safety system. Prompt action by an operator prevented a serious accident, but the Nuclear Regulatory Commission levied its largest fine ever against the operator of the reactor, citing the "most significant" safety implications since Three Mile Island. The Salem incident was noteworthy for three reasons. One was that a serious accident could have occurred under different circumstances--for example, if the plant had been operating at full instead of reduced power. The second was that the incident was thought by the nuclear industry to have had only "a negligible chance of occurring, on the order of once in a million reactor operating years" (Marshall, 1983:280). The third was that the same system failed again just three days later.

Neither the Ginna mishap nor the twin incidents at the Salem plant received the kind of press coverage that had accompanied the Three Mile Island (TMI) accident, but the continuing difficulties scarcely made matters any easier for the nuclear power industry. Indeed, the Ginna and Salem incidents--and possibly others--may ultimately prove to have fallout of a different sort. To whatever extent the TMI accident recedes from the public consciousness, related experiences may serve as reminders of the potential risks of nuclear electricity, and of the continued possibility of further accidents.

Nuclear Power and the Public: Beyond Intuition

With the onset of the 1980s, the nuclear industry found itself mired in serious troubles. Changing markets, shifts in international energy trade and performance far below expectation were the visible sources of its economic woes and cascading projections. But these were not the sole sources. Rising public criticism added complications to the already uncertain climate. Through legislative action, judicial proceedings and direct agitation, public opposition would eventually produce serious licensing and construction delays, increasing the costs of nuclear development both directly and indirectly.

Over the course of several decades, public concerns over domestic nuclear power have evolved through a series of polarized issues. Beginning with questions over local siting decisions, concerns shifted to nuclear safety more generally, and then to the issues of proliferation safeguards and radioactive waste disposal. The process of evolving criticism has resulted in a succession of saliencies; first one issue has come to public attention, to be replaced by another and then by still another. In running its course, the nuclear debate has now gone full circle, touching on all aspects of the nuclear fuel cycle. Some issues appear to have been settled, while others have merely faded from public consciousness, and still others linger on as key concerns. This entire evolutionary process has been characterized as a many-headed hydra--no sooner has one issue lost the spotlight of controversy than two others spring up to take its place (Hohenemser et al., 1977).

Despite the shifts in specific public concerns, several key issues appear to have solidified, withstanding the test of time. Principal among these are concerns over reactor safety and the risk of catastrophic accidents, the local siting of nuclear facilities, and the disposal of radioactive wastes.

Each of these issues has been the subject of detailed scientific and technical study. Indeed, scientific and technical matters have dominated the attention of experts on both sides of the nuclear debate: What, for example, are the probabilities of a serious reactor meltdown? How many deaths and new cases of cancer would result from such a meltdown? What is the health risk from living in the vicinity of a nuclear plant? What are the best technical means for storing radioactive wastes?

Answers to such scientific and technical questions, of course, are essential to nuclear program development--and much has been learned about the "objective" risks and benefits associated with nuclear power. Largely overlooked in past discussions, however, has been the "subjective" side of the technical questions--the side that is the focus of the present volume. How much risk is the public willing to accept to enjoy the benefits of further nuclear development? Who is willing to have a nuclear plant--or a nuclear waste repository--located in his/her community? Are there really critical masses?

The problem is not that these questions have been forgotten entirely. Instead they have generally been addressed only in an intuitive or unsystematic way--and often, ironically, by scientists and engineers whose "technical" work is both rigorous and systematic.

There is no law of nature, however, that requires the scientific method to be abandoned merely because questions of human behavior are involved. In the words of the second Ford Foundation Energy Study, *Energy: The Next Twenty Years*, "Social science research to identify and explore policy options and their impacts is . . . as important as the hard science and engineering research" (Ford Foundation Study Group, 1979:51). We are in full agreement: the social and political issues seem to us to deserve the same kind of rigorous, systematic investigation that has been devoted to the technical issues.

PUBLIC REACTIONS TO NUCLEAR POWER : THE EVIDENCE

Our concern with public acceptability of nuclear power leads us directly to the material making up the bulk of this book--empirical evidence gathered through traditional social scientific methods. The chapters presenting this evidence are organized into four parts. Part One begins with a global assessment of public reactions to nuclear power, followed in Part Two with a focus on the psychological and sociological bases of these reactions. Part Three shifts the focus to local issues, which currently include some of the more difficult social and political problems. Part Four presents statements from persons who represent the leading institutional actors in the nuclear debate: government, industry and public interest groups.

The Larger Picture

Chapter 2, by William Rankin, Stanley Nealey and Barbara Melber, provides an overview of the fluctuations in public support for nuclear power over the past decade. Drawing upon a variety of important national data sources, the chapter shows that support and opposition did not follow a consistently smooth pattern. The trend data show that nuclear power was quite widely accepted in the early 1970s, although the picture had become blurred by the early 1980s. The idea of a "nearby" nuclear facility evidently began to be viewed with reservations by the middle of the 1970s, but the general idea of nuclear power development was still quite strongly supported at that time. There was a particularly noticeable drop in public favorability, however, immediately following the Three Mile Island accident.

Perhaps in part because of the rise of the alternative energy movement, and in part because of the rising popularity of "cutting back" more generally, it has been hypothesized that Americans view nuclear power to be in polar opposition to energy conservation. Chapter 3, by Eugene Rosa, Marvin Olsen and Don Dillman, asks whether that is in fact the case. Summarizing the results of a major regional study, the authors conclude that increased opposition to nuclear power cannot be explained simply in terms of increased support for conservation. In addition, their analysis shows that the overall opinion picture is considerably more complex than is sometimes assumed. Sizable fractions of the public favor both nuclear power and energy conservation, and a significant minority express opposition to both. These findings have important implications for future energy policy options, and they indicate that present complexities are greater than would have been assumed on the basis of the common arguments in the nuclear power debate.

The Bases of Public Perception and Attitude

In Chapter 4, Allan Mazur examines the influence of the media on public attitudes. As Mazur notes, the nuclear debate is one of a broad class of technological controversies. His chapter provides a comparative context for the fluctuations of public support and opposition, and it concludes that specific media-worthy events have had a clear influence on the public stance toward nuclear technology. Press coverage of the Three Mile Island accident appears to have been a particularly significant factor in influencing public response to the accident--but *not* necessarily because the news media were lacking in balance in their treatment of the accident. Rather, the effects of the press coverage--even balanced coverage--apparently reflected underlying concerns about specific characteristics of the nuclear power industry, as well as being related to several features of the TMI accident itself.

Chapter 5, by Paul Slovic, Baruch Fischhoff and Sarah Lichtenstein, draws from the rich tradition of research on risk assessment to summarize some of the major reasons why people fear nuclear power as much as they do. After a careful examination of existing studies, the authors conclude that members of the general public tend to rate nuclear power as having a far higher risk than do technical experts, but that the data cannot be explained on the basis of public "irrationality." Indeed, the evidence suggests instead that technical experts are often prone to make the same kinds of errors in judgment as do members of the general public.

In Chapter 6, Robert Mitchell summarizes what may be the most detailed analysis yet undertaken with a national sample of post-TMI attitudes toward nuclear power. In particular, Mitchell looks for evidence that some segment of the population may be reacting to nuclear power with particularly irrational impulses. After a detailed analysis, he concludes that it is possible to explain a large portion of the variation in public attitudes toward nuclear power. However, consistent with the conclusion of Slovic and his colleagues, Mitchell finds that arguments about the "irrationality" of the public apparently have very little evidence to stand upon.

Whose Back Yard?

Concerns over local siting are addressed in the next section. Chapter 7, by Barbara Farhar-Pilgrim and William Freudenburg, compares attitudes toward nuclear power with attitudes toward other energy supply technologies, particularly coal and solar power. The authors go on to assess public receptivity to the local siting of nuclear power plants. Drawing from a broad range of available studies, they conclude that nuclear power tends to be less popular than any other energy supply option except imported oil. They note further that the relative unpopularity of nuclear power is particularly clear when the facilities are intended for a person's own back yard.

For whatever other effects it may have had, the accident at Three Mile Island allowed researchers to examine the effects of a nuclear accident on a nearby community. The accident, in effect, changed potential risk and local siting objections into a reality for the residents around Harrisburg, Pennsylvania. In Chapter 8, Cynthia Flynn--who was studying the Three Mile Island area even before the accident occurred--provides an overview of the local impacts of the mishap. She also summarizes the effects of the TMI accident on 11 other nuclear reactor sites that were being studied under a Nuclear Regulatory Commission contract at the same time. One of the central conclusions of her chapter is that, while the incident was measurably stressful for a number of persons living in the vicinity of the ill-fated reactor, it appears that the national reverberations from the accident may have been far more significant than were the local effects.

Of all the facilities that might be located in someone's back yard, nuclear waste facilities may be the most unpopular. Chapter 9, by Dorothy Zinberg, summarizes the history of nuclear waste planning from the standpoint of public concerns. In an analysis that has increasingly clear implications for the future of nuclear power, she suggests that many of the current problems of the nuclear waste industry may be direct reactions to some of the actions taken earlier by the same industry.

Speaking on Behalf of the Public

Needless to say, the three main institutional actors in the nuclear power debate--the federal government, the nuclear industry, and organized critics of the technology--frequently differ in their assessments of public opinion. Complicating matters further is the fact that each often claims to be speaking on behalf of the public good. Accordingly, the next three chapters provide representative viewpoints from each of these powerful actors. They are followed by a fourth chapter that summarizes the public's own views, as revealed in survey results.

Chapter 10 is by W. Kenneth Davis, who served during the first two years of the Reagan Administration as the second-highest official in the Department of Energy, and who has since gone on to become the Chairman of the Atomic Industrial Forum. Davis was quite influential in the development of the official Reagan Administration policy toward nuclear power; his chapter provides a concise summary of the policy, and of the evidence and reasoning that were employed in developing it.

Chapter 11 is by a leading critic of the nuclear power industry--and of the Reagan Administration. Barry Commoner argues in this chapter that the costs of nuclear power industry regulations are high, but that they are anything but "excessive." Rather, he concludes, the increased regulatory burden of recent years is an altogether appropriate expression of the will of the people.

Chapter 12, by Robert Szalay, the Vice President of the Atomic Industrial Forum, presents a markedly different perspective. This chapter argues that while public perceptions can be altered by a sustained record of successful performance, such success depends crucially on improvements in what has historically been an inefficient regulatory process. He concludes his chapter with a discussion of the types of changes in the regulatory process that the nuclear industry feels could remove unnecessary burdens and costs without sacrificing safety.

Chapter 13, by Cora Bagley Marrett, offers yet another point of view. This chapter first discusses public attitudes toward nuclear power in the context of public confidence in science and technology more generally. The chapter then goes on to consider survey evidence on the broader public's views about the appropriate amount of influence to be exercised by the lay public--relative to the influence of technological experts--on issues such as nuclear power.

Finally, in the fourteenth and concluding chapter of this volume, the two of us review the themes that emerge from the volume. We also provide our assessment of the implications that the assembled evidence may have for nuclear power policies of the future.

ACKNOWLEDGEMENTS

While our work on this volume has not been without its difficulties, we have slowly come to realize that only one of our goals would be impossible to achieve. There is simply no way we could express our gratitude to all of the persons and institutions who helped to make this book a reality; at best we can only offer our special public thanks to the small handful whose help proved absolutely crucial. Foremost among them would have to be Robert F. Howell, Chairman of the Department of Rural Sociology, and James F. Short, Jr., Director of the Social Research Center, at Washington State University. Both of them provided substantial moral and financial support; without them there might not even have been a book.

Also at Washington State University, Gladys Birch has been a valuable asset, taking care of many important details in addition to most of the typesetting. Timothy Jones and Carrie Lee guided the delicate final stages of the book's preparation. Richard Rossi was highly resourceful in producing the volume's graphics; Lela Odell, Marilyn Howell and Louise Scott assisted with proofreading, manuscript typing and good-humored tolerance of the book's many demands. We suspect that all of the above probably deserve raises.

A number of other persons also deserve special recognition. At the American Association for the Advancement of Science, Joellen Fritsche has been a genuine pleasure to work with, and we are deeply indebted to her for the patience and assistance she provided. Mosey Hosseinpour of the Battelle Human Affairs Research Centers produced titles, subtitles and much of the other lettering, doing so in admirable and helpful fashion. Melinda Renner of the Atomic Industrial Forum went far beyond the call of duty, educating the two of us on how one really goes about putting an index together; she gave the book's index an order and rationality it could not have enjoyed without her help. The actual job of compiling the final index, an often-onerous task, was carefully and cheerfully completed by Nanette Flynn and Timothy Jones.

We also need to offer a public word of thanks to the volume's authors. Their cooperation has been absolutely first-rate. When we began this project, we were told two things--one was that editing a book is far more work than it seems to be, and the other was that authors can't be trusted. We have found the first bit of advice to be true beyond our wildest expectations, but the second simply does not apply to the group of authors with whom we have worked. Every one of them has been prompt, helpful and professional. Given that they are a distinguished and busy group of people--and given the number of requests they were asked to fulfill--we are particularly impressed, and particularly grateful.

Most of the chapters in this book were originally presented at a symposium of the 1982 meeting of the American Association for the Advancement of Science (AAAS), and all author and editor royalties are being donated to support the ongoing activities of the AAAS. The sponsorship of the U.S. Rural Sociological Society was a key factor in making the initial symposium possible, as was the backing of the American Sociological Association and of Section K (Social, Political and Economic Sciences) of the AAAS. Co-sponsors of the session included AAAS Section T (Information, Computing and Communication) and the International Association for Impact Assessment. We appreciate the backing of all of these sponsors and cosponsors, and we hope the final result lives up to their expectations.

FOOTNOTES

[1]One of the reasons for the apparent cost advantage was a substantial subsidy from the manufacturer to the utility. The Oyster Creek plant and several other early reactors had been sold on "turnkey" contracts--so called because the purchasing utility was guaranteed that the plant would be

completed for a specific price, and needed to do little more than "turn the key" to put the reactor into operation. Any differences between the quoted prices and the "real costs" were thus paid for by the manufacturers, not the utilities. Later orders--basically those placed from 1966 on--were to include no such guarantees.

[2]The U.S. Department of Energy generally expresses its projections for coal-fired electricity generation in terms of quads of energy consumed rather than in terms of overall generating capacity. (A quad is quadrillion British Thermal Units, or BTUs; see also Footnote b of Table 2.) In the interest of comparability across years, we have based our coal calculations on the quads-of-consumption figures, rather than on generating capacities (see Footnote c of Table 2). To allow comparisons with the figures for nuclear power, we then converted the quads-of-consumption figures into the generating capacity totals reported in Table 2 and Figure 2. In the interest of consistency, all generating capacity conversions were performed with a single conversion factor (0.05 quads per gigawatt of generating capacity), even in cases where the reports being cited used differing conversion factors of their own. The details of our calculations are reported in Footnote c of Table 2.

REFERENCES

Bupp, Irvin C. and Jean-Claude Derian
1981 *The Failed Promise of Nuclear Power: The Story of Light Water.* New York: Basic Books.

Commoner, Barry
1984 "The Public Interest in Nuclear Power." Pp. 267-294 in William R. Freudenburg and Eugene A. Rosa (eds.), *Public Reactions to Nuclear Power: Are There Critical Masses?* Boulder, CO: Westview Press/American Association for the Advancement of Science.

Cone, B. W., D. L. Brenchley, V. L. Brix, M. L. Brown, K. E. Cochran, P. D. Cohn, R. J. Cole, M. G. Curry, R. Davidson, J. Easterling, J. C. Emery, A. G. Fassbender, J. S. Fattorini, Jr., B. Gordon, H. Harty, D. Lenerz, A. R. Maurizi, R. Mazzucchi, C. McClain, D. D. Moore, J. H. Maxwell, W. J. Sheppard, S. Solomon and P. Sommers
1980 *An Analysis of Federal Incentives Used to Stimulate Energy Production* (Revised). Richland, WA: Pacific Northwest Laboratory, U.S. Department of Energy.

Congressional Research Service
1977 *Project Interdependence: U.S. and World*

Energy Outlook Through 1990. Washington, D.C.: Library of Congress.

Cook, Earl
1976 *Man, Energy, Society.* San Francisco: W. H. Freeman and Co.

Davis, W. Kenneth
1984 "Nuclear Power Under the Reagan Administration." Pp. 257-265 in William R. Freudenburg and Eugene A. Rosa (eds.), *Public Reactions to Nuclear Power: Are There Critical Masses?* Boulder, CO: Westview Press/American Association for the Advancement of Science.

Dupree, Walter G., Jr. and John S. Corsentino
1975 *United States Energy Through the Year 2000 (Revised).* Washington, D.C.: U.S. Bureau of Mines, Department of Interior (December).

Dupree, Walter G., Jr. and James A. West
1972 *United States Energy Through the Year 2000.* Washington, D.C.: U.S. Department of Interior (December).

Electric Power Monthly
1982 "Prologue: Nuclear Power Development." *Electric Power Monthly* (#2, February):xi-xvi.

Ford Foundation Study Group
1979 *Energy: The Next Twenty Years.* Cambridge, MA: Ballinger.

Freudenburg, William R. and Eugene A. Rosa (eds.)
1984 *Public Reactions to Nuclear Power: Are There Critical Masses?* Boulder, CO: Westview Press/American Association for the Advancement of Science.

Hohenemser, Christoph, Roger Kasperson and Robert Kates
1977 "The Distrust of Nuclear Power." *Science* 196: 25-34.

Komanoff, Charles
1981 *Power Plant Cost Escalation.* New York: Komanoff Energy Associates.

Lovins, Amory B.
1976 "Energy Strategy: The Road not Taken?" *Foreign Affairs* 55 (#1, October):65-96.

Marshall, Eliot
1983 "The Salem Case: A Failure of Nuclear Logic." *Science* 220 (April 15):280-282.

Nelkin, Dorothy
1971 *Nuclear Power and Its Critics.* Ithaca, NY: Cornell University Press.

Pelham, Ann
1981 *Energy Policy* (Second Edition). Washington, D.C.: Congressional Quarterly, Inc.

Roberts, Barry, Andrew Reynolds and Gene Clark
1982 *U.S. Commercial Nuclear Power: Historical*

Perspective, Current Status, and Outlook. Washington, D.C.: U.S. Energy Information Administration, Office of Coal, Nuclear, Electric and Alternate Fuels.

Schumacher, E. F.
1973 *Small is Beautiful: Economics as if People Mattered.* New York: Harper and Row.

Shapley, Deborah
1977 "Reactor Safety: Independence of Rasmussen Study Doubted." *Science* 197 (July 1):29-31.

Slovic, Paul, Baruch Fischhoff and Sarah Lichtenstein
1984 "Perception and Acceptability of Risk From Energy Systems." Pp. 115-136 in William R. Freudenburg and Eugene A. Rosa (eds.), *Public Reactions to Nuclear Power: Are There Critical Masses?* Boulder, CO: Westview Press/American Association for the Advancement of Science.

Szalay, Robert A.
1984 "A Nuclear Industry View of the Regulatory Climate." Pp. 295-306 in William R. Freudenburg and Eugene A. Rosa (eds.), *Public Reactions to Nuclear Power: Are There Critical Masses?* Boulder, CO: Westview Press/American Association for the Advancement of Science.

U.S. Atomic Energy Commission
1972 *Nuclear Power: 1973-2000.* Washington, D.C.: U.S. Government Printing Office.
1974 *Nuclear Power Growth: 1974-2000.* Washington, D.C.: U.S. Government Printing Office.
1975 *Reactor Safety Study: An Assessment of Accident Risks in U.S. Commercial Nuclear Power Plants.* Washington, D.C.: U.S. Nuclear Regulatory Commission (WASH-1400).

U.S. Department of Energy
1977 *Inventory of Power Plants in the United States.* Washington, D.C.: U.S. Department of Energy (December).
1979 *National Energy Plan II, Appendix B: U.S. Energy Projections.* Washington, D.C.: U.S. Government Printing Office.
1981 *Energy Projections to the Year 2000: A Supplement to the National Energy Policy Plan.* Washington, D.C.: U.S. Department of Energy.
1983 *U.S. Central Station Nuclear Electric Generating Units: Significant Milestones (Status as of October 1, 1982).* Washington, D.C.: U.S. Department of Energy, Office of Converter Reactor Deployment.

U.S. Department of Interior
1972 *United States Energy: A Summary Review.*

Washington, D.C.: U.S. Government Printing Office (January).

U.S. Energy Information Administration

1979 *Annual Report to Congress 1978, Volume Three: Forecasts.* Washington, D.C.: U.S. Department of Energy, National Energy Information Center.

1980 *Annual Report to Congress, 1979, Volume Three: Projections.* Washington D.C.: U.S. Department of Energy, National Energy Information Center.

1981 *Federal Support for Nuclear Power: Reactor Design and the Fuel Cycle.* Washington, D.C.: U.S. Energy Information Administration, Office of Economic Analysis.

1982 *1981 Annual Report to Congress, Volume Three: Projections.* Washington, D.C.: U.S. Department of Energy, National Energy Information Center.

1983 *1982 Annual Energy Outlook.* Washington, D.C.: U.S. Energy Information Administration, Office of Energy Markets and End Use.

U.S. Energy Research and Development Administration

1975 *A National Plan for Energy Research, Development and Demonstration: Creating Energy Choices for the Future.* Washington, D.C.: U.S. Government Printing Office (ERDA-48).

U.S. Federal Energy Administration

1974 *Project Independence Blueprint Final Task Force Report: Nuclear Energy.* Washington, D.C.: U.S. Government Printing Office.

U.S. Federal Power Commission

1971 *The 1970 National Power Survey: A Report by the Federal Power Commission.* Washington, D.C.: U.S. Government Printing Office.

Weinberg, Alvin M.

1972 "Social Institutions and Nuclear Energy." *Science* 177:27-34.

1976 "The Maturity and Future of Nuclear Energy." *American Scientist* 64:16-21.

Wermiel, Stephen

1982 "High Court Faces Big Nuclear-Power Cases, Including Ruling on California Restrictions." *The Wall Street Journal* (November 26):13.

Part 1

The Larger Picture

William L. Rankin,
Stanley M. Nealey, Barbara Desow Melber

2. Overview of National Attitudes Toward Nuclear Energy: A Longitudinal Analysis

INTRODUCTION

The continued development of nuclear power is now an important social issue, but this has not always been the case. As Rosa and Freudenburg (1984) point out in Chapter 1 of this volume, the fervor of the present-day debate has not always followed nuclear power. While earlier examples of controversy can be cited, the debate over nuclear power appears to have begun in earnest in 1969 or 1970 (Ebbin and Kasper, 1974) following the construction of approximately 25 nuclear power plants in the late 1960s, the debate over the National Environmental Policy Act, and movements like Earth Day. Subsequently, the debate has become more heated, leading some observers to label the current situation as a controversy or conflict--or even as a fight (Schmidt and Bodansky, 1976) or rebellion (Lewis, 1972).

Yet the increase in fervor may or may not represent changes in the attitudes of the general public toward nuclear power, since as Mazur (1984) notes in Chapter 4, the persons who become activists on an issue will often differ significantly from the "average" American citizen. To examine trends in the attitudes of the broader public, one must draw instead upon representative national surveys, combining studies in a way that permits a longitudinal analysis--one that examines changes over time.

Pp. 41-67 in William R. Freudenburg and Eugene A. Rosa, (eds., 1984) *Public Reactions to Nuclear Power: Are There Critical Masses?*

The importance of representative surveys can be seen from the fact that spokespersons on all sides of the nuclear issue often claim to be speaking for "the public." Many such claims can be found in the nuclear controversy, but one has only to look at other chapters in this book to see that this is the case. For example, in Chapter 10 Davis (1984) suggests that the Reagan Administration's policy toward nuclear power is consistent with public thinking on the matter. Indeed, the Atomic Energy Act of 1954, which was passed by the Congress that represents the American public politically, mandated that nuclear power be given a chance to prove its viability, and each Congress since then has appropriated funds for research and development on nuclear power. On the other hand, in Chapter 11 Commoner (1984) concludes that he is speaking for the public, and presents the argument that the development of nuclear power is not in the public interest.

But who is "the public?" Even a casual examination of this question uncovers the existence of several publics that are interested in nuclear power issues. These publics include, for example, the U.S. population as a whole, demographic subsets of this population, opinion leaders in business and industry, ratepayers in a given utility district, special interest groups, and local support and opposition groups. Thus there are numerous publics, and indeed, each of the spokespersons referred to above may have been speaking for one or more of them. The problem seems to be that the public to which one is referring is not often made clear.

In this chapter, we would like to provide a longitudinal analysis of public attitudes toward nuclear power, where the public is defined to be the adult population in the United States. This is the public that is sampled in national opinion polls, and the one that is eligible to vote in national elections.

Is this an important public to examine in the nuclear power controversy? As discussed by Freudenburg and Rosa (1984b) in the concluding chapter of this volume, the link between public attitudes and political decisions is unclear. Yet as they point out, political and administrative decisions must operate within the broad boundaries established by public opinion. Thus the adult U.S. public is important because of its influence in setting boundaries on broad national policy toward nuclear power. Subsets of the U.S. public would need to be examined for, say, regional policy decisions (see Chapter 3, by Rosa et al., 1984, regarding the western United States) or local siting decisions (see Chapter 7, by Farhar-Pilgrim and Freudenburg, 1984, regarding publics near potential nuclear power plant sites). When we speak of the public in this chapter, however, we are referring to the adult public of the United States as it is represented by the samples selected by national public opinion research firms.

Much is already known about the nuclear power attitudes of this public. Melber et al. (1977) collected and summarized 27 national surveys about nuclear power that had been conducted prior to the summer of 1977. Two general types of questions were used by survey firms to probe nuclear power attitudes. The first asked respondents whether they generally favored or opposed building more nuclear power plants. The second type of question asked whether the respondent favored or opposed the building of a nuclear power plant "nearby" (or within 5 to 20 miles of the respondent's home).

The survey data clearly indicated that a majority of the public favored the general use of nuclear power. For example, the national probability surveys analyzed for the report, which were primarily conducted in 1975 and 1976 by Louis Harris and Associates, Inc., and by Cambridge Reports, Inc., indicated that approximately 60% of the public supported nuclear power, with support levels ranging from 45% to 80%. Approximately 23% of the public opposed nuclear power, with opposition levels ranging from 6% to 35%, and approximately 17% of the respondents were undecided, with undecided levels ranging from 11% to 32%.

As might be expected, however, a higher percentage of the public favored nuclear power in general than favored having nuclear power plants built near their residences. In national surveys conducted by Becker Research Corporation and by Response Analysis Corporation from 1970 through 1976, the mean level of support for building a plant nearby was approximately 52%, with support levels ranging from 42% to 67%; the mean opposition level was 32%, with opposition levels ranging from 21% to 45%; and the average level of undecided responses was 16%, with undecided levels ranging from 0% to 27%.

Thus the U.S. public favored nuclear power during that time period. There was almost a three-to-one favorability toward the general issue of additional power plant construction, and on the question regarding a nuclear plant nearby the public favored such construction about 1.5 to 1. A major question regarding these attitudes is whether they were changing over time. Up through 1976 this did not seem to be the case. The Melber et al. analysis of survey data collected by five national research firms from 1971 through 1976 did not indicate any clear trend over time in support or opposition toward the general question of nuclear power. There was some indication, however, that attitudes toward local nuclear power plants were changing. Data collected by one survey organization found that support for a nearby plant dropped from about 57% in 1971 to about 49% in 1976, while opposition to a nearby plant increased from about 25% in 1971 to 38% in 1976. Those who were undecided in their attitudes dropped from about 18% to about 13% in the same time period (Melber et al., 1977). Thus it appears that general attitudes toward nuclear power remained quite stable through 1976, whereas acceptance of a plant built nearby decreased.

Since 1976, however, a great deal has happened that may have influenced public attitudes toward nuclear power. An increased belief in an energy shortage and foreign energy supply disruptions may have made public attitudes more positive toward nuclear power. On the other hand, reactor accidents and a continued controversy over nuclear waste management may have made attitudes more negative toward nuclear power. The most notable nuclear incident since 1976 was the Three Mile Island (TMI) accident, which occurred in late March and early April of 1979. As will be discussed in detail later, the TMI accident did have a significant effect on public attitudes toward nuclear power development--enough so that the results presented here are centered around pre- and post-TMI attitudes.

Because of the numerous events that could have changed public attitudes, Rankin et al. (1981) located and summarized additional national nuclear power surveys in order to extend the Melber et al. (1977) analysis. These surveys were conducted up to July 1981, and will be combined with pre-1977 data in this chapter to provide a longitudinal analysis of public attitudes toward nuclear power.

The remainder of the chapter consists of three sections. First, in the Survey Methodology section, a brief description of the surveys and the survey identification scheme is presented. Then in the section on Public Attitudes, the approach to evaluating the different types of attitude questions and the survey results are presented. The final section, Summary and Discussion, briefly summarizes the survey results and then discusses the implications of those results for future changes in public attitudes toward nuclear power.

SURVEY METHODOLOGY

Procedure for Acquiring Survey Data

This effort was dependent on survey data that had been collected by survey research organizations for their clients. No new data were collected solely for inclusion in this analysis. We have made major efforts to assemble relevant survey data at three different times over the past five years--in 1977, 1979 and 1981. In general, every sort of organization that might be interested in nuclear attitudinal surveys was contacted to determine whether they knew of such material. Organizations contacted included survey research firms, utility companies, nuclear industries, professional and trade organizations, pro- and antinuclear initiative groups, environmental groups, and academic groups. In addition, the *Gallup Opinion Index, Current Opinion*, and *Public Opinion Quarterly* were used to identify additional sources of survey data.

Across all data collection efforts, the above procedure for acquiring survey data resulted in the procurement of 228 surveys that in some way dealt with nuclear power. Of the 228 surveys, 130 were national surveys, 55 were state surveys, and the remaining 43 sampled from a more restricted geographical area (e.g., a utility district, a city, or some region around a nuclear power plant). The following report deals only with national surveys conducted by nationally known survey organizations.

TABLE 1
ABBREVIATIONS USED IN THIS CHAPTER FOR THE SURVEY ORGANIZATIONS

Survey Organization	Abbreviation
Associates for Research in Behavior, Inc.	ARB
Becker Research Corporation	Becker
Cambridge Reports, Inc.	Cambridge
Gallup Opinion Index; Gallup Poll	Gallup
Louis Harris and Associates, Inc.	Harris
NBC News/Associated Press	NBC
Response Analysis Corporation	RAC
Resources for the Future	RFF
University of Michigan, Institute for Social Research	UM

Most of the surveys discussed in this paper were conducted by an interviewer in the respondent's home. The selection of particular respondents for interviewing in these surveys is a complex process. It involves several steps, each of which includes a random component; the steps move from the selection of geographical sampling areas to the selection of households within these areas to the selection of a specific individual in the household. The remainder of the surveys were conducted over the telephone using a random digit dialing process. The surveys typically included between 1000 and 2000 respondents--samples of sufficient size to represent the national population.

In addition to variations in geographic area, sample size and data collection method, the surveys also differed on general questionnaire content. Some surveys dealt only with nuclear power, some dealt with several energy technologies including nuclear power, and others had only a small percentage of nuclear-related items. Finally, the surveys differed in the specific questions that were used to elicit nuclear-related beliefs and attitudes. The influence of wording differences on responses will be discussed where appropriate.

Method for Referring to Surveys

In order to refer to the surveys in a consistent manner throughout this chapter, the following system will be used. First, we will refer to the organizations that conducted the surveys, not to the groups that sponsored them. This is done for comparability and anonymity. Second, the survey organizations' names will be abbreviated or made into an acronym (e.g., Harris, Cambridge or RAC--see Table 1). Third, the date when the survey data were collected (not the date when the report was issued) will be placed in parentheses following the survey organization's name or acronym in the form of (year/month). Thus "Harris (78/10)" indicates that Louis Harris and Associates, Inc., conducted a national survey in October 1978.

PUBLIC ATTITUDES TOWARD NUCLEAR POWER

Introduction

Several question types have been used to assess public attitudes toward nuclear power. One type of question has asked whether the respondent favors or opposes the construction of more nuclear power plants. Numerous Harris and Cambridge surveys have assessed public attitudes with this type of question, so that ample data points are available for assessing changes in attitudes and for examining the effects of the accident at Three Mile Island. A second question type has asked whether the respondent favors the construction of a nuclear power plant nearby (or within a specified distance). Three different survey organizations have used the same question regarding acceptance of local power plant construction at different times, allowing a longitudinal assessment of local plant construction attitudes since 1971.

While data regarding the two types of attitudes mentioned above constitute the major longitudinal analyses that follow, several other question types have been used by

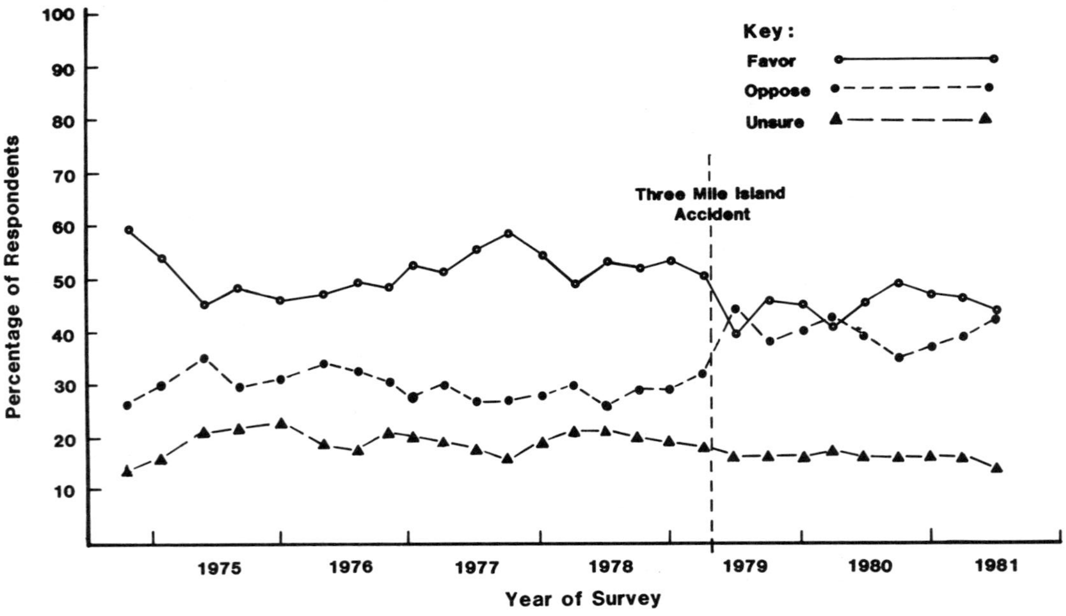

Figure 1. Construction of more Nuclear Plants--Trends Over Time

ITEM: "Do you favor or oppose the construction of more nuclear power plants ?" (Cambridge)

survey organizations for eliciting attitudes toward nuclear power since the TMI accident. These data, while only available for approximately a two-year period, complement the two question types above. Instead of asking whether the respondent favors or opposes the present state of affairs regarding nuclear power (the construction of more nuclear power plants), these questions ask whether the respondent favors or opposes measures to restrict nuclear power (permanent closure of all nuclear power plants, reduced operation or short-term plant closure, and operation of only those plants currently in existence).

General Attitudes Toward Nuclear Power Plant Construction

Data regarding general attitudes toward nuclear power plant construction are available from 26 Cambridge surveys conducted from September 1974 through June 1981, and from 21 Harris surveys conducted from March 1975 through March 1981. Cambridge asked its respondents, "Do you favor or oppose the construction of more nuclear power plants?" Harris asked a very similar question: "In general, do you favor or oppose the building of more nuclear power plants in the United States?"

The data for the Cambridge surveys are presented in Figure 1. Note that there was fluctuation in support and opposition toward nuclear power from 1974 up until the Three Mile Island accident. Although differences of just three or four percentage points between surveys are statistically significant because of the large sample size, there is no apparent long-term change prior to the TMI accident. Regression analyses run on the support, opposition, and undecided categories for the data points prior to TMI showed no significant upward or downward slope to the data.[1] Levels of support ranged from 48% to 58% (average = 51.3%, standard deviation = 3.9%), levels of opposition ranged from 26% to 35% (average = 29.8%, standard deviation = 2.5%), and levels of uncertainty ranged from 14% to 23% (average = 19.2%, standard deviation = 2.3%).[2] Note that for all surveys prior to TMI, the support levels were always higher than opposition levels by at least 10%.

The Three Mile Island accident, however, appears to have affected the relative stability of these attitudes.

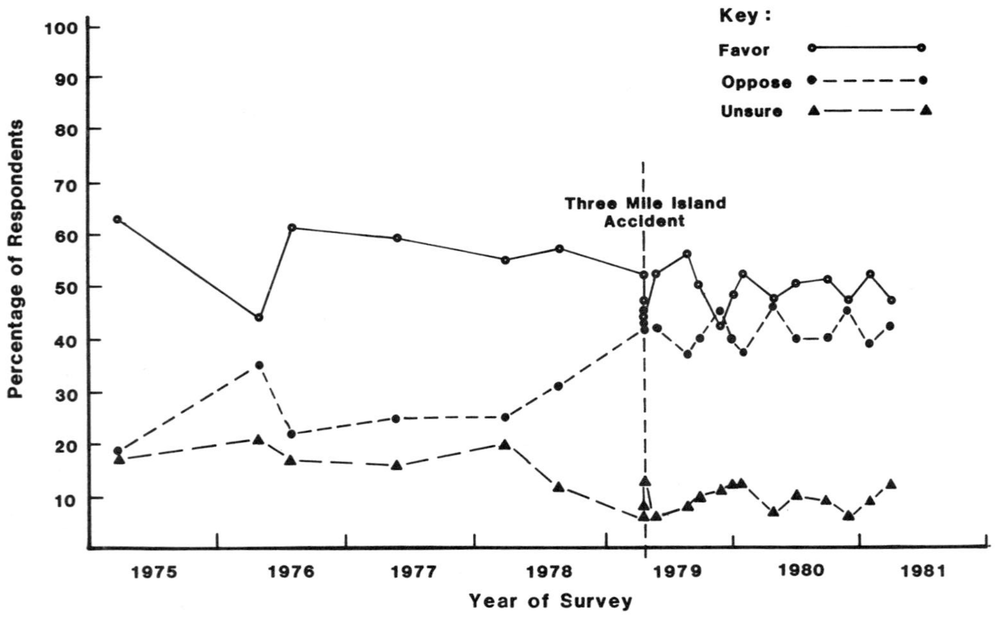

Figure 2. Construction of More Nuclear Plants -- Trends Over Time

ITEM: "In general , do you favor or oppose the building of more nuclear power plants in the United States?" (Harris)

In the first quarterly survey following the accident, Cambridge (79/6) found that opposition (44%) exceeded support (39%)--the first time this had occurred in the history of Cambridge surveys. The Cambridge survey that immediately preceded the accident (79/3) had found 50% support and 32% opposition. There was no apparent change, however, in the level of uncertainty. Although there was some attitude "rebound" toward pre-TMI levels by the time of the Cambridge (79/7) survey, the rebound has never been complete.

Regression analyses on the post-TMI data again found no significant slope. The levels of support ranged from 39% to 54% (average = 44.7%, standard deviation = 2.8%). Levels of opposition ranged from 36% to 44% (average = 39.6%, standard deviation = 2.8%), and levels of uncertainty ranged from 13% to 16% (average = 15.9%, standard deviation = 0.8%).

The differences in average support, opposition, and uncertainty levels between the pre- and post-TMI data points are all statistically significant (t-test, $p < .001$).[3] Following the accident, there were statistically significant decreases in average support levels (6.6%) and average uncertainty levels (3.3%), and a significant increase in average opposition (9.8%) to the construction of more nuclear power plants.

Although it is hard to infer causality from non-experimental data, the Cambridge findings strongly suggest that the TMI accident had a significant effect on attitudes. First, the fact that the data exhibited zero slope before and after the accident, but significantly differed in average levels, strongly suggests that the accident (or something else that happened from March through June 1979) affected attitudes (Campbell and Stanley, 1963). Second, for the first time since Cambridge began measuring nuclear attitudes, opposition levels exceeded support levels. This has in fact happened twice since the accident.

Data collected by Harris support this claim for attitude change due to the Three Mile Island accident (see Figure 2). With the exception of the Harris (76/4) data, levels of support, opposition, and uncertainty were relatively stable prior to TMI. The Harris (76/4) data appear to be noticeably lower than the other Harris pre-TMI data. The 44% support found in this survey is highly discrepant from the support levels found in the other pre-TMI surveys, which ranged around

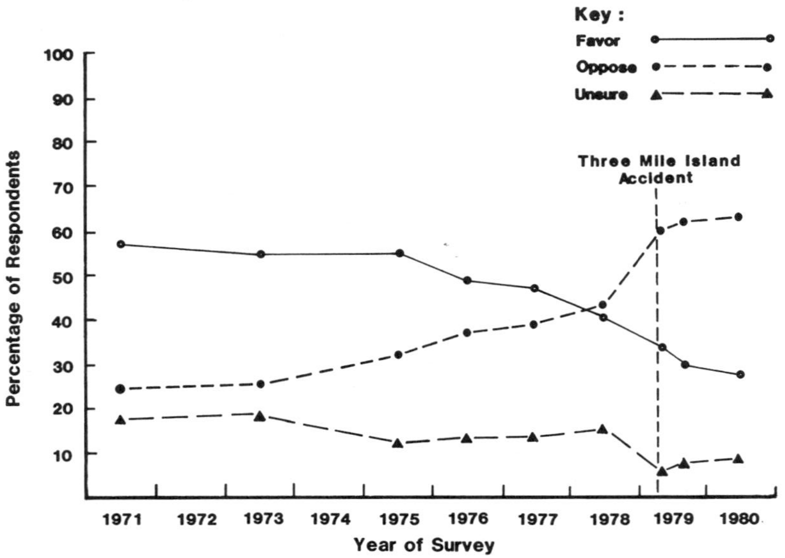

Figure 3. Trends in Support and Opposition Toward Construction of Local Nuclear Power Plants

ITEM: "Suppose your local electric company said it wanted to build a nuclear power plant in this area. Would building such a plant be all right with you, or would you be against it?" (Becker, RAC and ARB)

60%. Similarly, the opposition level for Harris (76/4) is discrepant from other pre-TMI opposition levels. Several suggestions have been made as to why this discrepancy occurred; they generally involve nuclear-related incidents around the time of the survey. However, the fact that similar changes were not found in the Cambridge (76/3) data tends to argue against such reasoning. The Harris (76/4) data may simply represent a sampling anomaly of no real significance. In the following discussion, however, we will take the more conservative course of including these data points.

For the period before the TMI accident, support levels ranged from 44% to 63% (average = 56.5%, standard deviation = 6.8%). Opposition levels ranged from 19% to 35% (average = 26.2%, standard deviation = 5.9%), and uncertainty ranged from 12% to 20% (average = 17.3%, standard deviation = 2.4%). Regression analyses on pre-TMI data also showed no significant trends in support, opposition, and uncertainty levels.

The Harris data also suggest strongly that the Three Mile Island accident affected attitudes. For one thing, the pattern of attitudes became quite variable. For another, opposition levels exceeded support levels in several of the post-TMI surveys, while this had never been the case in the Harris surveys. Finally, the average support, opposition, and uncertainty levels differed significantly between the pre- and post-TMI surveys. Support decreased an average of 7.4% (to an average of 49.0%, with a standard deviation of 3.6%). Opposition increased an average of 15.6% (to an average of 41.8%, with a standard deviation of 3.3%), and uncertainty decreased an average of 8.0% (to an average of 9.3%, with a standard deviation of 2.4%). Combined with the Cambridge data, these findings strongly suggest that TMI had a causal effect in changing public attitudes toward nuclear power.

Attitudes Toward Local Nuclear Power Plant Construction

The Cambridge and Harris questions discussed above were broadly worded so as to probe a respondent's attitude toward the general U.S. policy of building more nuclear power plants. Other attitude questions have probed the willingness of a respondent to allow a nuclear power plant to be built near his or her residence. Figure 3 shows the results from one specific question about attitudes toward nearby plant

TABLE 2
PERCENTAGE OF SUPPORT, OPPOSITION AND UNCERTAINTY TOWARD CONSTRUCTION OF A NUCLEAR POWER PLANT WITHIN FIVE MILES OF RESPONDENT'S COMMUNITY

	Favor	Oppose	Uncertain
Gallup (76/6)[a]	42	45	13
Harris (78/10)[b]	36	55	7
Gallup (79/4)[a]	33	60	7
Harris (80/1)[b]	42	56	9

[a]"As of today, how do you feel about the construction of a nuclear power plant in this area--that is, within five miles of here? Would you be against the construction of such a plant in your area, or not?"

[b]"Do you favor or oppose having a nuclear power plant within five miles of your community?"

construction that has been asked since 1971. These data were collected for the same sponsor but by three different research organizations from 1971 through 1980--Becker, RAC, and ARB. These data serve as the basis for longitudinal analysis. Other relevant data will be presented following the discussion of trends.

Becker conducted the first three surveys presented in Figure 3, RAC conducted the middle three surveys, and ARB conducted the three most recent surveys. In all nine surveys, the question read, "Suppose your local electric company said it wanted to build a nuclear power plant in this area. Would building such a plant be all right with you, or would you be against it?"

The data indicate that support for local nuclear power plant construction decreased, while opposition increased, through the 1970s. Regression analysis showed that support decreased significantly ($p < .05$)--an average decrease of 3.4% per year from 1971 through 1980. The regression line for opposition levels increased significantly from 1971 through

1980 at a rate of 4.6% per year. The slope of the regression line for the undecided responses did not differ significantly from zero. The pre-TMI and post-TMI data, analyzed separately, both had zero slope, but a *t*-test comparison of the pre- and post-TMI data (averages = 15.7% and 7.7%, respectively) showed a significant decline in the mean values ($p < .001$). Thus the TMI accident may have caused fewer people to be undecided about their attitudes toward local nuclear power plant construction.

The data discussed above could be questioned regarding the fact that they were collected by three different survey organizations. Most importantly, the changes in public attitudes tend to correspond with changes in the survey organizations by the survey sponsor. However, other survey data exist which lend strong evidence to the conclusion that there is presently more opposition than support regarding local nuclear power plant construction.

Gallup (76/6; 79/4) and Harris (78/10; 80/1) both collected data on acceptance of a nuclear power plant located within five miles of the respondent's area (see Table 2). The Gallup (76/6) survey found that opposition (45%) was greater than support (42%), although not significantly. However, in the three surveys conducted in 1978, 1979 and 1980, opposition (average = 57.0%) was significantly higher than support (average = 37.0%). The undecided levels for all four surveys (average = 9.0%) were quite comparable to those presented in Figure 3 from 1976 through 1980.

In summary, support for local nuclear power plant construction decreased, while opposition increased, through the 1970s. While support was stronger than opposition by about two to one in the early 1970s, the situation has now reversed. There is now majority opposition toward the construction of a local nuclear power plant.

Attitudes Regarding Restrictions on Nuclear Power Plants

The data presented in the two preceding sections have indicated that a plurality to a majority of the U.S. public favors the construction of more nuclear power plants in the United States, but that a majority of the respondents do not want the plants built near their communities. Thus the

TABLE 3
PERCENTAGE OF SUPPORT FOR THREE ALTERNATIVES FOR NUCLEAR POWER PLANT OPERATION

	RFF[a] (80/1)	UM[b] (Average of five Surveys, 1980)
Build more	23	31
Operate only current	47	45
Close down	20	15
Don't know/no answer	11	9

[a]"With which statement about the use of nuclear power in the United States do you most agree?"

[b]Respondents to select alternative that most reflects their attitude.

general support for nuclear power appears to be "soft," at least with regard to siting issues. In order to gauge the strength of the public's general attitude toward nuclear power, it is important to look at the public's willingness to support various restrictions on nuclear power.

In general, three different types of questions have been used to probe attitudes regarding restrictions on nuclear power; they ask respondents about operating only those plants already built, cutting back the operation of current plants, and permanently closing all plants. Responses to these three types of questions are discussed below.

RFF (80/1) and UM (80/1; 80/4; 80/6; 80/9; 80/11) have asked respondents which of three choices about nuclear power they favor most--building more plants, operating only the current plants, or closing down all existing nuclear power plants (see Table 3). Across all six surveys, there was plurality support (average = 45.2%) for operating only those plants that have been built. RFF (80/1) found that 23% of the public favored building more plants, 20% favored closing down all existing plants, and 11% could not select among the three choices. The UM surveys, however, found more support than did RFF for building more plants. Averaging across the five UM surveys, there was significantly more support for building more plants (average = 31.2%) than there was for closing down all plants (average = 15.0%).

Other survey organizations have not provided respondents with three choices regarding nuclear power, but instead have asked respondents whether they favor shutting down all nuclear power plants at this time or as soon as possible (see Table 4). All nine surveys since April 1979 that asked this question found majority opposition toward permanently shutting down all nuclear power plants. Even during the Three Mile Island accident, Gallup (79/4) and Harris (79/4) found that the public strongly opposed shutting down all plants. Averaging across the seven surveys conducted since the TMI accident in 1979, there was an average of 16.0% support for closing down all plants, 75.3% opposition toward closing all plants, and 8.6% were undecided. Thus the U.S. public does not favor shutting down existing nuclear power plants.

However, there is more public support for shutting down nuclear power plants for an indefinite time period until more is known about nuclear power plant safety (see Table 5). The NBC (79/4) and Harris (79/4; 79/5; 80/12) surveys found comparable results. Averaging across all four surveys, 53.3% of the public favored continued power plant operation, 42.8% favored closing down all plants until more is known about power plant safety, and 4.0% were uncertain.

If the question put to respondents is less restrictive than shutting down plants--that is, "cutting back" on operations--there is plurality to majority support for the restriction (see Table 6). The Gallup surveys have shown great fluctuation from 1976 through 1980 on this attitude item. In Gallup (76/6), 40% favored cutting back operations until more strict regulations could be put into practice, 34% believed that the plants were safe enough with present safety regulations to allow continued operation, and 26% were undecided. Immediately following the TMI accident, however, Gallup (79/4) found that a 66% majority of the public favored cutting back operations, 24% favored continued operations, and 10% were

TABLE 4
PERCENTAGE OF SUPPORT, OPPOSITION AND UNCERTAINTY TOWARD THE TOTAL AND PERMANENT CLOSURE OF ALL NUCLEAR POWER PLANTS

	Favor	Oppose	Uncertain
Gallup (79/4)[a]	25	64	11
Harris (79/4)[b]	15	79	6
RFF (80/1)[c]	20	69	11
UM (80/1)[d]	15	77	8
UM (80/4)[d]	17	74	9
UM (80/6)[d]	14	77	9
UM (80/9)[d]	13	78	9
UM (80/11)[d]	16	74	9
Harris (80/12)[b]	17	78	5

[a]"Would you favor or oppose shutting down all nuclear plants at this time?"

[b]"Do you approve or disapprove of the following policies for handling nuclear power in this country?--All nuclear power plants should be shut down permanently and no more allowed to be built."

[c]"We should stop building nuclear plants including those under construction and shut down the existing ones as soon as possible."

[d]"Close down all nuclear plants."

TABLE 5
PERCENTAGE OF SUPPORT, OPPOSITION AND UNCERTAINTY TOWARD CLOSING DOWN NUCLEAR POWER PLANTS

	NBC[a]	Harris[b]		
	(79/4)	(79/4)	(79/5)	(80/12)
Close down	43	40	43	45
Don't close down	51	57	54	51
Not sure	6	3	3	4

[a]"Should all nuclear power plants be closed down until questions about safety are answered?"

[b]"Do you approve or disapprove the following policies for handling nuclear power in this country?--All nuclear power plants in the country should be closed down until the federal government knows more about the safety risks involved in them."

TABLE 6
PERCENTAGE OF SUPPORT, OPPOSITION AND UNCERTAINTY TOWARD CUTTING BACK THE OPERATION OF NUCLEAR POWER PLANTS UNTIL MORE STRICT REGULATIONS CAN BE PUT INTO PRACTICE

	Gallup[a]			
	(76/6)	(79/4)	(79/6)	(80/1)
Safe enough	34	24	34	30
Cut back operations	40	66	40	55
Not sure	26	10	26	15

[a]"Do you feel that nuclear power plants operating today are safe enough with the present safety regulations, or do you feel that their operations should be cut back until more strict regulations can be put into practice?"

undecided. Two months later, however, the attitudes were exactly the same as in June 1976. Then by January 1980, they had again reversed themselves so that a 55% majority favored cutting back operations. Nonetheless, since 1976 there has always been at least plurality support for cutting back on the operation of nuclear power plants until more strict regulations can be put into practice.

In summary, about three quarters of the public opposes permanently closing all nuclear power plants. There is less strong (but still slight majority) opposition to closing all plants until questions of safety are answered. However, there is plurality to majority support for cutting back on the operation of nuclear power plants until more strict safety regulations can be put into place. When given a choice among three alternatives, over a 40% plurality of the public favors operating only the current plants, about 30% of the public believes that more plants should be built in addition to the operation of current plants, and about 15% believe that all nuclear plants should be closed down.

Beliefs Affecting Attitudes Toward Nuclear Power

In order to predict changes in nuclear power attitudes, it is not only necessary to know the history of those attitudes and how they have changed; it is also very important to know what beliefs about nuclear power influence nuclear power attitudes. Melber et al. (1977) used discriminant analysis to predict the general attitudes on the basis of nuclear power beliefs. The data set used was formed by combining two Harris (75/4; 76/7) surveys. Rankin et al. (1981) used regression analysis to predict a respondent's attitude toward constructing a local power plant by using nuclear beliefs from the ARB (80/6) survey data. Although the surveys did not use comparable belief items, the findings are still somewhat similar.

Melber et al. (1977) found that the best predictor of general nuclear power attitudes was the respondent's belief about power plant safety. The second best predictor was one's acceptance of nuclear power as a function of the cost of nuclear-generated electricity. The third best predictor was one's belief as to whether nuclear power is a reliable form of energy for the United States in the long run. The fourth best predictor was another belief about the cost of electricity from nuclear power, the fifth best predictor was a belief about pollution from nuclear power, and the sixth best predictor was one's belief about the magnitude of the radioactive waste disposal problem. Other variables also entered the prediction equation, but with increasingly less influence.

Rankin et al. (1981) used multiple regression analysis to predict local power plant acceptance using nuclear power beliefs. They found that the strongest determinant of nuclear attitude was, again, one's belief about nuclear power plant safety. Of almost equal importance was one's belief about the need for nuclear power to free the U.S. from relying on Arab oil. Of less importance in determining local power plant acceptance were the following (from most to least important): a belief as to whether the government does a good job checking on the safety of nuclear plants; confidence in the government's ability to see to it that nuclear plants are built safely; a belief about the cost of nuclear-generated electricity; a belief about whether nuclear power plant equipment is well designed and safe; concern about radioactive waste disposal; and confidence in nuclear scientists and engineers.

In summary, beliefs about the safety of nuclear power plants are the most important factors in influencing nuclear power attitudes. These are followed in importance by beliefs regarding the economics of nuclear power and by beliefs about nuclear power being a reliable long-term energy source that can help free the U.S. from dependence on foreign energy sources. Beliefs about nuclear power plant pollution and radioactive waste disposal also have some influence on nuclear power attitudes.

SUMMARY AND DISCUSSION

Summary

A plurality to a majority of the public supported the general concept of constructing more nuclear power plants from 1971 through April 1979. Immediately following the Three Mile Island accident in April 1979, opposition was stronger than support for a short period of time. In

1980-81, there was generally more support than opposition for constructing additional nuclear power plants in the United States, but support had become significantly lower and opposition had become significantly higher than was the case before the TMI accident.

In the early 1970s, the public supported the construction of a local nuclear power plant by a two-to-one margin. This attitude gradually changed during the 1970s, so that opposition now outweighs support by about two to one. These changes in attitudes were apparent even before TMI.

The public has also shown some willingness to support restrictions on nuclear power. A plurality to a majority of the public favors cutting back nuclear operations until more strict safety regulations can be put into place. However, a slight majority of the public opposes closing down nuclear power plants until certain safety questions have been answered. In addition, a large majority of the public opposes shutting down all nuclear power plants. When given three alternatives to choose from, about a 45% plurality of the public favors operating only existing nuclear power plants, about 30% favor building more plants, about 15% favor shutting down all plants, and the remainder are undecided.

In analyzing the influence of specific beliefs on attitudes toward nuclear power, we have found beliefs about the safety of nuclear power plants to be the most important by far. Beliefs about the economics of nuclear power were also important, as were beliefs about nuclear power being a reliable long-term energy supply that can help free the U.S. from foreign energy sources. Finally, beliefs about pollution from nuclear power plants and about the seriousness of the waste disposal problem also influence nuclear attitudes.

Discussion

Much is available in the way of survey data that bear on the public's views toward nuclear power and its continued development. Of importance now are the conclusions that can be drawn with regard to the future of nuclear power development. First, we wish to draw the obvious but very important conclusion that nuclear-related beliefs and attitudes can change. Support for local plant construction decreased gradually and significantly through the 1970s, while opposition increased. Attitudes toward general nuclear power plant construction remained relatively stable, with minor fluctuations, until the accident at TMI. At that time, attitudes became less pronuclear and more antinuclear. Thus significant events have shown the ability to influence beliefs and attitudes toward nuclear power.

This leads to a second and equally obvious conclusion that these beliefs and attitudes will likely change in the future if significant nuclear-related events occur. What might these events be, and what effects would they be likely to have? Our research has shown that reactor safety concerns, energy supply concerns, and economic concerns are the largest determinants of nuclear attitudes. Thus future reactor accidents could have a further negative impact on public acceptance of nuclear power, especially if any accidents were to occur within several years of TMI. On the other hand, if no major reactor accidents occur over the next several years, the TMI accident may be gradually forgotten, and belief in a history of safe reactor operation could increase.

This change toward more positive attitudes would be even more likely to occur if two other events were to happen. One is that additional research be conducted on reactor safety, because the belief that the government is acting to guarantee reactor safety is a secondary determinant of nuclear attitudes. Second is that the government be perceived as strongly regulating the safe construction and operation of nuclear power plants, since this belief was also shown to be a secondary determinant of attitudes toward nuclear power. With regard to safety-related beliefs and their effects, however, we would have to conclude that it would be much easier for nuclear attitudes suddenly to become significantly more antinuclear because of one large accident (or a series of smaller accidents) than it would be for nuclear attitudes to become significantly more pronuclear, whether suddenly or as a longer-term result of safe operations coupled with strict regulation and safety-related research.

Sudden or gradual changes in a pronuclear direction are more likely to result from events related to energy supply, since our analysis found that nuclear attitudes are related to such issues. However, Melber et al. (1977) found that one's nuclear attitude is not related to one's belief about whether a general energy shortage exists, although Rankin et al. (1981)

found that one's nuclear attitude is related to one's energy shortage concerns if the shortages deal with energy independence issues. Thus it may be that only certain types of energy supply issues will influence nuclear attitudes.

Because nuclear power is likely to be evaluated relative to other energy sources, advances or setbacks in the development of these sources could have an impact on the relative favorability of nuclear power. If solar electricity production were to achieve technological breakthroughs with regard to cost, for example, so that it became cost-competitive with nuclear power, there appears to be little doubt that the solar option would be favored unless other strongly negative conditions prevailed.

In the public's mind, however, coal and nuclear plants are more likely to be viewed as the two major possibilities for present-day power plant construction. In addition, public acceptance of coal plants has been increasing over the past several years, while public acceptance of nuclear plants has been decreasing. Thus events that would enhance public beliefs about coal plants would increase public acceptance of a local coal plant relative to acceptance of a local nuclear plant. Such enhancement could come through technological breakthroughs--for example, a low-cost desulfurization process--or through regulatory changes such as a lowering of air pollution standards that would make coal more economically attractive than nuclear power. On the other hand, technological discoveries or regulatory changes that would increase the safety or lower the cost of nuclear power relative to coal plants would increase nuclear power's relative attractiveness. At least at this time, however, most persons would rather have a coal plant than a nuclear plant built in their area.

The preceding paragraph has speculated about future choices regarding the type of power plant that will be acceptable to the public. What about the continued operation of existing nuclear power plants, and the licensing and operation of plants already under construction? We conclude that the public has strongly indicated its attitude that operating plants should continue to operate. This attitude is likely held for two main reasons that have been shown to be related to nuclear power attitude--that the energy is needed, and that the economic investment is too important simply to discard. It is likely that the public holds almost the same attitude toward other nuclear plants that are well into the construction phase. This leads to the final conclusion: Despite the public's recent hesitation toward nuclear power, the larger the U.S. nuclear industry becomes--both in terms of the relative amount of energy being produced, and in terms of economic investment--the less likely it is that the public will be willing to forego the nuclear option completely.

ACKNOWLEDGEMENTS

The original document from which these data were taken was prepared for the Waste Management Systems Studies Program of the Pacific Northwest Laboratory of the U.S. Department of Energy under contract DE-AC06-76RLO-1830. The authors would like to thank the Department of Energy for supporting this research.

FOOTNOTES

[1]Regression analysis is a statistical technique used to simplify the presentation of data. In Figure 1, for example, the variation in the percentage of respondents who favored nuclear power from 1974 through 1978 makes it hard to determine, through visual inspection alone, whether the percentage was increasing or staying about the same. Regression analysis determines which straight line drawn through the data points best illustrates the overall trend of the data. The "slope" of the line can be upward or downward, or the line can be level, in which case it is said to have "zero slope." A statistical test is used to determine whether the slope of the line is significantly greater or less than zero. If the slope of the line is not statistically different from zero, then one variable is not significantly related to the other. In the present case, for example, zero slope means that attitudes did not show a statistically interpretable trend over time.

[2]The standard deviation is a measure of how widely the individual data points vary around the average value (mean) of all data pints combined. Approximately 70% of all data points are within one standard deviation above or below the mean; approximately 95% of all the data points are within two standard deviations above or below the mean.

[3]The *t*-test is used to determine whether the differences found between the mean values of two sets of data are simply due to chance or are "real" (i.e., nonrandom) differences between the data sets. The statement "$p < .001$" reads that the

probability (*p*) is less than one in one thousand (.001) that the observed differences between the sets of data are due to chance variation. The common practice is to accept any observed differences where $p < .05$ as being "statistically significant"--i.e., probably "real"--since there is only a 5% likelihood that these differences would be due to chance variation.

REFERENCES

Campbell, Donald T. and Julian C. Stanley
1963 *Experimental and Quasi-Experimental Designs for Research.* Chicago: Rand McNally.

Commoner, Barry
1984 "The Public Interest in Nuclear Power." Pp. 267-294 in William R. Freudenburg and Eugene A. Rosa (eds.), *Public Reactions to Nuclear Power: Are There Critical Masses?* Boulder, CO: Westview Press/American Association for the Advancement of Science.

Davis, W. Kenneth
1984 "Nuclear Power Under the Reagan Administration." Pp. 257-265 in William R. Freudenburg and Eugene A. Rosa (eds.), *Public Reactions to Nuclear Power: Are There Critical Masses?* Boulder, CO: Westview Press/American Association for the Advancement of Science.

Ebbin, Stephen and Raphael Kasper
1974 *Citizens Groups and the Nuclear Power Controversy.* Cambridge, MA: M.I.T. Press.

Farhar-Pilgrim, Barbara and William R. Freudenburg
1984 "Nuclear Energy in Perspective: A Comparative Assessment of the Public View." Pp. 183-203 in William R. Freudenburg and Eugene A. Rosa (eds.), *Public Reactions to Nuclear Power: Are There Critical Masses?* Boulder, CO: Westview Press/American Association for the Advancement of Science.

Freudenburg, William R. and Eugene A. Rosa (eds.)
1984a *Public Reactions to Nuclear Power: Are There Critical Masses?* Boulder, CO: Westview Press/American Association for the Advancement of Science.
1984b "Are the Masses Critical?" Pp. 331-348 in William R. Freudenburg and Eugene A. Rosa (eds.), *Public Reactions to Nuclear Power: Are There Critical Masses?* Boulder, CO: Westview Press/American Association for the Advancement of Science.

Lewis, Richard S.
1972 *The Nuclear-Power Rebellion: Citizens vs. the Atomic Industrial Establishment.* New York: Viking Press.

Mazur, Allan
1984 "Media Influences on Public Attitudes Toward Nuclear Power." Pp. 97-114 in William R. Freudenburg and Eugene A. Rosa (eds.), *Public Reactions to Nuclear Power: Are There Critical Masses?* Boulder, CO: Westview Press/American Association for the Advancement of Science.

Melber, Barbara D., Stanley M. Nealey, Joy Hammersla and William L. Rankin
1977 *Nuclear Power and the Public: Analysis of Collected Survey Research.* Seattle, WA: Battelle Human Affairs Research Centers (PNL-2430).

Rankin, William L., Barbara D. Melber, Thomas D. Overcast and Stanley M. Nealey
1981 *Nuclear Power and the Public: An Update of Collected Survey Research on Nuclear Power.* Seattle, WA: Battelle Human Affairs Research Centers (PNL-4048 and BHARC-400/81/027).

Rosa, Eugene A. and William R. Freudenburg
1984 "Nuclear Power at the Crossroads." Pp. 3-37 in William R. Freudenburg and Eugene A. Rosa (eds.), *Public Reactions to Nuclear Power: Are There Critical Masses?* Boulder, CO: Westview Press/American Association for the Advancement of Science.

Rosa, Eugene A., Marvin E. Olsen and Don A. Dillman
1984 "Public Views Toward National Energy Policy Strategies: Polarization or Compromise?" Pp. 69-93 in William R. Freudenburg and Eugene A. Rosa (eds.), *Public Reactions to Nuclear Power: Are There Critical Masses?* Boulder, CO: Westview Press/American Association for the Advancement of Science.

Schmidt, Fred H. and David Bodansky
1976 *The Fight over Nuclear Power.* San Francisco: Albion Publishing Co.

Eugene A. Rosa,
Marvin E. Olsen, Don A. Dillman

3. Public Views Toward National Energy Policy Strategies: Polarization or Compromise?

INTRODUCTION

The scientific and technical community, sharply divided over nuclear energy, has been engaged in a lengthy and often heated debate over the role of nuclear energy in meeting the nation's future energy needs. But while it is often assumed that the U.S. public is similarly divided over the nuclear option, previous work has not examined this assumption directly. Is the general public, in mirror reflection of the debate among experts, also sharply divided over the nuclear option?

To address this question properly, we must first recognize the larger context within which the nuclear debate takes place. The debate over nuclear energy does not stand in isolation, but is part of a far broader and more fundamental controversy over an optimum strategy for solving the nation's energy predicament. At the root of this broader controversy is the deeper question: Should the United States meet its future energy needs primarily through increased production or through decreased energy demand?

At one extreme in this broader controversy are those who argue that economic growth is synonymous with energy growth, emphasizing the historical link between national levels of economic activity and energy consumption. To ensure a

Pp. 69-93 in William R. Freudenburg and Eugene A. Rosa (eds., 1984)
Public Reactions to Nuclear Power: Are There Critical Masses?

continuation of economic growth, they argue, national policy should provide incentives for increased production, aiming toward a steady increase in the available supply of energy. Although increased production could be achieved from several alternative energy sources, nuclear power is usually viewed as the cornerstone of this position.

Adherents of the opposite position argue that energy-consuming practices in the United States result in the waste of vast amounts of energy resources and in serious environmental harm. They feel that the role of energy in economic prosperity is not rigid, arguing instead that economic growth and other national goals can be achieved with far lower energy inputs than in the past. In this view, national energy policy should emphasize a reduction in energy demand through improved efficiencies and other conservation measures. The resulting reduction in energy consumption would obviate the need for the expansion of nuclear energy.

The debate over nuclear energy, then, can be viewed as an offshoot of the larger debate over fundamental energy policy strategies. But this does not tell the whole story. The central figures in the national energy policy debate--scientists, engineers, energy company executives, public officials, and legislators--are often sharply divided over optimum energy strategies, and they have typically assumed that the public is similarly divided. Indeed, this assumption--that public sentiment is highly polarized, in mirror reflection of the polarization among energy experts--has become orthodoxy in the energy policy community.[1] Related assumptions are that the public's interests are more or less adequately represented by the active participants in the debate, and that the sharply divided nature of public sentiment will prolong the nuclear stalemate. In the words of Bupp and Derian:

> The opposition to nuclear power reveals a deep cleavage in Western society. Contrary to the assumptions of government and business leaders, the opposition is not likely to disappear when the facts are established and commonly understood. Resolution of the nuclear safety controversy depends less on whether the political and economic leadership of the industrial world is correct in its collective assessment of nuclear power than it does on whether

> this judgment is accepted as legitimate by their constituencies (Bupp and Derian, 1981:130).

Polarized debates, however, often ignore alternative or compromise positions that may be crucial to resolving controversy. The underlying debate over the broad strategy for resolving the national energy predicament is no exception. As one comprehensive policy study observes, "The best hope for achieving a workable national energy policy, in fact, lies in the strong likelihood that a large number of U.S. citizens fall in the broad spectrum *between* these opposing attitudes. Therein rests our optimism about achieving a nationwide consensus on energy policy" (Schurr et al., 1979:408).

In this context, the *actual* extent of public polarization over broad energy policy, and the extent to which that polarization is reflected in the nuclear debate, should be matters of considerable interest. Knowing the actual degree of polarization will enable us to make a more accurate assessment of the prospects for ending the nuclear stalemate. A sharply divided public will be more likely to prolong the stalemate, whereas prospects for a resolution are likely to be improved with a less polarized public.

In this chapter, we treat this issue as an empirical question, asking whether the orthodox view is supported by the evidence. Our analysis is devoted to four specific, researchable questions:

- Are public attitudes sharply divided over the choice between nuclear power and other energy options, especially conservation?
- If the public is so divided, is the division a reflection of the polarized debate in energy policy circles?
- Do most people prefer producing our way out of the nation's energy predicament primarily through the expansion of nuclear power?
- Alternatively, do most people favor reducing energy demand through an emphasis on conservation?

Locating the position of nuclear power in the controversy over broad policy strategy leads to four possible options for

FIGURE 1
A TYPOLOGY OF GENERAL PUBLIC ENERGY PREFERENCES

		Nuclear Choice	
		Oppose or Neutral	Favor or Strongly Favor
Conservation Choice	Oppose (Less than 4.0 on index of three items)	Neither No Strong Policy Preference	Pronuclear Nuclear Solution Only
	Favor (4.0 or more on index)	Proconservation Conservation Solution Only	Both Both Nuclear and Conservation

energy policy: (1) support for nuclear power and rejection of conservation; (2) support for conservation and rejection of nuclear power; (3) support for both conservation and nuclear power; and (4) support for neither (see Figure 1). For discussion purposes, it is convenient to refer to the positions as being *pronuclear, proconservation, both,* and *neither,* respectively.

EVIDENCE AND ANALYSIS

Public views toward nuclear power are most frequently assessed with national survey or issue-specific poll data[2] (see for example Chapter 2 of this volume, by Rankin and his colleagues, 1984, and Chapter 7, by Farhar-Pilgrim and Freudenburg, 1984). Often those polled are asked to respond to a dichotomous choice, such as "Do you favor or oppose the construction of more nuclear power plants?" Asking the question in this way may produce results that may make the public appear to be more polarized than it actually is. For example, recent data showing the public to be almost evenly divided on the question of whether or not to build more nuclear plants--with roughly 45% on each side--may be due in part to the way in which the question was asked. With a wider range of choices, or with the possibility of compromise positions, public responses may turn out to be less sharply divided.

National surveys and issue-specific poll data have other limitations that restrict their usefulness for addressing the research questions we have posed. They often limit the opportunity for making an *in-depth* examination of the social characteristics--such as demographic background factors--of the persons holding the various policy positions. Nor do they usually permit examination of several attitudes or preferences simultaneously. In this chapter we examine in detail the results of a recent survey that allows us to overcome some of these shortcomings. The survey, entitled "Energy Directions," was conducted in the spring of 1981 in ten western states and in the comparative eastern state of Pennsylvania. The sample was drawn from a population of 19 million households, or nearly 24% of all households in the United States.[3]

TABLE 1
PERCENT OF RESPONDENTS WHO FAVOR OR STRONGLY FAVOR TAKING SPECIFIED ACTIONS AS A WAY OF MEETING FUTURE U.S. ENERGY NEEDS

	Percent		
Choice	Favor	Strongly Favor	Total
More use of solar energy	40.0	52.5	92.5
More exploration for oil in the United States	50.4	39.6	90.0
More use of wind energy	49.1	39.4	88.5
More use of western coal	50.0	21.2	71.2
More use of oil from western shale	53.1	16.9	70.0
Reduce energy use in homes	51.1	17.5	68.6
Reduce energy use in business and industry	41.1	15.4	55.4
Reduce energy use in individual travel	41.8	11.3	53.1
More use of nuclear power	29.3	16.6	45.9

Nuclear Power and Conservation

Where in general do the people in the "Energy Directions" study stand on nuclear power? Support for nuclear power was measured with a single question that asked whether respondents strongly favored, favored, were neutral toward, opposed, or strongly opposed more use of nuclear power as a way of helping meet our country's future energy needs. Our data show 46% favoring more use of nuclear power, with 31% being opposed and 23% being neutral. While attracting a plurality of support, nuclear power is still opposed by a sizable minority.

Public support for nuclear power appears to be considerably weaker when it is compared with other production options or with conservation. Table 1 compares support for nuclear power with eight other energy policy options, each of which was asked with identical response categories.

Compared to the other options, nuclear power is the least-favored choice. The five other energy production options overwhelm nuclear energy in popularity, attracting a sizable majority of public support. Ninety-two percent favor solar energy, 90% approve of further exploration for U.S. oil, 89% support the use of wind energy, and 70% agree to the development of western coal or oil shale. Furthermore, all three conservation items attract at least a majority of favorable responses. Sixty-nine percent favor reduction of energy use in homes, 56% favor reduction of energy use in business and industry, and 53% of the public is apparently even willing to forego some personal travel before it accepts nuclear power.[4]

PUBLIC STANCES ON THE FOUR POLICY OPTIONS

To address the specific research questions posed at the outset, we cross-classified responses to the nuclear power and conservation questions to produce the four-category typology shown earlier in Figure 1. With this typology respondents can be categorized according to their position on each of the four possible policy options.

TABLE 2
PREFERENCE FOR EACH OF THE
FOUR ENERGY POLICY POSITIONS AMONG
WESTERN REGION, PENNSYLVANIA RESPONDENTS,
AND A SEPARATE NATIONAL SAMPLE

	Percent Taking Each Policy Position			
Policy Position	Criterion of 3.7[a]	Criterion of 4.0[a]	Average	CEQ Study[b]
Western Region				
Pronuclear	25%	32%	29%	28%
Proconservation	34%	26%	30%	34%
Both	22%	15%	18%	14%
Neither	19%	27%	23%	24%
Pennsylvania				
Pronuclear	17%	22%	19%	
Pronconservation	29%	27%	33%	
Both	17%	12%	15%	
Neither	28%	40%	34%	

[a]Mean of summed responses to each conservation item where 1 = strongly oppose, 2 = oppose, 3 = neutral, 4 = favor, and 5 = strongly favor.

[b]Data from the study conducted for the U.S. Council on Environmental Quality by Roper and Cantril with a national probability sample of adults 18 years and older, January-March 1980. (See Chapter 6 of this volume, by Mitchell, 1984, for a further description of the study.) Instructions to respondents were: "Now, I am going to read you some phrases that describe different kinds of interests people have. As I read each one, would you please tell me whether it definitely applies to you, or only somewhat, or not at all?" Included in the seven phrases read were (1) Someone who is antinuclear, and (2) Someone who is pronuclear. Six categories of responses resulted with the following percentages: (1) 19% definitely antinuclear; (2) 15% somewhat antinuclear; (3) 14% both (somewhat anti- and somewhat pro-); (4) 24% neither; (5) 15% somewhat pronuclear; and (6) 13% definitely pronuclear. The percentages presented in the table were arrived at by combining the definitely and somewhat antinuclear, and the definitely and somewhat pronuclear categories.

To arrive at this categorization, it was necessary to index the responses to the three conservation items. This was done by scoring responses to each item as follows: 1 = strongly oppose; 2 = oppose; 3 = neutral; 4 = favor; and 5 = strongly favor. Respondents who averaged 4.0 or greater are considered to be favorable toward conservation. However, use of the 4.0 criterion represents a rather stringent requirement, inasmuch as compilation of several items inevitably results in regression toward the mean. Therefore we also consider a slightly less stringent criterion of 3.7 on the conservation index in the discussion that follows.

The proportions of respondents who fall into each of the four energy policy categories, using both the 3.7 and 4.0 criteria, are shown in Table 2.

It is evident that the sizes of the various categories are affected by the criterion that is used. In the western region, using the lower 3.7 criterion, the proconservation category is largest with 34%, followed by the pronuclear category with 25%, support for both with 22%, and support for neither with 19%. With the higher 4.0 criterion, the pronuclear category becomes the largest with 32%, followed by neither with 27%, proconservation with 26%, and both with 15%. In Pennsylvania, slightly more people fall into the proconservation category and fewer people fall into the pronuclear category under either criterion--a finding that may reflect the continued aftermath of the Three Mile Island accident. Since reasonable arguments can be made for using both of these criteria for identifying people who are proconservation, it is useful to look at the averages of the two criteria, which are also reported in Table 2. Examined from this perspective, the proconservation and pronuclear categories are about equal in size in the western region, while the neither category is somewhat smaller and the both category is the smallest. In Pennsylvania, the proconservation and neither categories predominate with about equal-size memberships, followed by the pronuclear category and then by a relatively smaller both category.

If we also allow for a margin of error around each of these figures, given the possibility of sampling variations, our safest overall conclusion is that all four energy policy positions are well represented both in the western region and in Pennsylvania, with each category containing between one-sixth and one-third of the total population. It is also apparent that the combined conservation-nuclear position is somewhat less popular than the others.

Our results become even more interesting when they are compared to a national probability sample of adult households taken one year earlier by the U.S. Council on Environmental Quality (Mitchell, 1980). Although questions asked in these two studies had vastly different wording, the percentages of people in the respective response categories are closely comparable across the two studies. Allowing again for a margin of error due to sampling variations, the results may be considered essentially identical. Thus the sizable proportion of the public in each of the four categories is apparently not a regional phenomenon, nor necessarily a function of one sample point in time.

Category Characteristics

Since the energy policy positions represented by our four categories all attract considerable numbers of supporters, our next concern is to describe the major demographic and socioeconomic characteristics of the members of each category. The descriptive characteristics examined here are sex, age, education, occupation, annual household income, type of residence, home ownership status, and length of time in the present residence.

To simplify the data presentation, two limitations are imposed throughout. First, only data for the more stringent 4.0 criterion for conservers are reported. We also conducted all of these analyses using the 3.7 criterion, but discovered that the characteristics of the members of each category were approximately the same regardless of the criterion level used. Second, only data for the western region are reported, since it was the primary concern of this study. With only a few minor exceptions, the characteristics of the category members are approximately the same in Pennsylvania as in the West.

Data describing the members of each policy category in the western region in terms of the above eight factors are given in Table 3. No tests of statistical significance are reported since even small differences tend to be significant at a high level of confidence in samples of this size. We also omit coefficients to indicate the strengths of the relationships between the set of four categories and each descriptive factor, since we are interested in differences between the categories rather than in overall correlations of the four-category typology with the descriptive factors.

Category Profiles

Who are the people that hold each of the policy positions? Table 3 enables us to sketch profiles of the adherents to each position on the basis of their sociodemographic backgrounds. Pronuclear persons tend to be predominantly men, somewhat older, fairly high in educational attainment, predominantly in manual and clerical occupations, of moderately high income, and living in single-family homes that they have owned for considerable periods of time. The profile of persons in the both category is quite similar, although this group tends to be slightly younger, somewhat more educated, even more predominantly in the manual and clerical occupations, and earning slightly higher incomes.

These profiles must be resketched considerably when looking at the proconservation position. The conservation supporters include many more women and young people, as well as people who are better educated but who have somewhat lower incomes. Members of this group are also more likely to be living in rented multiple-family housing and to be more mobile geographically. Members of the neither category have a mixed profile; in some ways they most resemble the proconservation people, and in other ways the people taking the pronuclear position. Similar to proconservationists, they are more likely to be young and female. Similar to the pronuclear respondents, many have a high school education or less, hold manual occupations, have low to middle incomes, and live in single-family residences that they own.

In general, those who hold proconservation and pronuclear positions display a number of fairly distinctive characteristics that set them off from the rest of the population. Proconservationists are most notably young people with high educations and occupations, but with moderate incomes, while pronuclear persons are most notably men with lower-status jobs but high incomes who own their single-family homes. In contrast, persons in the both and neither categories are more representative of the total population, except that those in

TABLE 3
CHARACTERISTICS OF RESPONDENTS FAVORING EACH POLICY POSITION IN THE WESTERN REGION, USING THE 4.0 CRITERION FOR CONSERVERS

	Pro-Nuclear	Both	Pro-Conservation	Favor Neither
Sex				
Male	74%	75%	51%	56%
Female	26%	25%	49%	44%
Age				
Under 35	17%	19%	43%	35%
35 - 44	17%	18%	22%	21%
45 - 54	20%	18%	16%	16%
55 - 64	26%	24%	9%	14%
65 and older	21%	21%	10%	14%
Education				
Less than 12 years	12%	9%	7%	13%
High school graduate	26%	23%	16%	29%
Some college	24%	30%	30%	32%
College graduate	18%	16%	19%	13%
Graduate school	20%	22%	29%	13%
Occupation				
Manual	31%	25%	24%	35%
Clerical and sales	21%	26%	22%	24%
Managerial	17%	18%	10%	14%
Professional	28%	30%	40%	23%
Homemakers and students	3%	2%	4%	4%
Household Income				
Under $10,000	12%	10%	15%	19%
$10,000 - $19,999	21%	19%	25%	25%
$20,000 - $29,999	29%	30%	25%	25%
$30,000 - $39,999	11%	18%	17%	18%
$40,000 or higher	27%	24%	18%	13%
Type of Residence				
Single family	62%	62%	59%	63%
Multifamily	18%	22%	32%	22%
Other	20%	16%	9%	15%
Ownership Status				
Own	80%	76%	63%	71%
Rent	19%	23%	36%	28%
Length of Residence				
1 - 5 years	45%	49%	66%	50%
6 - 10 years	16%	19%	14%	23%
11 or more years	40%	32%	20%	27%

the latter category tend to have somewhat lower socioeconomic statuses.

Energy Opinions

We might reasonably expect persons in the four energy policy categories to hold relatively divergent views concerning the seriousness of the energy situation and the desirability of developing other energy sources. The validity of those expectations is examined in this section. Again, only data for the 4.0 conserver criterion and the western region are reported here, as shown in Table 4 and discussed below.

Seriousness of the U.S. Energy Situation. Nine-tenths of the proconservationists agree that the U.S. energy situation is either serious or very serious, whereas this view is held by only about three-fourths of the nuclear power supporters. Interestingly, however, persons in the combined category tend to agree with the proconservationists rather than with the pronuclear persons on this issue, while those in the neither category tend to agree with the nuclear supporters. In other words, although large majorities of the respondents in all four categories accept the fact that the United States is facing a serious energy problem, persons who favor increased efforts at conservation (regardless of their attitudes toward nuclear power development) are more likely to hold this view than those who do not favor conservation (regardless of their positions on nuclear energy).

Development of Other Energy Sources. As we have already seen in Table 1, nuclear energy is the least favored of the energy production options considered, while the other five options are favored by a clear majority of the respondents. Does this pattern of results hold for the four policy categories? The data in Table 4 show one striking consistency with the overall pattern. Regardless of policy position, there is overwhelming support for the further development of solar energy, with percentages ranging from 90% to 96%. In contrast, persons in these energy policy categories are sharply divided over the desirability of coal development. Less than half of the conservation supporters favor this option, while four-fifths of the nuclear supporters do. Persons in the both category are also relatively strong believers in the benefits of coal, while support for coal development is less pronounced among those in the neither category.

TABLE 4
ENERGY OPINIONS OF THE MEMBERS OF THE FOUR ENERGY POLICY CATEGORIES IN THE WESTERN REGION, USING THE 4.0 CRITERION FOR CONSERVATIONISTS

	Pro-nuclear	Both	Pro-conservation	Neither
Seriousness of the U.S. energy situation				
Serious	40%	39%	35%	48%
Very serious	33%	53%	56%	28%
Total	73%	92%	91%	75%
Favor development of other energy sources				
Solar	90%	95%	96%	90%
Coal	80%	74%	47%	60%
Domestic oil	94%	91%	79%	85%
Oil shale	79%	72%	57%	59%

Further development of domestic oil resources is very strongly endorsed by persons in the pronuclear and both categories, and favored slightly less by those in the neither category, and to an even lesser extent by proconservationists--although even those persons give relatively marked support to this energy option. Finally, oil shale development is favored by roughly three-fourths of those in the pronuclear and both categories, and by somewhat over half of the respondents in the proconservation and neither categories.

Two interesting generalizations can be drawn from these energy opinions. First, as suggested above, support for conservation efforts is markedly related to one's belief about the seriousness of the energy problem, so that persons in the proconservation and both categories tend to hold similar views on this question. In contrast, persons in the both category tend to side with the nuclear supporters in strongly favoring further development of all sources of energy, while more persons in the proconservation and neither categories express doubts about the wisdom of developing some energy sources. Secondly, in all four categories, large majorities favor increased development of all of these energy sources--with the single exception being proconservationists with regard to coal. Even persons who support neither conservation nor nuclear energy give rather strong endorsement to these other energy sources, indicating that they are not as negatively disposed toward energy development as one might assume.

Energy Conservation

Logic suggests that members of the proconservation group should express stronger support of conservation programs and be more willing to adopt conservation practices than persons in the pronuclear and neither categories--both of whom say they oppose or are neutral toward increased emphasis on conservation as a means of meeting our national energy needs. Since persons in the both category do favor conservation, however, they should resemble the proconservationists in their conservation views and actions. Table 5 allows us to examine this expectation.

Support of Conservation Programs. The "Energy Directions" questionnaire listed several kinds of relatively demanding conservation programs and asked respondents

TABLE 5
ENERGY CONSERVATION VIEWS AND ACTIONS OF THE MEMBERS OF THE FOUR ENERGY POLICY CATEGORIES IN THE WESTERN REGION, USING THE 4.0 CRITERION FOR CONSERVERS

	Pro-Nuclear	Both	Pro-Conservation	Favor Neither
Support Conservation Programs				
Require manufacturers to make energy efficient appliances	75%	92%	89%	86%
Provide larger tax credits for home conservation actions	76%	82%	89%	81%
Change building codes and mortgage requirements to encourage conservation	76%	86%	89%	79%
Provide larger tax credits for home solar heating and cooling	69%	83%	87%	76%
Keep the 55 MPH speed limit	54%	72%	79%	65%
Require utilities to raise their rates with increased consumption	54%	65%	75%	60%
Require home thermostats to be no higher than 65° in winter	26%	45%	53%	28%
Require all homes to pass an energy audit	27%	36%	40%	32%
Place higher taxes on gasoline	12%	17%	28%	13%

TABLE 5 (Continued)

	Pro-Nuclear	Both	Pro-Conservation	Favor Neither
Discourage building homes away from towns and cities to lessen travel	15%	23%	24%	14%
Could Reduce Home Energy Consumption by 25% if Necessary				
Probably	36%	49%	46%	44%
Definitely	15%	19%	23%	16%
Total	49%	68%	70%	59%
Had a Home Energy Audit				
Yes	9%	9%	8%	8%
Household Conservation Actions Taken				
Caulk and weatherstrip the house	63%	58%	52%	53%
Install ceiling insulation	58%	53%	44%	45%
Double-pane windows	24%	29%	23%	26%
Storm doors	22%	20%	18%	19%
Set thermostat at 65° or lower	47%	58%	67%	50%
Set water heater at 130° or lower	63%	63%	58%	58%
Close off unused rooms	59%	62%	64%	60%

whether or not they favored each one. The most notable fact about their responses is the high level of agreement across all four policy categories. As expected, people in the proconservation and both categories score virtually the same on most of the items, nuclear supporters have somewhat lower scores on all of the items, and those in the neither category tend to fall somewhat in between. But most of those category differences are relatively minor in comparison with the wide variation in support for the various conservation programs.

Several programs are favored by large majorities of the people in all four categories. These include requiring manufacturers to produce more energy efficient appliances, providing larger tax credits for energy-conserving home improvements, changing building codes and mortgage requirements to encourage new types of energy-saving housing, providing larger tax credits for installing home solar heating and cooling systems, keeping the 55 MPH speed limit, and requiring utilities to raise their rates as levels of consumption rise. All of these programs contain at least some mandatory elements, and none of them rely on free market principles or on public relations tactics. Yet a majority of the people who oppose or are neutral toward conservation as a general energy policy for the future nevertheless support these stringent conservation programs. Apparently their general policy position on energy conservation does not apply to many specific conservation measures.

At the same time, several other programs are rejected by a majority of the respondents in all categories, regardless of their position on conservation policies. These rejected programs include (1) requiring home thermostats to be set no higher than 65° in winter,[5] (2) requiring all homes to pass an energy audit, (3) placing higher taxes on gasoline, and (4) discouraging the building of homes away from towns and cities as a means of lessening travel distances. The common feature of these rejected programs is that they all would directly touch people's personal lifestyles and restrict their freedom of choice and action. In contrast, most of the accepted programs contained "macro" or structural constraints rather than personal ones (although the speed limit, a personal constraint, is an exception). Even people who believe that conservation should be our primary response to the energy problem nevertheless tend to reject constraints that impinge directly on their personal autonomy.

Reducing Home Energy Consumption by 25%. To measure people's personal commitment to energy conservation, we posed this hypothetical question: "If you were asked to reduce your energy consumption during the entire next year by one-fourth--that is, 25% less than you now consume--do you feel you could do it?" Nearly half of the respondents in all four categories said "probably," and another one-sixth to one-fifth said "definitely." Proconservationists were more likely than others to give a positive response to this question, but large majorities of persons in the both and neither categories also did, and even among pronuclear persons, almost half gave a positive reply. In short, a large proportion of the people in this country apparently feel that they can make a significant reduction in their energy use, and this feeling is largely unrelated to their position on energy conservation policies.

Home Energy Audits. Having a home energy audit is often a critical first step toward taking household conservation actions. However, less than one-tenth of all of the respondents in this study have taken that step, regardless of their overall energy policy position.

Household Conservation Actions. With five of the seven actions examined here, people in the pronuclear and neither categories--who are opposed or neutral toward a general policy of energy conservation as a means of meeting our energy needs--are more likely than people in the proconservation category to have taken such actions in their own home. Only on the actions of turning down the thermostat and closing off unused rooms do proconservationists score higher than others. Persons in the both category also tend to score high on most of these conservation actions. In other words, even when people are opposed to energy conservation as an energy policy, they are very likely to report taking household conservation actions. Apparently they are not rejecting the idea of conserving energy, but just disagree with the proposal to make it our national energy policy. The lower levels of conservation actions among proconservationists, meanwhile, are probably explained by their relatively modest incomes, nonhomeownership status, and frequent mobility, rather than by any kind of objection to taking household conservation actions.

The apparent lesson to be learned from this analysis of energy conservation views and actions is that people's broad policy positions--such as favoring or opposing conservation as a national energy policy--have only minor effects on their attitudes toward specific energy conservation programs, their willingness to reduce their own energy consumption, and their own adoption of household energy-conserving actions. From this we might conclude that the presumed basic dispute between proponents of "supply" versus "demand" energy strategies is probably more a debate over broad ideologies and policy strategies than one over the importance of conserving energy.

SUMMARY AND CONCLUSIONS

We can now return to the original question that prompted this study: Is the public as sharply divided over nuclear power as the prevailing orthodoxy in energy policy circles asserts? Since we divided the question into four parts, we address each in turn:

- About 60% of the U.S. public is polarized in the controversy over nuclear energy versus conservation as a national energy policy, with the two sides of the issue receiving equal support. At the same time, about one-fifth of the public wants to pursue both energy options and another one-fifth opposes both.

- The underlying issue of increased energy production versus reduced consumption cannot be reduced to a simple dichotomy in the public viewpoint. At least 40% of the public is committed to taking neither of these broad options.

- A substantial majority of the public prefers to develop all other energy sources before going further with nuclear development. Almost all respondents favor more use of solar energy, regardless of their position on the nuclear/conservation controversy, and large majorities also favor greater development of other energy sources such as coal and oil shale.

- At the same time, support for energy conservation is also very strong among the respondents, regardless of their positions on the nuclear energy issue. Although only about half of the public thinks that energy conservation should be the foundation of national energy policy, large minorities of people support a variety of stringent conservation program proposals, and sizable numbers report taking conservation actions in their homes.

The principal conclusion to be drawn from our analysis is that the controversy between expanding nuclear energy and increasing energy conservation is considerably more complicated than it is often assumed to be. Contrary to what appears to be the orthodox view in the energy policy community, the public is not composed of two opposing camps. Rather, the public's energy policy preferences consist of a blend of acceptable energy supply sources and conservation measures. Solar energy, attracting virtually no serious opposition to its further development, is a particularly acceptable source. The public also wants to see the expansion of other energy sources, such as coal, oil and oil shale, but is not eager to see any further construction of nuclear power plants. At the same time, the public takes energy conservation quite seriously, would like the federal government to establish a variety of effective energy conservation programs, and reports having taken a number of energy conservation actions already.

Implications for National Energy Policy

Our principal conclusion--that the public is less polarized over nuclear power than is commonly assumed--might lead one to conclude that the public climate is now propitious for an accelerated expansion of nuclear power. In our judgment, this would be a misreading of the evidence. Nuclear power does not attract unequivocal support from the public. Energy conservation, meanwhile, has apparently caught on with many Americans who find it far more acceptable than the nuclear option.

This evidence suggests that a national policy which emphasizes differences between nuclear power and conservation in strikingly oppositional terms seems destined to gain less public support than a policy which makes room for both options. If the public resources for further development of nuclear power come at the expense of conservation programs, this is not likely to attract widespread public support. Indeed, the evidence we have examined suggests the likelihood of just the opposite effect. Devoting major efforts toward developing nuclear power at the expense of conservation may very well prolong the high level of opposition to nuclear power.

A necessary condition for ending the nuclear stalemate is the eventual resolution of the perennial problems that have plagued this technology--problems of reactor safety, risks associated with low-level doses of radiation, and the problem of radioactive waste disposal. Added to these, skyrocketing costs and construction delays will need to be brought under control. The likelihood that all of these problems can be solved in the near future is not great, whatever may be the enthusiasm of the national administration and the nuclear industry.

Even if these problems were solved, that would not necessarily open the way for the unbridled expansion of nuclear energy. The importance of public sentiment, the theme underscored in this volume, cannot be ignored. National energy policy can either prolong the nuclear stalemate or contribute to its end, depending on the way in which the public viewpoint is considered in the process of policy implementation. To continue to ignore the public will be to ignore an important condition for ending the nuclear stalemate.

Given these circumstances, what is a reasonable strategy for creating a national consensus on energy policy? Since the perennial problems facing the nuclear industry persist, and since there is a significant amount of continuing public opposition to nuclear power, a policy calling for rapid nuclear expansion may be ill-advised. At the same time, however, there is a high level of support for conservation programs, and many Americans already appear to be taking conservation actions. One effective policy strategy, then, might be to buy the nation time for resolving the key features of the nuclear debate, through renewed energy conservation efforts, including a continuation of government programs that are effective (Rosa, 1978). These efforts might profitably be coupled with a cautious and limited--but definitely not strong--emphasis on further expansion of nuclear energy.

ACKNOWLEDGEMENTS

This paper resulted from research conducted under Washington State University Agricultural Research Center Project 0538, contributing to Western Region Project W-159, "The Consequences of Energy Conservation for Western Region Households." Additional support from the Western Rural Development Center, Oregon State University, Corvallis, Oregon, is gratefully acknowledged.

FOOTNOTES

[1]All three recent comprehensive national energy policy studies assert the existence of this polarization, and go on to outline the contours of the extreme positions (National Academy of Sciences, 1980; Ford Foundation Study Group, 1979; Schurr et al., 1979), although the Ford Foundation Study Group (1979:79) also notes, "The truth probably lies somewhere between these extreme views." In the letter of transmittal for the final report from the Committee on Nuclear and Alternative Energy Systems, Phillip Handler, then chairman of the National Research Council and president of the National Academy of Sciences, made a special point of noting that committee members began the study sharply polarized over nuclear energy, and that, "four years later, that polarization persists, and many of the same positions are still regularly defended" (National Academy of Sciences, 1980: vi).

[2]The difference between a poll and a survey lies in the nature of the questions asked and in some of the data analysis procedures, not in sampling techniques. Polls typically ask relatively straightforward opinion and attitude questions, and limit their reports to descriptive findings. Surveys generally explore topics in greater detail and depth, usually with the goal of explaining the underlying causes of the attitudes or actions being studied.

[3]The survey was implemented through the Agricultural Experiment Stations of the ten participating states in the western region--Arizona, California, Colorado, Idaho, Montana, Nevada, Oregon, Utah, Washington and Wyoming--and the station in the eastern state, Pennsylvania. It was conducted under Western Region Project W-159, "Consequences of Energy Conservation Policies for Western Region Households," with additional support from the Western Rural Development Center located at Oregon State University, Corvallis, Oregon. The

questionnaires were mailed to a total of 17,213 households--15,047 in the ten-state western region, and 2166 in Pennsylvania. A disproportionate stratified sampling technique was used, with 50% of the contacts in each state being with metropolitan households and 50% non-metropolitan households. The Total Design Method for conducting mail surveys was followed (Dillman, 1978), yielding a total of 9725 usable questionnaires, or an overall response rate of 56%. Weighting procedures were followed that ensured regional representativeness of all reported percentages and other measures. Details of the weighting procedures can be found in Rosa and Miethe (1981), and complete methodological details of the study are reported in Makela et al. (1982).

[4]This finding is all the more remarkable given that several recent studies have found reductions in personal transportation to be the least popular form of conservation with the American public (see Farhar et al., 1980).

[5]A bare majority of the conservationists support this measure, but overall, its support is well below 50%.

REFERENCES

Bupp, Irvin C. and Jean-Claude Derian
1981 *The Failed Promise of Nuclear Power: The Story of Light Water* (paperback edition). New York: Basic Books. (Originally published as *Light Water: How the Nuclear Dream Dissolved,* 1978).

Dillman, Don A.
1978 *Mail and Telephone Surveys: The Total Design Method*. New York: John Wiley and Sons.

Farhar, Barbara C., Charles T. Unseld, Rebecca Vories and Robin Crews
1980 "Public Opinion About Energy." *Annual Review of Energy* 5:141-172.

Farhar-Pilgrim, Barbara and William R. Freudenburg
1984 "Nuclear Energy in Perspective: A Comparative Assessment of the Public View." Pp. 183-203 in William R. Freudenburg and Eugene A. Rosa (eds.), *Public Reactions to Nuclear Power: Are There Critical Masses?* Boulder, CO: Westview Press/American Association for the Advancement of Science.

Ford Foundation Study Group
1979 *Energy: The Next Twenty Years*. Cambridge, MA: Ballinger.

Freudenburg, William R. and Eugene A. Rosa (eds.)
1984 *Public Reactions to Nuclear Power: Are There Critical Masses?* Boulder, CO: Westview Press/American Association for the Advancement of Science.

Makela, Carole, LaRae B. Chatelain, Don A. Dillman, Joye J. Dillman and Patricia A. Tripple
1982 "Energy Directions for the United States: A Western Perspective." Corvallis, OR: Western Rural Development Center.

Mitchell, Robert C.
1980 *Public Opinion on Environmental Issues: Results of a National Opinion Survey.* Washington, D.C.: President's Council on Environmental Quality.
1984 "Rationality and Irrationality in the Public's Perception of Nuclear Power." Pp. 135-179 in William R. Freudenburg and Eugene A. Rosa (eds.), *Public Reactions to Nuclear Power: Are There Critical Masses?* Boulder, CO: Westview Press/American Association for the Advancement of Science.

National Academy of Sciences
1980 *Energy in Transition: 1985-2010.* Final Report of the Committee on Nuclear and Alternative Energy Systems. San Francisco: W. H. Freeman and Co.

Rankin, William L., Stanley M. Nealey and Barbara D. Melber
1984 "Overview of National Attitudes Toward Nuclear Energy: A Longitudinal Analysis." Pp. 41-67 in William R. Freudenburg and Eugene A. Rosa (eds.), *Public Reactions to Nuclear Power: Are There Critical Masses?* Boulder, CO: Westview Press/American Association for the Advancement of Science.

Rosa, Eugene
1978 "The Public and the Energy Problem." *The Bulletin of the Atomic Scientists* 34:5-7.

Rosa, Eugene and Terance Miethe
1981 *Stratified Sampling and Weighting for Statistical Inference: A Case Example From a Large Mail Survey.* Pullman, WA: Social Research Center and Department of Sociology, Washington State University.

Schurr, Sam H., Joel Darmstadter, Harry Perry, William Ramsay and Milton Russell
1979 *Energy in America's Future: The Choices Before Us. A Study of the RFF National Energy Strategies Staff.* Baltimore: Johns Hopkins University Press.

Part 2

The Bases of Public Perceptions and Attitudes

Allan Mazur

4. Media Influences on Public Attitudes Toward Nuclear Power

INTRODUCTION

The products of science and technology have increasingly become the objects of controversy, with nuclear power being the leading topic of debate in recent years. The controversy over nuclear power can thus be regarded as one example from a large class of technical controversies that includes debates over fluoridation, Laetrile, recombinant DNA, the antiballistic missile, the supersonic transport (SST) and others.

For any given controversy, public attitudes toward the technology in question fluctuate over time, and dramatic shifts can sometimes take place in the proportions of the public favoring or opposing the technology. This pattern is clearly illustrated in Chapter 2 by Rankin and his colleagues (1984), where public opposition to nuclear power rose markedly after the accident at Three Mile Island. Other fluctuations in opinion both preceded and followed the accident.

What accounts for these fluctuations in public sentiment toward nuclear power? The goal of this chapter is to address this question, examining it within the context of other technical controversies and focusing particularly on the role of the media in shaping public attitudes.

Pp. 97-114 in William R. Freudenburg and Eugene A. Rosa (eds., 1984) *Public Reactions to Nuclear Power: Are There Critical Masses?*

SIMILARITIES ACROSS TECHNICAL CONTROVERSIES

Each technical controversy, of course, has its own unique features, and impressive differences exist between expensive and complex technologies such as nuclear power and the SST, on the one hand, and the cheap and simple addition of fluoride to drinking water, on the other. Nonetheless, there are striking similarities across these controversies; the similarities can be used as a basis for making meaningful comparisons among them and for understanding social influences common to them all. What follows is a highly condensed treatment; a fuller discussion can be found in *The Dynamics of Technical Controversy* (Mazur, 1981a).

In each case, the focal point of dispute is a product or process of science or technology, yet these controversies invariably have political, religious or other ideological implications as well. Some (not all) of the principal participants in each controversy are expert technologists or scientists. They appear on both sides of each issue, disagreeing not only on the proper policy to follow but also on relevant factual questions that seem to the puzzled lay public as if they should be matters of "objective" science. Even the rhetoric of partisans is similar across controversies.

Almost invariably, two distinct sides emerge in any technical controversy that has escalated to the point of widespread public attention. It is usually convenient and accurate to label one of these the "establishment" position, and the other the "challenge" position, which opposes that of the establishment. The establishment position is associated with some combination of government offices, perhaps the military, corporate industry, and professional organizations; the challenge side is associated with voluntary organizations such as environmental and consumer groups, or ad hoc groups formed specifically to promote a given protest or a set of related protests. The establishment side usually supports the technology while the challenge side opposes it, although there are occasional reversals as in the case of Laetrile.

Activists and the Wider Public

In describing public adherence to one side or another, it is crucial to differentiate between active participants in the controversy and the more passive members of the wider public who simply express their views in a referendum or in response to a question on an opinion poll, or who spend a day listening to rock music at a demonstration. The activists are a small and non-representative portion of the total population.

Most activists on the establishment side have become involved through the occupational activity of their workday jobs--for example, employees of the nuclear industry or of regulatory agencies. There are professionals on the challenge side as well, including writers, lawyers and lobbyists, but many challenge activists work for little or no pay.

These volunteer activists are from the higher strata of society, usually middle age or older, and are often active in community affairs. They are knowledgeable about the technology they oppose, and they consider its hazards to outweigh its benefits. They express their opposition within the context of larger ideological concerns: antifluoridationists fear the power of central government to impose mass medication; antinuclear activists are concerned about the degradation of the environment and corporate control of society. The challengers of each technology have a distinct political cast: antifluoridationists are usually conservative, while antinuclear activists are usually liberal. In contrast, members of the general public are usually neither knowledgeable nor concerned about technical controversies, and when they do take a position it is rarely correlated with their other political or ideological concerns (see Chapter 6 of this volume, by Mitchell, 1984, for corroborating evidence).

The Mass Media

The mass media are the primary link between active participants in a controversy and the wider public. A few recognized spokespersons for the establishment and challenge sides supply most of the information reported by major national news outlets such as *The New York Times* and *The Washington Post*, *Time* and *Newsweek*, the wire services, and television network news. The general public learns of the controversy either directly from the national media or from regional media that pick up and relay the national stories, sometimes supplemented by local sources (Figure 1). Thus

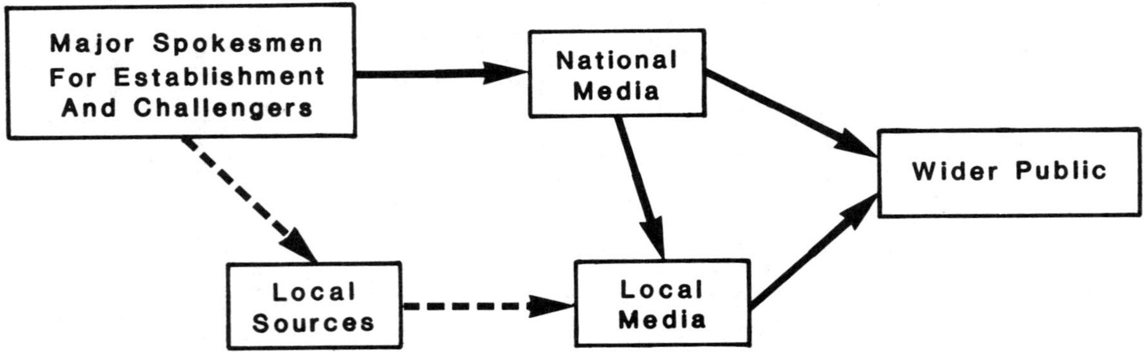

Figure 1. Flow of Information from Activists to the Wider Public.

information flows to the public through a narrow channel that is regulated by a small number of activists and media people.

The minutes of a half-hour television news program are preallocated to the world, national or local news, regular features, editorials, and advertisements. Newspapers and news magazines preallocate their page space in a similar way, with the responsibility for each section being given to an editor and associated personnel. These are stable formats, matched to the production organization, and they are changed only for unusual circumstances. Thus both the print and the electronic media have predetermined "news holes" that must be filled for each edition. The selection of those events of the day to be included or excluded, and the space and placement allocated to the included items, reflect a reasonably objective appraisal by editors of which among these events are the most "newsworthy." Nonetheless, other factors obviously intervene, such as the "human interest" in a particular item. The pre-existing working relationship between a news source and a reporter may also facilitate the placement of an item.

The Three Mile Island accident was obviously a newsworthy event, yet the quantity of coverage given to it far surpassed what was given two months later to the nation's worst airline accident, the crash of a DC-10 that killed 274 people. Among the factors contributing to the inordinate quantity of coverage were these: The power plant accident occurred at a time of public concern with nuclear power, so media people were sensitized to the issue and easily attracted to the event. By a quirk of timing, the antinuclear movie *The China Syndrome* was released to theaters across the nation just days before the accident. The event itself had great human interest--the week-long struggle with the bubble, the heroics of the nuclear engineers in averting disaster, the entry of the President, and the exit of the frightened populace--all of this had the drama of a soap opera, to be followed day after day. In addition, the plant site in Pennsylvania was easily accessible to reporters in nearby New York and Washington (Sandman and Paden, 1979). Each of these factors encouraged high coverage.

The quantity of media coverage given to a technical controversy can vary greatly from year to year. In the

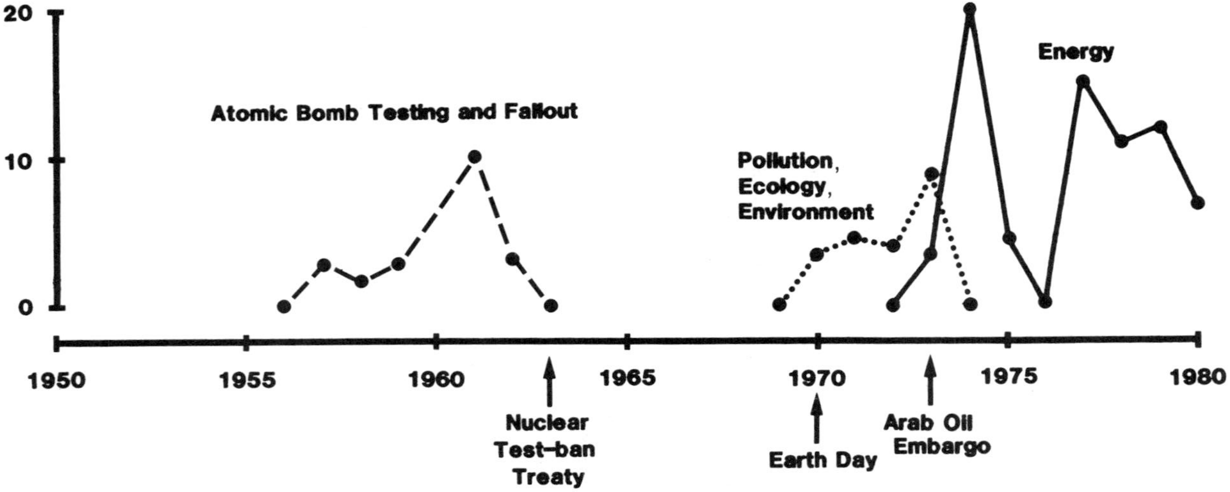

Figure 2. Large National Issues Related To Nuclear Power

Percentage of Gallup Poll Respondents Naming a Given Issue as "The Most Important Problem Facing the Country Today"

controversies I have studied, including nuclear power, these yearly fluctuations vary with the yearly level of activity by challengers. To a great extent, this covariance is simply due to media reporting of challenger activity. The more demonstrations, interventions and referenda in a given year, the more coverage. However, the link between activism and media coverage works in both directions, since challengers are more likely to make protests during periods when the media are responsive. At least one form of active protest--bomb threats against nuclear energy facilities--directly follows fluctuations in media coverage of nuclear power (Mazur, 1982). Similarly the proponents generate protechnology propaganda during these same periods when they are most likely to receive coverage. The symbiotic relationship between activism and media coverage was well illustrated during the months following the Three Mile Island accident, when the media showed unsurpassed receptivity to stories about nuclear power. Activists on both sides of the controversy spent a great deal of effort in feeding the hungry press until it was satiated.

Larger National Issues

Activists who are involved in a controversy as part of their occupational roles, such as employees of the nuclear industry or of environmental groups, may persist in these activities as a normal part of their routine working life. In contrast, volunteer activists must be sustained by their ideological concerns, the interest of the mass media and the social support of their comrades--all of which are transitory. The volunteer activists, more than occupational activists, require a momentum, a supportive "mood of the times," to maintain their commitment to the controversy in the face of competing demands on their resources.

Most of us have an intuitive sense that there are times when protest is "in the air"--as was the case for nuclear power in 1979 and 1980--and other times when it is not, when there is little enthusiasm for challenges or demonstrations.

If we look at the long histories of controversy over fluoridation and nuclear power (see, e.g., Figure 2), we can distinguish periods of waxing and waning protest. The periods of rising concern coincide with times of strong

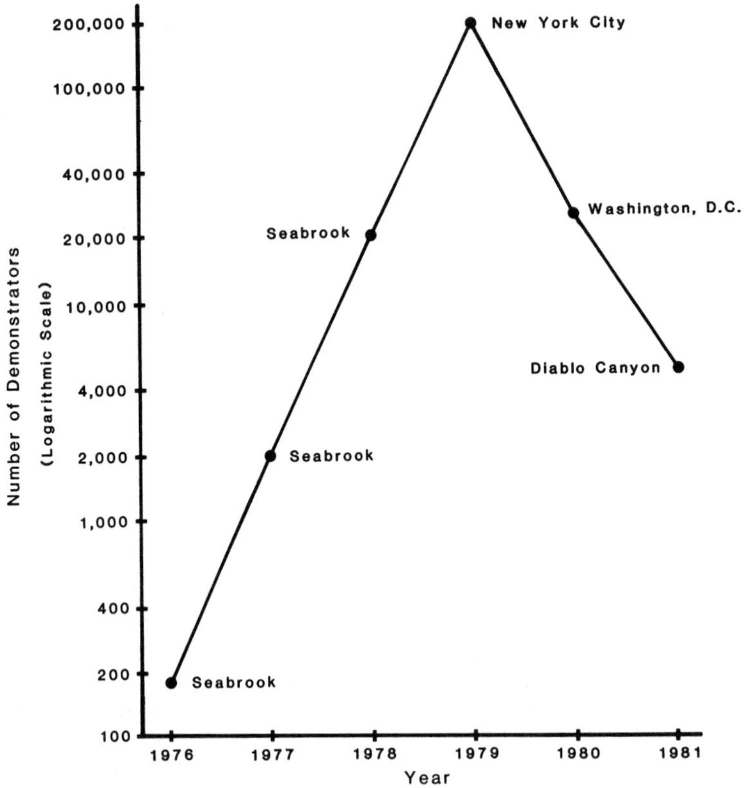

Figure 3. Largest Antinuclear Power Demonstration in Each Year

Note: Diablo Canyon protest of 1979 drew 20–25,000 people.
Source: The New York Times Index.

national interest in larger issues related to the technology under protest.

The first protests against nuclear power plants, in the early 1960s, coincided with national concern about atomic bomb testing and fallout. At that time, the rhetoric of protest specifically referred to radioactive fallout. When the United States and Russia signed a nuclear test-ban treaty in 1963, the protests against nuclear plants essentially ceased until the late 1960s, when they rose again as part of the environmental movement. As that concern diminished in the early 1970s, the Arab oil embargo of 1973 set off our national concern with energy.

We may visualize the nuclear power controversy as a surfer riding successive waves that are large national issues--first the fallout wave, then the environmental wave, and then the energy wave. Similarly, the fluoridation controversy "rode" the national concerns over communism and the environment. As each wave diminishes, the challengers fall unless they can catch another wave.

It is easy, of course, to look back over the course of a controversy and "fit" its peaks with various larger issues that were prominent at the time, since there is no shortage of candidate issues. To avoid the worst excesses of post hoc theorizing, I have set some methodological rules for the identification of these larger pertinent issues. First, I consider only those issues that are prominent enough to register on the periodic Gallup polls which ask, "What is the most important problem facing the country today?" This means there will be fewer than ten issues for a given sampling. Second, I require an obvious connection between the national issue and the technical controversy. Third, I require political compatibility between the technical controversy and the national issue. Thus national concern about communist subversion is an issue of the political right and explains the activity of conservative antifluoridationists, but it cannot explain the activity of antinuclear protestors on the political left.

If these larger national issues provide the momentum that sustains the interests of volunteer activists and the media in the technology under protest, then we would expect the protest to diminish as its larger issue recedes (Figure 3). Most recently, the antinuclear power movement has ridden the

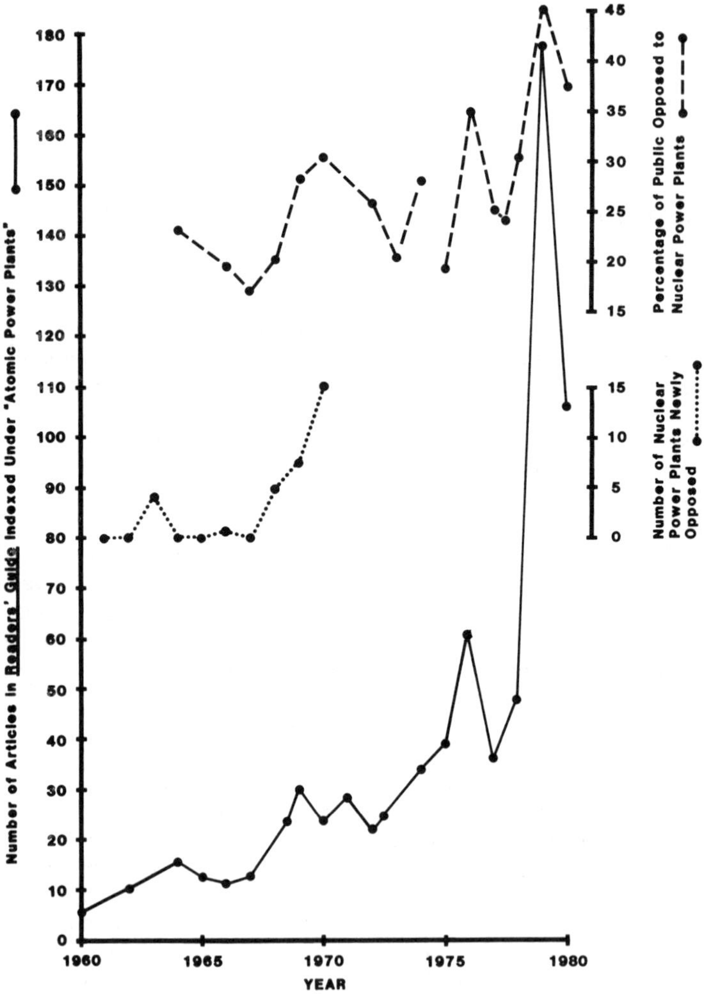

Figure 4. The Nuclear Power Plant Controversy

energy issue, which is now receding as a public concern according to Gallup and other opinion polls (Rosa, 1978; Harris, 1981). The nuclear power protest should diminish in parallel. Perhaps the unexpectedly low turnout at Diablo Canyon in September 1981 is symptomatic of the decline. The nuclear protest will be quiet in the near future unless there is a resurgent public concern with energy, or with another large issue related to nuclear power development.

The best candidate for a replacement issue is the rising public concern over nuclear arms, which is quite strong in Europe and may soon register on the American Gallup Poll of most important problems (see also the discussion in Chapter 11 of this volume, by Commoner, 1984). Nuclear weapons and nuclear power reactors have remained separate as issues since the early 1960s, however, perhaps because some of the major American spokespersons for arms control are supporters of nuclear power (Holden, 1982). My guess is that rising concern over nuclear war will not help the nuclear power protest much, but will shift the energies of liberal activists toward the MX and B-1, thus reducing the resources applied against power plants.[1]

MEDIA COVERAGE AFFECTS THE WIDER PUBLIC

The nation becomes a spectator to a technical controversy through the press and television, particularly during those periods when protest activity and media coverage are intense. It appears that as the quantity of coverage increases, public attitudes toward the technology (as measured in opinion polls) become increasingly *negative*. This is illustrated in Figure 4, which compares yearly fluctuations in magazine coverage of nuclear power with public opposition to nuclear power plants. The trends show corresponding peaks and valleys. A similar pattern appears in the fluoridation controversy (Figure 5).

These trend data are crude. The accident at Three Mile Island allows a finer view of the link between media coverage and public opinion, because in the year following the accident the Harris Poll took numerous opinion surveys, closely spaced in time (Mitchell, 1980). This fine-grained opinion

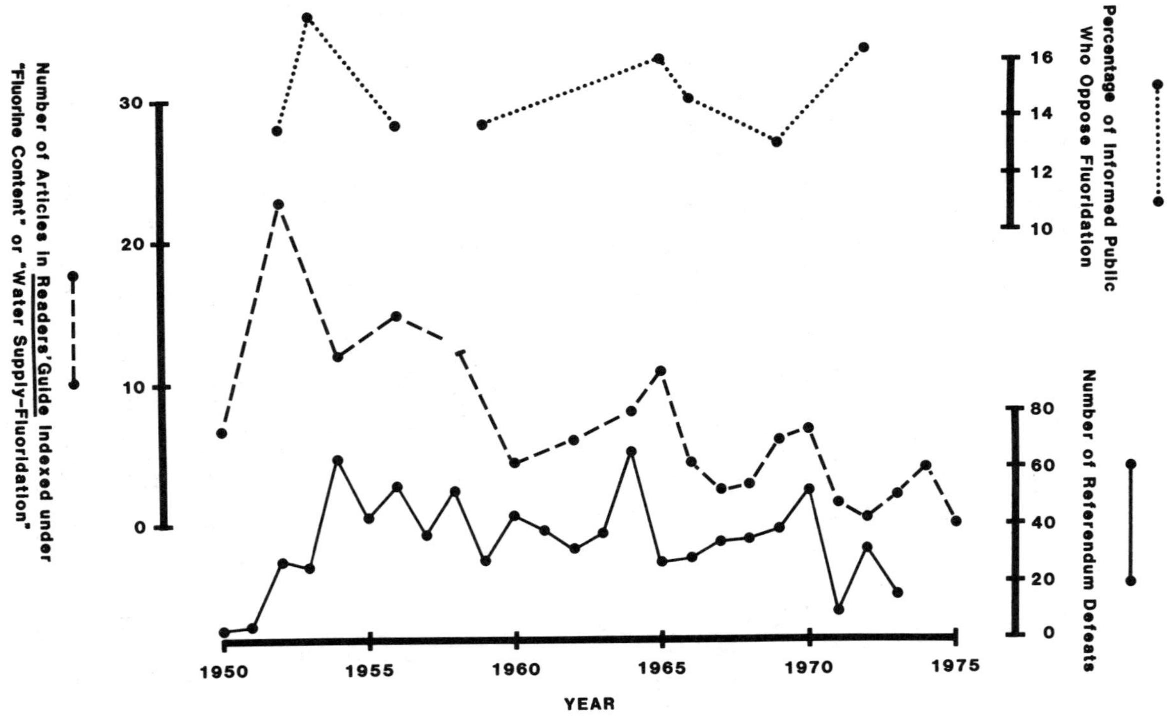

Figure 5. The Fluoridation Controversy

trend can be compared to (smoothed) weekly fluctuations in coverage of the accident on television network news, in *The New York Times*, and in the major news magazines, as shown in Figure 6.

The accident began on March 28, 1979, and in the week following almost 40% of television network evening news was devoted to it. Coverage in the news magazines was necessarily delayed by one week, but both *Time* and *Newsweek* ran cover stories in April. By June, the story had disappeared from the news magazines, and it appeared only in occasional short pieces on television until about October. At that time, there was a second, much smaller, rise in coverage to report the final work of the Kemeny Commission, which had been appointed by President Carter to investigate the accident. The Commission's report was released at the end of October, but the media had been anticipating it, reporting related events throughout October.

The proportion of the public opposing the building of more nuclear power plants rose sharply after the first burst of coverage (also see Chapter 2 of this volume, by Rankin and his colleagues, 1984). This is hardly surprising, since the specter of the accident would be expected to increase opposition regardless of any independent effect of the quantity of coverage. However, one would not expect on this basis alone that support for nuclear power would rebound within two months, as soon as the media coverage had fallen away--yet that is what happened. Furthermore, a clear short-term increase in public opposition appeared again during October and November, falling off in December, coinciding perfectly with the secondary peak of media coverage at the time of the Kemeny Commission's final work. The parallelism between these trends supports my contention that public opposition is a function of the quantity of media coverage.

Why does public opposition increase as media coverage increases, even in cases such as fluoridation where the media do not carry an obvious bias against the technology? Perhaps the prominence given to disputes between technical experts over the risks of the technology makes it appear dangerous to the public, as noted by Slovic and his colleagues (1984) in Chapter 5 of this volume. Persons experimentally exposed to both positive and negative arguments about fluoridation were more likely to oppose it than were persons

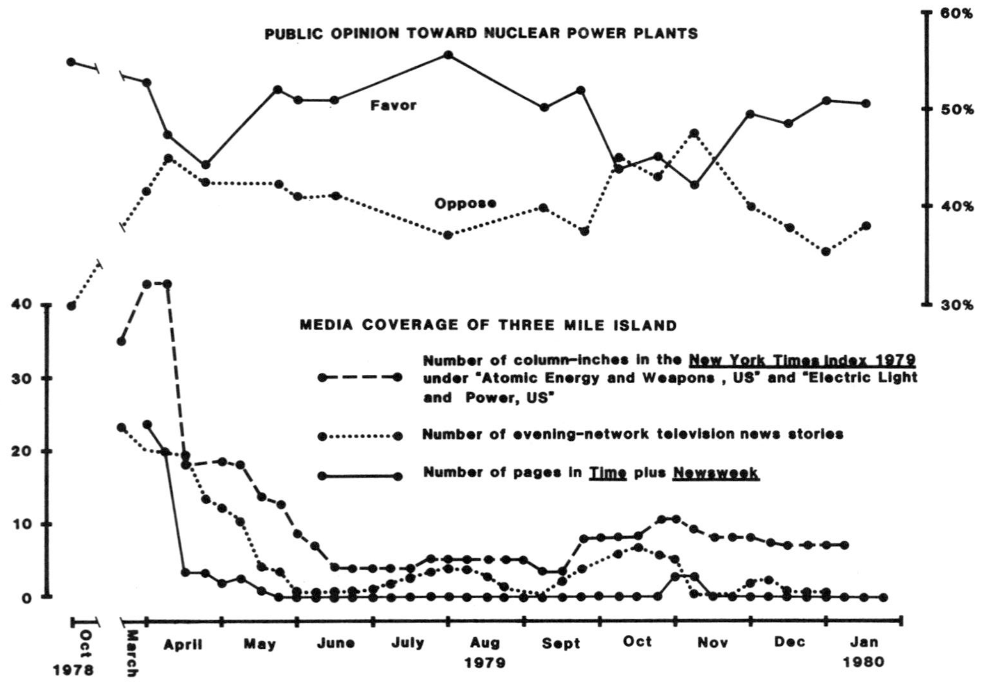

Figure 6. Public Opinion Toward Nuclear Power Plants and Media Coverage of the Three Mile Island Accident

who had not seen any of the arguments at all (Mueller, 1968). Fluoridation is more likely to be defeated in a referendum when there has been heated debate than when the campaign has been relatively quiet (Crain et al., 1969). During a local controversy over a proposed nuclear waste storage facility, residents who had heard or read about the controversy were more likely to oppose the facility and to consider it unsafe than were residents who had not heard about the controversy (Mazur and Conant, 1978). If doubt is raised about the safety of the technology, many in the public prefer to err on the side of safety, as if saying, "When in doubt, reject the technology--better safe than sorry" (Sapolsky, 1968).

THE DILEMMA OF RESPONSIBLE COVERAGE

In simpler times, the news media could be viewed as a passive reporter of daily events, so long as journalists' opinions were restricted to editorials. Increasingly we have come to see the media as an active shaper of the events that are reported. The press and television have certainly been full-fledged participants in the nuclear power controversy. Could they be anything else?

If public attitudes toward nuclear power are influenced by the simple quantity of media coverage, how does one report the controversy without at the same time affecting it? Certainly there are instances where one could argue whether particular journalistic practices were improper or not (President's Commission on the Accident at Three Mile Island, 1979), but the dilemma is deeper than that. My own recent study of newspaper reporting in the fluoridation controversy shows that even an ostensibly objective, even-handed story about the pros and cons of the technology tends to shift readers toward opposition (Mazur, 1981b).

My conclusions set me at odds with some other contributors to this volume. Chapters 10 and 12, by Davis (1984) and Szalay (1984), both reflect the long-standing belief of nuclear proponents that public opposition would fall away "if only the public knew the facts." This belief persists despite abundant research showing that *attitudes* toward nuclear power have little relationship to *knowledge* about it (Mazur, 1981a). But worse, for the proponents' point of view, is this: the more that they attempt to fill the media with stories about the low risks and high benefits of nuclear power, the more the media are bound to carry the opposition story as well. And the consequence of this heightened media coverage--even though it might be balanced or slightly pro-nuclear--is that public opposition will *increase*, not decrease. If the proponents of nuclear power wish to serve their own interests, the evidence suggests, the less said the better.

FOOTNOTES

[1]As this is being written in February 1983, it is possible to assess the predictions of the above two paragraphs. The Gallup and other polls show that energy has virtually disappeared as a public concern, while there has been rising concern over nuclear war. American nuclear plant proponents such as Hans Bethe have coalesced with opponents such as the Union of Concerned Scientists (UCS) in rising opposition toward the Reagan buildup of nuclear weapons. National protest against nuclear power plants has diminished, as predicted. The UCS newsletter of January 6, 1983, says of the power plant protest: "All seems quiet, so the attention of the American people and the media has moved on to other issues."

REFERENCES

Commoner, Barry

1984 "The Public Interest in Nuclear Power." Pp. 267-294 in William R. Freudenburg and Eugene A. Rosa (eds.), *Public Reactions to Nuclear Power: Are There Critical Masses?* Boulder, CO: Westview Press/American Association for the Advancement of Science.

Crain, Robert L., Elihu Katz and Donald B. Rosenthal

1969 *The Politics of Community Conflict.* Indianapolis: Bobbs-Merrill.

Davis, W. Kenneth

1984 "Nuclear Power Under the Reagan Administration." Pp. 257-265 in William R. Freudenburg and Eugene A. Rosa (eds.), *Public Reactions to Nuclear Power: Are There Critical Masses?* Boulder, CO: Westview Press/American Association for the Advancement of Science.

Freudenburg, William R. and Eugene A. Rosa (eds.)
1984 *Public Reactions to Nuclear Power: Are There Critical Masses?* Boulder, CO: Westview Press/American Association for the Advancement of Science.

Harris, Louis
1981 "Inflation Seen as Most Important Problem Facing Country." *The Harris Survey* 42 (May 25).

Holden, Constance
1982 "Antinuclear Movement Gains Momentum." *Science* 215 (February 12):878-880.

Mazur, Allan
1981a *The Dynamics of Technical Controversy* Washington, D.C.: Communications Press.
1981b "Unsuspected Bias in the Evenhanded Reporting of Technical Controversies." Unpublished paper. Syracuse, NY: Department of Sociology, Syracuse University.
1982 "Bomb Threats and the Mass Media: Evidence for a Theory of Suggestion." *American Sociological Review* 47 (#3, June):407-411.

Mazur, Allan and Beverlie Conant
1978 "Opposition to a Local Nuclear Waste Repository." *Social Studies of Science* 8:235-43.

Mitchell, Robert C.
1980 "Public Opinion and Nuclear Power Before and After Three Mile Island." *Resources* (January-April):5-7.
1984 "Rationality and Irrationality in the Public's Perception of Nuclear Power." Pp. 137-179 in William R. Freudenburg and Eugene A. Rosa (eds.), *Public Reactions to Nuclear Power: Are There Critical Masses?* Boulder, CO: Westview Press/American Association fo the Advancement of Science.

Mueller, John
1968 "Fluoridation Attitude Change." *American Journal of Public Health* 58:1876.

President's Commission on the Accident at Three Mile Island
1979 *The Accident at Three Mile Island: Report of the Public's Right to Information Task Force.* Washington, D.C.: U.S. Government Printing Office.

Rankin, William L., Stanley M. Nealey and Barbara D. Melber
1984 "Overview of National Attitudes Toward Nuclear Energy: A Longitudinal Analysis." Pp. 41-67 in William R. Freudenburg and Eugene A. Rosa (eds.), *Public Reactions to Nuclear Power: Are There Critical Masses?* Boulder, CO: Westview Press/American Association for the Advancement of Science.

Rosa, Eugene
1978 "The Public and the Energy Problem." *Bulletin of the Atomic Scientists* 34:5-7.

Sandman, Peter and M. Paden
1979 "At Three Mile Island." *Columbia Journalism Review* (July/August):43-58.

Sapolsky, Harvey
1968 "Science, Voters, and the Fluoridation Controversy." *Science* 162:427.

Slovic, Paul, Baruch Fischhoff and Sarah Lichtenstein
1984 "Perception and Acceptability of Risk from Energy Systems." Pp. 115-135 in William R. Freudenburg and Eugene A. Rosa (eds.), *Public Reactions to Nuclear Power: Are There Critical Masses?* Boulder, CO: Westview Press/American Association fo the Advancement of Science.

Szalay, Robert A.
1984 "A Nuclear Industry View of the Regulatory Climate." Pp. 295-306 in William R. Freudenburg and Eugene A. Rosa (eds.), *Public Reactions to Nuclear Power: Are There Critical Masses?* Boulder, CO: Westview Press/American Association for the Advancement of Science.

Paul Slovic,
Baruch Fischhoff, Sarah Lichtenstein

5. Perception and Acceptability of Risk from Energy Systems

INTRODUCTION

Over the next few decades, the success of energy production policies will depend vitally on public attitudes. Gradually it has become recognized that energy decisions cannot be determined by technical criteria alone. Social, psychological and political issues are crucial, and involve such questions as: "What kinds of risks should be accepted in exchange for what kinds of benefits? With how much uncertainty of specific kinds does the public care to live? How does one weigh the substantial routine impact of some technologies (for example, burning coal) with the small chance of a big disaster associated with others?" (Holdren, 1976:22).

Despite the importance of these questions, we lack knowledge about the social and psychological factors (goals, values, criteria, etc.) that determine public responses to technological risks in general or to risks from energy systems in particular. This is less because the problems in this area are difficult (which they are) than because very little time, effort, and research funding have been applied to them. As Rosa and Freudenburg (1984) note in the introductory chapter of this volume, one key reason for this neglect is the fact that scientists and policy makers have been slow to recognize the importance of public attitudes and perceptions, and have tended to view nuclear power development as being solely a technical matter, divorced from social considerations.

Pp. 115-135 in William R. Freudenburg and Eugene A. Rosa (eds., 1984)
Public Reactions to Nuclear Power: Are There Critical Masses?

Fortunately, a flurry of research activity in recent years has provided the beginnings of insight into the socio-psychological dynamics of societal risk taking. What follows is a brief review of that work. It starts with a discussion of the difficulties that human beings experience when attempting to estimate risks. With this as background, the remainder of the chapter discusses the perception and acceptance of risks from energy systems, with particular emphasis being placed on the public's response to nuclear power.

COPING INTELLECTUALLY WITH RISK

Evaluation of the risks from various energy systems requires, of experts and lay people alike, an appreciation of the probabilistic nature of the world and an ability to think intelligently about unlikely but consequential events. As Weinberg (1976:21) noted in the context of nuclear power, ". . . we certainly accept on faith that our human intellect is capable of dealing with this new source of energy." Recently, however, the faith of many who study human judgment and decision processes has been shaken.

Consider, for example, probabilistic reasoning. Due to its importance in decision making, the question of how people assess the probabilities of uncertain events has been a focus of research interest. This research indicates that even intelligent people systematically violate the principles of rational decision making when judging probabilities, making predictions, or otherwise attempting to cope with uncertainty. Frequently, these violations can be traced to the use of judgmental heuristics--mental strategies by which people reduce difficult judgments to simpler ones (Tversky and Kahneman, 1974). These heuristics are useful guides in some circumstances, but in others they lead to large and persistent biases with serious implications for decision making.

Availability Bias

This is not the place to pursue a full discussion of heuristics and biases in probabilistic thinking. Extensive reviews are available in a number of articles (Slovic, Fischhoff and Lichtenstein, 1977; Slovic, Kunreuther and White, 1974; Tversky and Kahneman, 1974). However, one heuristic bears mention here because of its special relevance to energy decisions. This is the "availability heuristic," whereby an event is judged to be likely or frequent if instances of it are easy to imagine or recall. Generally, frequent events are easier to recall than less frequent events, and likely occurrences are easier to imagine than unlikely ones. Thus availability is often an appropriate cue for judging frequency and probability. However, availability is also affected by numerous factors unrelated to likelihood. As a result, reliance on it may lead people to exaggerate the probabilities of events that are particularly recent, vivid, or emotionally salient.

The notion of availability is potentially one of the most important ideas for helping us to understand the distortions that occur in our perceptions of risks. For example, in discussing flood plain residents, Kates writes:

> A major limitation to human ability to use improved flood hazard information is a basic reliance on experience. Men on flood plains appear to be very much prisoners of their experience . . . . Recently experienced floods appear to set an upward bound to the size of loss with which managers believe they ought to be concerned (Kates, 1962: 140).

Kates attributes much of the difficulty in improving flood control to the "inability of individuals to conceptualize floods that have never occurred" (Kates, 1962:92). He observes that in making forecasts of future flood potential, individuals "are strongly conditioned by their immediate past and limit their extrapolation to simplified constructs, seeing the future as a mirror of that past" (Kates, 1962:88). In this regard, it is interesting that the purchase of earthquake insurance increases sharply after a quake, and then decreases steadily as the memories become less vivid (Steinbrugge et al., 1969).

Availability bias is illustrated by several recent studies in which college students and members of the League of Women Voters were asked to judge the frequency of various causes of death, such as smallpox, tornadoes and heart disease (Lichtenstein et al., 1978). In one study, they were first told the annual death toll for motor vehicle accidents in the United States (50,000) and then asked to estimate the frequencies of 40 other causes of death. In another study,

TABLE 1
BIAS IN JUDGED FREQUENCY OF DEATH

Most Overestimated	Most Underestimated
All accidents	Smallpox vaccination
Motor vehicle accidents	Diabetes
Pregnancy, childbirth, and abortion	Stomach cancer
Tornadoes	Lightning
Flood	Stroke
Botulism	Tuberculosis
All cancer	Asthma
Fire and flames	Emphysema
Venomous bite or sting	
Homicide	

Source: Adapted from Lichtenstein et al., 1978.

participants were given two causes of death and were asked to judge which of the two was more frequent.

Both studies showed people's judgments to be moderately accurate in a global sense, that is, people usually knew which were the most and least frequent lethal events. Within this global picture, however, people made serious misjudgments, many of which seemed to reflect availability bias. For example, accidents were judged to cause as many deaths as diseases, whereas diseases actually take about fifteen times as many lives. Homicides were incorrectly judged to be more frequent than diabetes and stomach cancer. Homicides were also judged to be about as frequent as strokes, although the latter actually claim about eleven times as many lives. Frequencies of death from botulism, tornadoes, and pregnancy (including childbirth and abortion) were also greatly overestimated.

Table 1 lists the lethal events whose frequencies were most poorly judged in our studies. In keeping with availability considerations, overestimated items were dramatic and sensational, whereas underestimated items tended to be unspectacular events that claim one victim at a time and are common in non-fatal form. A follow-up study showed that newspaper coverage of the various causes of death was biased in much the same way as were people's judgments (Combs and Slovic, 1979).

Overconfidence

A particularly pernicious aspect of heuristics is that people are typically very confident about judgments based on them. For example, in a follow-up to the study on causes of death, participants were asked to indicate the odds that they were correct in their judgments about which of two lethal events was more frequent (Fischhoff et al., 1977). Odds of 100:1 or greater were given often (25% of the time), but about one out of every eight answers associated with such extreme confidence was wrong. Fewer than 1 in 100 would have been wrong if the odds had been appropriate. About 30% of the judges gave odds greater than 50:1 to the incorrect assertion that homicides were more frequent than suicides. The psychological basis for this unwarranted certainty seems to be people's insensitivity to the tenuousness of the assumptions on which their judgments are based--in this case including the assumptions that are distorted by the availability heuristic. Such overconfidence is dangerous. It indicates that we often do not realize how little we know and how much additional information we need about the various problems we face.

Overconfidence manifests itself in other ways as well. A typical task in estimating failure rates or other uncertain quantities is to set upper and lower bounds so that there is a 98% chance that the true value lies between them. Experiments with diverse groups of people making many different kinds of judgments have shown that rather than 2% of true values falling outside the 98% confidence bounds, 20% to 50% do so (Lichtenstein et al., 1977). People think that they can estimate such values with much greater precision than is actually the case.

Unfortunately, experts seem as prone to overconfidence as lay people. Hynes and Vanmarcke (1976) asked seven "internationally known" geotechnical engineers to predict the height of an embankment that would cause a clay foundation to fail, and to specify confidence bounds around this estimate that were wide enough to have a 50% chance of enclosing the true failure height. None of the bounds specified by these experts actually did enclose the true height. The multimillion dollar Reactor Safety Study (U.S. Nuclear Regulatory Commission, 1975), in assessing the probability of a core melt in a nuclear reactor, used a procedure for setting confidence bounds that has been found in experiments to produce a high degree of overconfidence. Related problems led a recent review committee to conclude that the Reactor Safety Study greatly overestimated the precision with which it had assessed the probability of a core melt (U.S. Nuclear Regulatory Commission, 1978).

Another case in point is the 1976 collapse of the Teton Dam. The Committee on Government Operations has attributed this disaster to the unwarranted confidence of engineers, who were absolutely certain they had solved the many serious problems that arose during construction (Committee on Government Operations, 1976). In routine practice, failure probabilities are not even calculated for new dams, even though about 1 in 300 fails when the reservoir is first filled. Further anecdotal evidence of overconfidence may be found in many other technical risk assessments (Fischhoff, 1977). Some common ways in which experts may overlook or misjudge pathways to disaster include:

- *Failure to consider the ways in which human errors can affect technological systems.* Example: As Flynn's (1984) chapter in this volume notes, operators at Three Mile Island misdiagnosed the problems of the reactor and took inappropriate corrective actions. A minor incident thus became a major accident.

- *Overconfidence in current scientific knowledge.* Example: The harmful effects of X-rays went unrecognized until societal use had become widespread and largely uncontrolled.

- *Failure to comprehend the functioning of a technological system as a whole.* Example: The rupture of a liquid natural gas storage tank in Cleveland in 1944 resulted in 128 deaths, largely because no one had realized the need for a dike to contain spillage. The DC-10 failed in several early flights because none of its designers realized that decompression of the cargo compartment would destroy vital parts of the plane's control system running through it.

- *Slowness in detecting chronic, cumulative environmental effects.* Example: Although coal-mining accidents have long been recognized as one cost of operating fossil-fueled plants, the effects of acid rain on ecosystems were slow to be discovered.

- *Failure to anticipate human response to safety measures.* Example: The partial protection offered by dams and levees gives people a false sense of security and promotes development of the flood plain. When a rare flood does exceed the capacity of the dam, the damage may be considerably greater than if the flood plain had been unprotected.

Desire for Certainty

Every technology is a gamble of sorts, and like other gambles, it has an attractiveness that depends on the probability and size of its possible gains and losses. Both scientific experiments and casual observation show that people have difficulty thinking about and resolving the risk-benefit conflicts even in simple gambles. One way to reduce the anxiety that is generated by confronting uncertainty is to deny that uncertainty. The denial inherent in this anxiety-reducing search for certainty is thus an additional source of overconfidence. This type of denial is illustrated by people who, when faced with natural hazards, view their world either as perfectly safe or as predictable enough to preclude worry. Thus some flood victims interviewed by Kates (1962) flatly denied that floods could ever recur in their areas. Some thought (incorrectly) that new dams and reservoirs in the area would contain all potential floods, while others attributed previous floods to freak combinations of circumstances, unlikely to recur. Denial, of course, has its limits. Many people feel they cannot ignore the risks of nuclear power. For these people, the search for certainty is best satisfied by outlawing the risk.

Scientists and policy makers who point out the gambles involved in societal decisions are often resented for the anxiety they provoke. Borch (1968) noted how annoyed corporate managers get with consultants who give them the probabilities of possible events instead of telling them exactly what will happen. Just before a blue-ribbon panel of scientists reported that they were 95% certain that cyclamates do not cause cancer, U.S. Food and Drug Administration Commissioner Alexander Schmidt said, "I'm looking for a clean bill of health, not a wishy-washy, iffy answer on cyclamates" (Associated Press, 1976). Senator Edmund Muskie has called for "one-armed" scientists who do not respond "on the one hand, the evidence is so, but on the other hand . . ." when asked about the health effects of pollutants (David, 1975). In 1976, when people all over the country were demanding to know whether the swine flu vaccine was safe, the nature of their demands indicated that they were really trying to determine whether it was *perfectly* safe.

Perseverence of Beliefs

The difficulties of facing life as a gamble contribute to the polarization of opinions about hazards. For example, some people view nuclear power as being extraordinarily safe, while others view it as being a catastrophe in the making. It would be comforting to believe that these divergent beliefs would converge toward one "appropriate" view as new evidence was presented. Unfortunately, this is not likely to be the case. A great deal of research suggests that people's beliefs change slowly, and are extraordinarily persistent in the face of contradictory evidence (Ross, 1977). Once formed, initial impressions tend to structure and distort the way in which subsequent evidence is interpreted. New evidence appears to be reliable and informative if it is consistent with one's initial beliefs; contradictory evidence is dismissed as being unreliable, erroneous, and unrepresentative. Ross concluded his review of this phenomenon as follows:

> Erroneous impressions, theories, or data processing strategies, therefore, may not be changed through mere exposure to samples of new evidence. It is not contended, of course, that new evidence can *never* produce change--only that new evidence will produce *less* change than would be demanded by any logical or rational information-processing model (Ross, 1977:210).

Fallibility of Judgment

Our examination of risk perception leads to the following conclusions:

- Cognitive limitations, coupled with the anxieties generated by facing life as a gamble, cause uncertainty to be denied, risks to be distorted, and statements of fact to be believed with unwarranted confidence.

- Risk judgments are influenced (and sometimes biased) by the imaginability and memorability of hazards. Even for familiar risks, therefore, people may not have valid judgments.

- Disagreements about risk should not be expected to evaporate in the presence of "evidence." Definitive evidence, particularly about rare hazards, is difficult to obtain. Weaker information is likely to be interpreted in a way that reinforces existing beliefs.

Since it can be shown that even well-informed lay people have difficulty in judging risks accurately, it is tempting to conclude that the public should be removed from the decision-making process. The political ramifications of such a transfer of power to a technical elite are obvious. Indeed, it seems doubtful that such a massive disenfranchisement is feasible in any democratic society.

Furthermore, this transfer of decision making would seem to be misguided. For one thing, we have no assurance that experts' judgments are immune to biases once they are forced to go beyond documented evidence and rely on judgment. Although judgmental biases have most often been demonstrated with lay people, there is evidence that the cognitive functioning of experts is basically like that of anyone else, and that expert judgments are affected by the same types of cognitive limitations as are found among the general public.

In addition, in many if not most cases effective management of societal risks requires the cooperation of a large body of lay people. These people must agree to do without some things and accept substitutes for others; they must vote sensibly on ballot measures and elect legislators who will serve them as surrogate hazard managers; they must obey safety rules and use the legal system responsibly. Even if the experts were much better judges of risk than lay people, giving experts an exclusive franchise on decision making would merely substitute short-term efficiency for the long-term effort needed to create an informed citizenry.

FORECASTING PUBLIC RESPONSES TO NUCLEAR ENERGY

People respond to the hazards they perceive. The basic research cited above, supplemented by studies of perceptions of specific energy systems, could allow us to forecast public responses to those systems. To date, most studies of perceptions and attitudes toward energy systems have focused on nuclear power. In this section, we shall discuss some conclusions based on this research.

The General Problem

Even before the accident at Three Mile Island, the nuclear industry was foundering on the shoals of adverse public opinion. A sizable and tenacious opposition movement had been responsible for costly delays in the licensing and construction of new power plants in the United States and for political turmoil in several European nations.

The errant reactor at Three Mile Island stimulated a predictable immediate rise in antinuclear fervor. Any attempt to plan the role of nuclear power in the nation's energy future must consider the determinants of this opposition and anticipate its future course. One clue lies in recent research, which shows that the images of potential nuclear disasters in the minds of the antinuclear public are remarkably different from the assessments put forth by most technical experts. This section describes the images and speculates on their origins, permanence and implications.

Political Realities

Although questions of safety are pre-eminent in the nuclear debate, it is important to recognize that active opposition to nuclear power is an organized political movement which is fueled by many other concerns besides safety (Bronfman and Mattingly, 1976; Otway et al., 1978; Wilkes et al., 1978; see also the discussion by Mazur, 1984, in Chapter 4 of the present volume). While some nuclear opponents are motivated primarily by fear of routine or catastrophic radiation releases, others join the movement because they are disenchanted with growth, centralization, corporate dominance, technology, or government. These latter individuals may argue about safety because they view it as being the "Achilles' heel" of nuclear power. While the discussion that follows is not directly concerned with this larger political context, it does highlight the special qualities of nuclear power that cause (or allow) political opposition to be focused around considerations of risk.

Basic Perceptions

Opponents of nuclear power tend to believe both that its benefits are quite low and that its risks are unacceptably great (Fischhoff, Slovic, Lichtenstein, Read and Combs, 1978). On the benefit side, people do not see nuclear power as being a vital link in the meeting of basic energy needs (Pokorny, 1977). Many believe it to be merely a supplement to other sources of energy that are adequate themselves, or that could be made adequate by conservation.

On the risk side, nuclear power appears to evoke greater feelings of dread than almost any other technological activity (Fischhoff, Slovic, Lichtenstein, Read and Combs, 1978). Some have attributed this reaction to fear of radiation's invisible and irreversible contamination, threatening cancer and genetic damage. However, the use of diagnostic X-rays, another radiation technology that involves similar risks, is not similarly dreaded. If anything, people underestimate its risks. The difference may lie in another characteristic of nuclear power--its association with nuclear weaponry. As a result of its violent origins, nuclear power is viewed by people as a technology whose risks are uncontrollable, lethal, and potentially catastrophic--characteristics that are not present in people's perception of X-rays.

Research in which people are asked to describe their mental images of a nuclear accident and its consequences reveals the uncontrollable, lethal, and catastrophic qualities of perceived nuclear risks. There is a widely held expectation that a serious reactor accident is likely within one's lifetime and could result in hundreds of thousands, even millions, of deaths (Slovic et al., 1979). In addition, such an accident is expected to cause severe, irreparable environmental damage over a vast geographic area. These expectations contrast dramatically with the nuclear industry's official view that multiple safety systems will limit the damage in the extremely unlikely event of a major accident.

One inevitable consequence of this "perception gap" is uncertainty and distrust on the part of a public which suspects that the risks are incomparably greater than the experts' assessments (Kasper, 1979). The experts, in turn, question the rationality of the public and decry the "emotionalism" they see as blocking technological progress. Bitter and sometimes violent confrontations result.

Recognition of the perception gap has led many experts to claim that the public must be "educated" about the "real" risks from nuclear power. One public opinion analyst put the matter as follows:

> The biggest problem hindering a sophisticated judgment on this question is basic lack of knowledge and facts. Within this current attitudinal milieu, scare stories, confusion and irrationality often triumph. Only through careful education of facts and knowledge can the people know what the real choices are (Pokorny, 1977:12).

Our own view is that efforts to reduce the perception gap will face major obstacles. This pessimistic conclusion is based on two key aspects of the problem, one technical and one psychological.

The Technical Reality

The technical reality is that there are few "cut and dried facts" regarding the probabilities of serious reactor mishaps. The technology is so new and the probabilities in question are so small that risk estimates cannot be based on empirical observation. Instead, the assessments must be derived from complex mathematical models, such as the fault trees and event trees used in the Reactor Safety Study (U.S. Nuclear Regulatory Commission, 1975), to assess the probability and consequences of a loss-of-coolant accident. Despite an appearance of objectivity, risk assessments are inherently subjective. Someone, relying on judgment, must structure the analysis to determine the ways that failure might occur, their relative importance, and their logical interconnections.

The difficulties of performing risk assessments have led many critics to question the validity of the results (Bryan, 1974; Fischhoff, 1977; Primack, 1975). One major concern is that important initiating events or pathways to failure may be omitted, causing risks to be underestimated. If omissions are as common and difficult to detect as suggested earlier, then underestimation may be substantial. Another problem in assessing the reliability of reactor designs is the difficulty of taking proper account of "common-mode failures." In order to ensure greater safety, many technological systems are highly redundant: should one crucial part fail, there are others that are designed to do the same job or to limit the resulting damage. Since the probability of each part failing is very small, the probability of all parts failing (thereby creating a major disaster) should be miniscule. This reasoning is valid only if the various components are independent (so whatever causes one part to fail will not automatically cause the others to fail). "Common-mode failure" occurs when the independence assumption does not hold. For example, because electrical cables controlling the redundant safety systems at a reactor in Browns Ferry, Alabama, were not spatially separated, all five emergency core cooling systems were rendered inoperative by a single fire. Developing models that take proper account of such contingencies is a very difficult enterprise. The potential for omissions is complicated by the tendency for problems that are out of sight to be effectively out of mind, their omission unrecognized (Fischhoff, Slovic and Lichtenstein, 1978).

One critic's skepticism regarding the defensibility of assessments of rare catastrophes summarizes the technical problem concisely:

> The expert community is divided about the conceivable realism of probability estimates in the range of one in ten thousand to one in one billion per reactor year. I am among those who believe it to be impossible *in principle* to support numbers as small as these with convincing theoretical arguments . . . . The reason I hold this view is

> straightforward: Nuclear power systems are so complex that the probability the safety analysis contains serious errors . . . is so big as to render meaningless the tiny computed probability of accident (Holdren, 1976:21).

The Psychological Reality

Public fears of nuclear power should not be viewed as irrational. In part, these fears are fed by the realization that the facts are in dispute, and that experts have been wrong in the past, as when they irradiated enlarged tonsils or permitted people to witness A-bomb tests at close range. Furthermore, experts' errors often seem to be in the direction of underestimating risks. What one can criticize, perhaps, is the extent to which people's fundamental ways of thinking (such as reliance on the availability heuristic) lead them to a distorted view of such information as is presented. Certainly the risks from nuclear power would seem to be a prime candidate for availability bias because of the extensive media coverage they receive, and because of their association with the vivid and imaginable dangers of nuclear war. In contrast, the chronic, unspectacular effects of pollution associated with other energy sources may attract too little attention.

One disturbing implication of the availability heuristic is that any discussion of low-probability hazards, regardless of its content, may increase the memorability and imaginability of the hazards, and hence increase their perceived risks. This possibility poses a major barrier to open discussions regarding nuclear safety. Consider an engineer arguing the safety of disposing of nuclear wastes in a salt bed by pointing out the improbability of the various ways in which radioactivity could be accidentally released. Rather than reassuring the audience, the presentation might lead them to think, "I didn't realize there were that many things that could go wrong."

The availability heuristic magnifies fears of nuclear power by blurring the distinction between what is remotely possible and what is probable. As one nuclear proponent lamented, "When laymen discuss what *might* happen, they sometimes don't even bother to include the 'might'" (B. Cohen, 1974:36). Another analyst has elaborated a similar theme in the misinterpretation of "worst-case" scenarios:

> It often has made little difference how bizarre or improbable the assumption in such an analysis was, since one had only to show that some undesirable effect could occur at a probability level greater than zero. Opponents of a proposed operation could destroy it simply by exercising their imaginations to dream up a set of conditions which, although they might admittedly be extremely improbable, could lead to some undesirable results. With such attitudes prevalent, planning a given nuclear operation becomes . . . perilous (J. Cohen, 1972: 55).

Whereas the above discussion helps clarify the source of the perception gap between pronuclear experts and their lay opponents, it does not point unambiguously to one side or the other as having the most accurate appraisal of the overall risks from nuclear power. Although memorability and imaginability are capable of enhancing public fears, the inability to imagine all possible ways in which a system could fail might produce a false sense of security among technical experts. As a result, the identification of judgmental difficulties does not, in itself, afford an external criterion for closing the perception gap. The actual risks may never be known with great precision, and much new information will be subject to alternative interpretations, so the gap may be with us for a long time indeed. The Three Mile Island accident provides an example--it "proved" the possibility of a catastrophic meltdown to some, while to others it demonstrated the reliability of the multiple containment systems.

A Nuclear Future?

Are the strong fears and determined opposition to nuclear power likely to persist? Will nuclear power ever gain widespread public acceptance? Although answers to these questions are by no means clear, the public response to X-rays provides some clues. The almost universal acceptance of X-rays shows that a radiation technology can be tolerated once its use becomes familiar, its benefits clear, and its practitioners trusted.

Nerve gas provides an enlightening case study. Few human creations could be more dreaded or more potentially catastrophic than this deadly substance. In December of 1969, when the U.S. Army decided to transfer nerve gas from

Okinawa to the Umatilla Army Depot in Hermiston, Oregon, citizens of Oregon were outraged--except those in Hermiston. Whereas public opinion around the state was more than 90% in opposition, residents of Hermiston were 95% *in favor* of the transfer (United Press International, 1969; Bryerton, 1970). Several factors seem to have been crucial to Hermiston's acceptance of nerve gas. For one, munitions and toxic chemicals had been stored safely there since 1941, so the record was good and the presence of the hazard was familiar. Second, there were recognized economic benefits to the community from continued storage of hazardous substances at the depot, in addition to the feelings of satisfaction that some residents gained by doing something patriotic for the country. Finally, the responsible agency, the U.S. Army, was respected and trusted.

These examples illustrate the slow path through which nuclear power might gain acceptance. It requires an incontrovertible long-term safety record, a responsible agency that is respected and trusted, and a clear appreciation of benefit. In the aftermath of Three Mile Island, this path appears not only slow but unnavigable. A quicker path to acceptance, and one that may provide the only hope for the industry, could be forged by a severe energy shortage. Society has shown itself willing to accept increased risks in exchange for increased benefits. Brownouts, blackouts, or rationing of electricity would probably enhance the perceived need for nuclear power and increase public tolerance of its risks. One example of such a reaction is the oil crisis of 1973-74, which broke the resistance to offshore drilling, the Alaska pipeline, and shale oil development--all of which had previously been delayed because of environmental concerns. On the other hand, such crisis-induced acceptance of nuclear power may produce anxiety, stress and conflict in a population forced to tolerate what it perceives to be a great risk because of its addiction to the benefits of electricity.

ACCEPTANCE OF NON-NUCLEAR ENERGY SYSTEMS

The arguments presented above suggest that problems of public acceptance should be much less severe for non-nuclear sources of energy. Fossil fuels and hydroelectric systems are familiar and common, and are apparently perceived as being less risky than they actually are, although data are needed to test this speculation. Fossil, hydroelectric and solar energy systems have their origins in antiquity, and work via mechanisms (combustion, water force, and sunshine) that are familiar, natural and well understood. Accidents and fatalities with these systems tend to involve relatively few individuals, and those individuals tend to be spatially and socially isolated from the rest of society. Furthermore, the effects of such accidents are consummated in a fixed period of time, without the threat of lingering consequences. Observation of the recent failure of the Teton Dam in Idaho suggests that even such catastrophic hazards as the collapse of a hydroelectric dam will quickly be forgotten by those not directly involved, in contrast to the consequences of a reactor accident.

CONCLUSION

Management of nuclear power and alternative energy systems must be based on an understanding of people's thinking about risks. Our aim in this chapter has not been to document public opposition and fear of nuclear power, which are discussed extensively in several of the other chapters in this book. Instead we have attempted to point out that opposition stems both from the recognition of unresolved technical issues in the risk assessment process and from the fundamental thought processes that determine perceptions of risk.

Nuclear hazards are particularly memorable and imaginable, yet hardly amenable to empirical verification. Their special qualities blur the distinction between the possible and the probable and produce an immense gap between the views of most technical experts and those of a significant portion of the public. This gap must be acknowledged, and the difficulty of reducing it by educational programs or empirical demonstrations of safety must be recognized by planners and policy makers.

Despite the difficulties, attempts at education and communication must be pursued. To be truly productive, however, communication must be a two-way affair, predicated upon openness and mutual respect for the other side's intelligence. Nuclear power proponents must recognize that public opposition may stem from something other than ignorance and may be based in part on considerations that have little to do with health and safety risks. A proper communication program would attempt to identify these concerns so they may be discussed and debated openly.

In other words, the most appropriate goal of a communication program may not be to eradicate ignorance, but rather to reduce conflict and build trust and mutual respect among all sides of the nuclear issue. Toward that end, such a program should give high priority to designing an environment in which two-way communication and constructive debate can take place, and to identifying the proper issues to place on the agenda for such debates.

ACKNOWLEDGEMENTS

This chapter was originally published in Andrew Baum and Jerome E. Singer (eds.), *Advances in Environmental Psychology, Volume 3: Energy: Psychological Perspectives* (Hillsdale, NJ: Lawrence Erlbaum Associates, 1981) and is reprinted by permission.

REFERENCES

Associated Press
1976 "Doubts Linger on Cyclamate Risks." *Eugene Register-Guard* (January 14):A-9.

Borch, Karl
1968 *The Economics of Uncertainty.* Princeton, NJ: Princeton University Press.

Bronfman, Lois M. and T. J. Mattingly
1976 "Critical Mass: Politics, Technology, and the Public Interest." *Nuclear Safety* 17:539-549.

Bryan, William B.
1974 Testimony before the Subcommittee on State Energy Policy, Committee on Planning, Land Use, and Energy, California State Assembly, February 1.

Bryerton, Gene
1970 "Umatilla Army Depot--Is It a Step Toward Doomsday?" *Eugene Register-Guard* (January 11):C-1.

Cohen, Bernard L.
1974 "Perspectives on the Nuclear Debate." *Bulletin of the Atomic Scientists* 30:25-39.

Cohen, Jerry J.
1972 "A Case for Benefit-Risk Analysis." In H. J. Otway (ed.), *Risk vs. Benefit: Solution or Dream*. Los Alamos, NM: Los Alamos Scientific Laboratory, February, Report LA-4860-MS. (Available from the National Technical Information Service.)

Combs, Barbara and Paul Slovic
1979 "Newspaper Coverage of Causes of Death." *Journalism Quarterly* 56 (#4):837-843, 849.

Committee on Government Operations, U.S. House of Representatives
1976 *Teton Dam Disaster: Thirtieth Report by the Committee on Government Operations*. Washington, D.C.: U.S. Government Printing Office.

David, Edward E.
1975 "Editorial." *Science* 189:891.

Fischhoff, Baruch
1977 "Cost-Benefit Analysis and the Art of Motorcycle Maintenance." *Policy Sciences* 8:177-202.

Fischhoff, Baruch, Paul Slovic and Sarah Lichtenstein
1977 "Knowing with Certainty: The Appropriateness of Extreme Confidence." *Journal of Experimental Psychology: Human Perception and Performance* 3:552-564.
1978 "Fault Trees: Sensitivity of Estimated Failure Probabilities to Problem Representation." *Journal of Experimental Psychology: Human Perception and Performance* 4:330-344.

Fischhoff, Baruch, Paul Slovic, Sarah Lichtenstein, Stephen Read and Barbara Combs
1978 "How Safe is Safe Enough? A Psychometric Study of Attitudes Towards Technological Risks and Benefits." *Policy Sciences* 9:127-152.

Flynn, Cynthia
1984 "The Local Impacts of the Accident at Three Mile Island." Pp. 205-232 in William R. Freudenburg and Eugene A. Rosa (eds.), *Public Reactions to Nuclear Power: Are There Critical Masses?* Boulder, CO: Westview Press/American Association for the Advancement of Science.

Freudenburg, William R. and Eugene A. Rosa (eds.)
1984 *Public Reactions to Nuclear Power: Are There Critical Masses?* Boulder, CO: Westview Press/American Association for the Advancement of Science.

Holdren, John P.
1976 "The Nuclear Controversy and the Limitations of Decision Making by Experts." *Bulletin of the Atomic Scientists* 32:20-22.

Hynes, M. and Eric Vanmarcke
1976 "Reliability of Embankment Performance Predictions." *Proceedings of the ASCE Engineering Mechanics Division Specialty Conference.* Waterloo, Ontario, Canada: University of Waterloo Press.

Kasper, Raphael G.
1979 "Perceived Risk: Implications for Policy." In Gordon Goodman and William D. Rowe (eds.), *Energy Risk Management.* London, Great Britain: Academic Press.

Kates, Robert W.
1962 *Hazard and Choice Perception in Flood Plain Management.* Chicago, IL: Department of Geography, University of Chicago, Research Paper No. 78.

Lichtenstein, Sarah, Baruch Fischhoff and Lawrence D. Phillips
1977 "Calibration of Probabilities: The State of the Art." In Helmut Jungermann and Gerard de Zeeuw (eds.), *Decision Making and Change in Human Affairs.* Amsterdam, The Netherlands: D. Reidel.

Lichtenstein, Sarah, Paul Slovic, Baruch Fischhoff, Mark Layman and Barbara Combs
1978 "Judged Frequency of Lethal Events." *Journal of Experimental Psychology: Human Learning and Memory* 4:551-578.

Mazur, Allan
1984 "Media Influences on Public Attitudes Toward Nuclear Power." Pp. 97-114 in William R. Freudenburg and Eugene A. Rosa (eds.), *Public Reactions to Nuclear Power: Are There Critical Masses?* Boulder, CO: Westview Press/American Association for the Advancement of Science.

Otway, Harry J., D. Maurer and Kerry Thomas
1978 "Nuclear Power: The Question of Public Acceptance." *Futures* 10:109-118.

Pokorny, Gene
1977 *Energy Development: Attitudes and Beliefs at the Regional/National Levels.* Cambridge, MA: Cambridge Reports.

Primack, Joel
1975 "Nuclear Reactor Safety: An Introduction to the Issues." *Bulletin of the Atomic Scientists* 31:15-17.

Rosa, Eugene A. and William R. Freudenburg
1984 "Nuclear Power at the Crossroads." Pp. 3-37 in William R. Freudenburg and Eugene A. Rosa (eds.), *Public Reactions to Nuclear Power: Are*

There Critical Masses? Boulder, CO: Westview Press/American Association for the Advancement of Science.

Ross, Lee
1977 "The Intuitive Psychologist and His Shortcomings: Distortions in the Attribution Process." In Leonard Berkowitz (ed.), *Advances in Experimental Social Psychology.* New York: Academic Press.

Slovic, Paul, Baruch Fischhoff and Sarah Lichtenstein
1977 "Behavioral Decision Theory." *Annual Review of Psychology* 28:1-39.
1979 "Images of Disaster: Perception and Acceptance of Risks from Nuclear Power." In Gordon Goodman and William D. Rowe (eds.), *Energy Risk Management.* London, Great Britain: Academic Press.

Slovic, Paul, Howard Kunreuther, and Gilbert F. White
1974 "Decision Processes, Rationality, and Adjustment to Natural Hazards." In Gilbert F. White (ed.), *Natural Hazards, Local, National, and Global.* New York: Oxford University Press.

Steinbrugge, Karl V., F. E. McClure, and A. J. Snow
1969 *Studies in Seismicity and Earthquake Damage Statistics.* Washington, D.C.: U.S. Department of Commerce (COM-71-00053).

Tversky, Amos and Daniel Kahneman
1974 "Judgment Under Uncertainty: Heuristics and Biases." *Science* 185:1124-1131.

U.S. Nuclear Regulatory Commission
1975 *Reactor Safety Study: An Assessment of Accident Risks in U.S. Commercial Nuclear Power Plants.* Washington, D.C.: U.S. Nuclear Regulatory Commission (WASH-1400, NUREG-75/014).
1978 *Risk Assessment Review Group Report to the U.S. Nuclear Regulatory Commission.* Washington, D.C.: U.S. Nuclear Regulatory Commission (NUREG/CR-0400).

United Press International
1969 "Nerve Gas Fuss Ruffles Hermiston--But not as You'd Expect." *Eugene Register-Guard* (December 18):A-1.

Weinberg, Alvin M.
1976 "The Maturity and Future of Nuclear Energy." *American Scientist* 64:16-21.

Wilkes, John M., M. Lovington, R. Horne, F. Pulaski and R. Poole
1978 "Formation of Attitudes About Nuclear Power." Presented at the annual meetings of the Society for the Social Study of Science, Bloomington, Indiana.

Robert C. Mitchell

6. Rationality and Irrationality in the Public's Perception of Nuclear Power

Social scientists have advanced two explanations for the recent increases in opposition to nuclear power that are described in this volume's pages. According to the first approach, the "nuclear phobia" explanation, people's rejection of nuclear power is an emotional, uninformed response, resulting in large part from scare tactics used by antinuclear activists and/or from the tendency for television news to overdramatize the hazards of nuclear power. Some proponents of this view believe the public's basically irrational fear of nuclear power can be overcome by using insights derived from the psychotherapeutic treatment of people who suffer from other kinds of phobias. Some of them also interpret a consistent finding--the fact that women tend to have a greater aversion to nuclear power than do men--as resulting from a greater propensity on the part of women to be motivated by irrational factors (Kasperson et al., 1979:275).

The second or "lay rationality" explanation, by contrast, regards people's fears of nuclear power as being essentially rational, given the nature of human cognitive capacities and the particular type of risk posed by nuclear power. Proponents of this second explanation call for mutual dialogue between the pronuclear experts and the concerned public as the best way to bridge the perceptual gap between the two groups.

Pp. 137-179 in William R. Freudenburg and Eugene A. Rosa (eds., 1984) *Public Reactions to Nuclear Power: Are There Critical Masses?*

These two approaches are obviously very different in their assumptions and in their policy implications. This chapter compares the two, using data from a national survey on energy and environmental issues that was conducted in 1980. For two reasons, this endeavor will require a more detailed (and technical) methodological presentation than will be found in the other chapters of this volume. First, the survey being used was not specifically designed to test the two explanations; thus it is only through the use of certain simplifying assumptions, which have to be described and justified, that the explanations can be assessed with the data at hand. Second, the chapter draws on statistical techniques that make it possible to consider a number of possible explanatory factors simultaneously, seeing how well the nuclear phobia theory accounts for the data when the lay rationality theory is taken into account, and vice versa.

The chapter consists of three parts. In Part I, I summarize the two explanations and describe the roles played by rational and emotional arguments in the debate over nuclear power. Part II contains the details of my test of the two explanations. In this section of the chapter I outline a model of why people hold the views they do about nuclear power, derive hypotheses from each of the two approaches noted above, place these hypotheses in the context of other studies' findings, and test them. Part III summarizes my findings and discusses their implications.

I have tried to limit the technical discussion to Part II of this chapter. Those who do not wish to pursue the analytical details of the data analysis may wish to proceed directly to Part III from Part I. The principal findings to emerge in Part II are three in number: (1) Although factors associated with both theories help to account for people's aversion to nuclear power, the "everyday rationality" approach has greater explanatory power; (2) While women are more opposed to nuclear power than men, there is no evidence that they perceive it in a less rational manner; and (3) Women appear to regard nuclear power as an environmental issue while men view it as a scientific/technological issue; it is this difference in perspective that accounts for the greater opposition among women.

PART I: TWO EXPLANATIONS FOR THE OPPOSITION TO NUCLEAR POWER

Nuclear Phobia

Although press coverage during the 1950s about the peaceful uses of the atom emphasized its great potential to improve society and raised utopian expectations, the atom's dominant image--reinforced by the Cuban missile confrontation, the fallout debate, and classroom rehearsals for atomic attacks--continues to be one of unparalleled destruction. In *The Broken Connection,* psychiatrist Robert Lifton (1979) argues that the imagery of atomic weapons has had a profound subconscious effect on the human psyche. To live a meaningful life, people require a sense of continuity between life and death, which may be expressed in a variety of ways (including religious beliefs, living on through our children and their children, and living on through our influence on others). Nuclear weapons' destructive potential threatens this connection between life and death by introducing the profoundly unsettling threat of extinction, of apocalypse, of annihilation. While this imagery of extinction is ignored by most humans through processes of denial, Lifton believes it produces "a pervasive sense of vulnerability to annihilation" (1979:352).

It may also produce irrational opposition to nuclear power;[1] Lifton, for one, believes people's fear of nuclear power is an extension of their fear of nuclear weapons (1979: 385-6). Several other psychiatrists share this view. Philip Pahner says, "Clearly death symbolism is involved in the struggle [against nuclear power plants]" (1976:7). According to Robert DuPont, "The nuclear power industry has been virtually stopped in the U.S. because of fear" (1981a:14). DuPont characterizes this fear as phobic, by which he means an "ultimate irrational fear" that stems from unconscious motivations (1981b).

DuPont believes this phobia is exacerbated by the media's focus on fear in the coverage of the nuclear debate (1981a:1; see also Theberge, 1981) and by the efforts of nuclear opponents to encourage this response (DuPont,

1981a:2). In a hearing held by a subcommittee of the House of Representatives, DuPont and M. B. Gottlieb took the position that the presence of such emotional and irrational elements produces "fertile ground for the creation of misinformation and myth" (Gottlieb, 1981). According to them, only the removal of such fear will permit nuclear power to be judged on its merits (DuPont, 1981a:3).

Everyday Rationality

Researchers who take what I call the "everyday rationality approach" come from a different disciplinary setting than do those who espouse the irrationality approach (sociology or social psychology rather than psychiatry), and they use different methods (direct quantitative measurement of factors rather than intuitive or inferential judgments from in-depth studies of small samples). They attribute concern about the safety of nuclear power to universal cognitive limitations rather than to unconscious drives or ignorance.

One set of studies using this approach (Bowman and Fishbein, 1978; Otway et al., 1978; Thomas et al., 1980; Sundstrom et al., 1981) draws on the expectancy-value model of cognitive structure (Fishbein and Ajzen, 1975); this research uses survey data to examine people's beliefs about the attributes of various energy technologies, their evaluation of these beliefs (e.g., on a good-bad scale) and the consequences they expect to result from the implementation of the technologies. According to this approach, acceptance will be greater when respondents believe that desirable effects are likely and undesirable effects are unlikely. Out of a wide range of possible effects that have been considered in these studies, the most important determinant of an individual's attitudes appears to be the expected balance between the economic benefits (e.g., more jobs) and the hazards (e.g., radiation hazards, exposure to risks beyond the individual's control) of nuclear power.[2]

In a second set of studies, Paul Slovic and his colleagues asked several groups of people who were mostly opposed to nuclear power's expansion to evaluate the degree of benefit and risk associated with 30 different activities and technologies. The benefits of nuclear power appeared to be "unappreciated," its risks were judged to be extremely high, and people wanted it to be 29 times safer than they perceived it to be (Slovic et al., 1979:4). The groups' fatality estimates for an imagined maximum credible disaster also tended to be far in excess of those "considered reasonable by most technical experts" (Slovic et al., 1979:11).

Authors in this second group believe their findings reflect a rational perception of nuclear power. According to Sundstrom et al. (1981:188), the predictive success of the expectancy-value model "suggests that *rational processes* underlie decisions about acceptance of a nuclear power plant" (emphasis in the original). In like manner, Otway et al. (1978:117) say their findings suggest ". . . that people are 'rational'--in the sense of integrating information--in terms of their own subjective values, and choosing to behave (e.g. vote) in a way that is consistent with these values."

With regard to assertions by nuclear proponents that the risks associated with nuclear energy are orders of magnitude lower than other, more familiar risks, thus implying an irrational basis for the opposition to nuclear power by the public, Otway and colleagues make this observation:

> To expect people's attitudes toward a new technology to be primarily determined by statistical estimates of physical safety is a highly simplified, and incorrect model of human thought processes--it implies such a degree of "rationality" as to be itself irrational (Otway et al., 1978:117).

However, since Otway and his colleagues do not attempt to determine the factors that *lie behind* people's beliefs about the safety and risk of nuclear power, their empirical findings do not necessarily contradict the irrationality position.

This is not the case with Chapter 5 of this volume, by Paul Slovic and his colleagues (1984), who explicitly explore the thought processes that determine people's evaluation of nuclear risks. While they acknowledge that public fears are fed in part by the "realization that the facts are in dispute and that experts have been wrong in the past," they argue that nuclear power is associated with involuntary, unknown, uncontrollable, unfamiliar and potentially catastrophic risks--

not because of subliminal fears or phobias, but because people tend to apply their everyday intuitive inferential strategies to the issue. On the basis of their research they conclude that "Public fears of nuclear power should not be viewed as irrational" (Slovic et al., 1984:128).

The Nuclear Debate

Before I proceed to describe my test of the two alternative views, some comments on the actual use of rational and non-rational arguments and symbols in the debate over nuclear power are necessary to place these findings in perspective.

First, it is important to recognize that *both* sides in the debate believe "the facts" are on their side, and that both expend considerable effort in making factual arguments in the many forums available to them. Moreover, both use legal and scientific experts to make arguments for their side and to lend legitimacy to their contentions. The significant role of rational argument can be seen by examining antinuclear petitions and publications (such as *Critical Mass Journal, Not Man Apart*, and *No Nukes*, the book written by a group of Clamshell Alliance activists--Gyorgy, 1979).[3] As Marrett (1984) notes in Chapter 13 of this volume, moreover, the general public apparently perceives scientists to be divided over the merits of nuclear power.

Second, the antinuclear side of the debate does not necessarily have a monopoly on unconscious motivation. Appeals to fear and apocalyptic imagery are undeniably a feature of the movement's activities, as attested to by the death heads, mushroom clouds, and pictures of young children clinging to their mothers that are featured in some antinuclear posters, and by the strident, fear-provoking rhetoric used by some antinuclear leaders. On the pronuclear side, however, some appeals are based on factors with strong emotional overtones such as national security (Hoyle, 1977). Moreover, if Lifton is correct, a powerful unconscious factor--"the religion of nuclearism, in which we embrace the very aspects of our potential extermination as a source of salvation" (1979:43)--also lies behind pronuclear sentiments.

Third and finally, important elements on both sides of the issue believe that more than just technical concerns are involved. They see it as a debate over the direction American society should take in the future, as a debate about values. Many antinuclear activists believe that nuclear power is not only unsafe but inhumane, promoting a society where nature is exploited, societal institutions are centralized at the expense of local communities, the economy is dominated by large corporations, and individuals are alienated from the technology that sustains them. These considerations are often muted in the movement's outreach to the general public, however, because activists regard the safety issue as their natural point of contact with the public (see, e.g., Gyorgy, 1979). Values figure much more prominently in the movement's successful efforts to gain support from people sympathetic to other movements with which it shares strong value affinities--including movements for peace (Nelkin, 1981a), environmental protection (Mitchell, 1980a), women's rights (Nelkin, 1981b), Native American rights (Nelkin, 1981c) and alternative technologies (Morrison, 1980).

Those in favor of nuclear power do not ignore the value side of the debate either, although their appeals to values often take the form of attacks on what they believe to be the ideology of the antinuclear movement, such as its advocacy of a "no-growth" society (Hosmer, 1978; Nisbet, 1979). Other nuclear advocates link the expansion of nuclear power to economic security, and actively solicit the support of constituencies such as Blacks and labor (Logan and Nelkin, 1980) for whom this value is assumed to have special appeal.

In conclusion, appeals to fear undeniably play a role in the antinuclear movement, but these appeals must be viewed in the perspective of the debate as a whole. Both sides produce a great deal of informative material, both sides make value appeals, and neither has a monopoly on oversimplification and the use of emotion. As Mazur (1984) notes in Chapter 4 of this volume, much is available by way of information and analysis that could lead someone to be concerned about nuclear safety, or to be sanguine about it, apart from arguments based on emotional appeals.

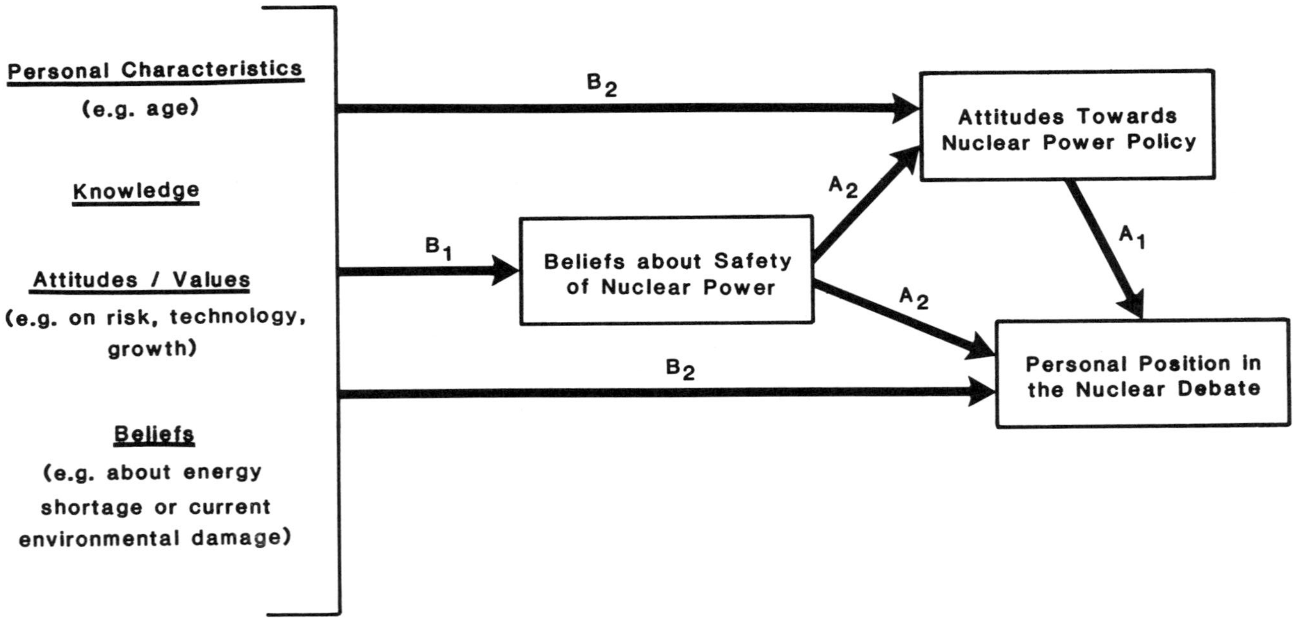

Figure 1. General Model of the Causes of Attitudes Towards Nuclear Power

PART II: A TEST OF THE TWO APPROACHES

Survey Data on Doomsday Fears and Knowledge

Although the researchers who advocate both of the above points of view cite evidence to support their conclusions, none of the contentions have been subjected to systematic empirical tests. Those who argue for the importance of unconscious fears in motivating nuclear opponents offer no systematic empirical evidence to support their views. They rely instead upon the professional insight of the psychiatrist, whose patient in this case is the larger public.[4] Those who assert that public concern is motivated by rational processes do use quantitative data, but either from select (not random) populations (Slovic et al., 1979, 1984) or without explicitly measuring irrationality (Sundstrom et al., 1981; Otway et al., 1978).

In this section I use data from a national survey of opinions about environmental and energy issues to test some hypotheses that I derive from the two approaches outlined above. As noted earlier, this part of the chapter may be skipped by readers who are not interested in the technical details of the analysis, since the main findings will be summarized in Part III. The survey was designed and analyzed by Resources for the Future (RFF) for the U.S. Council on Environmental Quality (Mitchell, 1980b). The fieldwork was conducted by Roper and Cantril, whose staff interviewed a probability sample of 1576 people for half an hour each in February and March of 1980. The questionnaire contains several items on nuclear power, in addition to questions on values, attitudes, knowledge and background characteristics.

The Model

Figure 1 summarizes the basic explanatory model I will estimate using the RFF data. It consists of three equations that use path analysis to treat attitudes toward nuclear safety, attitudes toward the nation's nuclear power program, and the respondents' positions on the nuclear debate, respectively, as depending on three sets of potential explanatory variables.[5] In this case I assume that someone's beliefs about the safety of nuclear power plants will affect his/her attitudes toward nuclear power. A second assumption, depicted by path A_1 in Figure 1, is that negative attitudes toward nuclear power cause people to think of themselves as opponents of the technology.

Nuclear safety plays a central role in the model because beliefs about safety have been shown to be the strongest predictors of people's attitudes and "behavioral intentions" toward nuclear power--e.g., the intention to vote against it in a referendum (Harris, 1978; Hensler and Hensler, 1979; Rankin and Nealey, 1978). My measure of beliefs about the safety of nuclear power, which is the second item in Table 1, below, is the most frequently used question on this topic.

Nuclear Phobia Hypotheses

The finding that people oppose nuclear power primarily because they believe it to be "unsafe" focuses our attention on what causes people to be more or less concerned about nuclear safety. There are three hypotheses about the causes of safety concerns that follow from the nuclear phobia approach described above and that are amenable to testing with these data. In what follows I present the hypotheses and review previous findings that are relevant to each of them.

> H_1 People who hold "exaggerated fears" about nuclear power will be more concerned about nuclear safety, other things being equal, than those who do not.

There are two studies that report tests of this hypothesis, although one of them is defective in its methodology. Kasperson and his colleagues (1979) interviewed 100 people at each of three nuclear plant sites. They found one out of four interviewees responded "with anxiety" to a sentence completion item with the stem: "When I think of the nuclear power plant, I feel ______." Moreover, twice as many women as men responded with anxiety. According to the authors, these data support the idea that displaced anxiety is an important cause of public concern over nuclear energy. They also state: "The linkage that many people make between nuclear plants and nuclear weapons (there is widespread, and ill-founded, concern that a plant will explode) may play a significant role in these sex differences" (Kasperson et al.,

1979:275). The problem with these inferences is that the authors did not analyze their data to see if those who gave anxious responses were in fact more concerned about nuclear energy than those who did not express anxiety. Whether women have a greater propensity to be motivated by irrational factors, as Kasperson and his colleagues imply (1979:275), will be explored in the analysis below.

The other study does not suffer from this defect. Hensler and Hensler surveyed a California sample of 884 people in 1976, one-fifth of whom spontaneously mentioned doomsday images of one kind or another when asked to say what comes to mind "when you hear the term 'nuclear energy' or 'nuclear power'" (1979:21). Although those who mentioned doomsday images were somewhat more likely to have a negative view of nuclear power, this belief did not emerge as an independent explanatory factor when other factors were "controlled," or held constant statistically, in their regression analyses. They conclude: "If doomsday images have any effect on evaluations of nuclear power plants it is minor" (1979:61).

> H_2 Those who are more knowledgeable about nuclear power and other energy issues will be less concerned about nuclear safety than those who are less knowledgeable.

Previous studies show no clear pattern on this hypothesis. Two studies have found somewhat greater support for nuclear power among the more knowledgeable respondents (Nealey and Rankin, 1978; Cole and Fiorentine, 1983)[6] while another found the reverse (Kasperson et al., 1979). Several have found no relationship or have declared the relationship to be insubstantial (Hensler and Hensler, 1979; Lounsbury et al., 1979) and one study of attitudes toward the Clinch River Breeder Reactor found no difference on a knowledge scale based on the facts emphasized by the supporters, but did find that, on a scale based on facts emphasized by the opponents, the opponents were more knowledgeable than the supporters (Clelland and Bremseth, 1980). Finally, in their studies of two Massachusetts state samples, Reed and Wilkes (1981) found that knowledge had an interaction effect with political ideology and confidence in environmentalists. For respondents with confidence in environmentalists (or who were liberal), greater knowledge was associated with less support for nuclear power, while the reverse was true for those lacking confidence in environmentalists (or who were conservative). Reed and Wilkes concluded that this finding supports a "selective perception" model, where beliefs mediate the effect of knowledge (Reed and Wilkes, 1981:4).

> H_3 The greater their formal education in years, the less people will be concerned about nuclear safety.

Since formal education seeks to inculcate both specific knowledge and a facility to use new knowledge in a critical fashion (Bishop, 1976), the last hypothesis based on the nuclear phobia approach is that education will be inversely correlated with irrational fears. Previous studies have found moderately high correlations between education and energy knowledge, as I do with the RFF data ($r = .39$ for men and .29 for women). Those studies using multivariate techniques to examine the relationship between education and nuclear attitudes, however, have failed thus far to find statistically believable effects.[7]

Lay Rationality Hypotheses

It is less obvious how to test the lay rationality view with the survey data. There is no direct way to learn from these data whether or not the respondents employ the kinds of judgmental heuristics and knowledge structures that Slovic and his associates believe to lie behind nuclear safety concerns. Moreover, Slovic and associates treat these strategies as human universals. They do not speculate about why some people use them to conclude that nuclear plants are unsafe, while other non-experts who presumably possess the same mental equipment reach the opposite conclusion.

Nevertheless, if the lay rationality approach is correct, people's judgments about nuclear power should be affected in a predictable fashion by their tastes or preferences. As James March has written, "Rational choice involves two kinds of guesses . . . . We try to imagine what will happen in the future as a result of our actions and we try to imagine how we shall evaluate what will happen" (1978:589). If this view is correct, we should be able to account for a statistically and substantively significant portion of the variance in attitudes toward nuclear safety and nuclear power by examining people's values and their general orientations toward risk. For example, lower safety concerns and greater acceptance of nuclear power should be found among people who are optimistic about the benign consequences of technology, who are not averse to externally imposed risks, who believe natural systems are inherently robust and exist primarily to serve human needs, who place a high value on national security, and who are less inclined to worry about the situation of future generations. Alternatively, if people react to nuclear safety and nuclear power on an irrational basis, their answers would be expected to follow a more random pattern, and the variance explained by values should be low, especially compared with the variance explained by irrational fears (H_1-H_3 above). These assumptions lead to the following hypotheses about each of the dependent variables in the model:

H_4 People's concerns about nuclear safety are a function of their values and their general concern about imposed risk.

H_5 People's views about nuclear power are a function of their values and their concern about nuclear safety.

H_6 People's positions on the nuclear debate are a function of their values, their views about nuclear power, and their concern about nuclear safety.

Previous studies offer some support for these hypotheses. According to Rankin and Nealey, who studied an Oregon sample using Rokeach's (1973) measure of values, "human values are strong determinants of one's nuclear power attitude" (1978:iii). Nuclear power attitudes have also been found to be negatively related to environmental values (Rankin and Nealey, 1978; Hensler and Hensler, 1979; Benedict et al., 1980; Clelland and Bremseth, 1980), equality concerns (Rankin and Nealey, 1978), and concerns about technology (Groth and Schutz, 1976; Hensler and Hensler, 1979; and Benedict et al., 1980). The attitudes have been found to be positively related to values dealing with a comfortable life, family security and national security (Rankin and Nealey, 1978).

TABLE 1
OVERALL TOTALS AND SEX DIFFERENCES
FOR MEASURES OF OPINION ON NUCLEAR POWER
(Percentages)

	Total	Men	Women	Difference W-M
Q.42 At the present time the United States has 70 nuclear power plants in operation, plus 91 more plants which are currently under construction. I am going to read you three statements about the use of nuclear power in the United States. With which statement do you most agree?				
We should continue to build more nuclear plants as needed	23%	33%	14%	-19%
No more new plants should be planned but we should continue to use the ones already in operation and finish those now under construction	47	45	48	3
We should stop building nuclear plants including those under construction and shut down the existing ones as soon as possible	20	15	25	10
Don't know	11	7	15	8
Q.52 All in all, from what you have heard or read, how safe are nuclear power plants that produce electric power--very safe, somewhat safe or not so safe?				
Very safe	15	23	8	-15
Somewhat safe	40	44	36	- 8
Not so safe	29	21	36	15
Dangerous (volunteered)	9	8	10	2
Don't know	7	4	10	6
Q.67 Now, I am going to read you some phrases that describe different kinds of interests people have. As I read each one, would you please tell me whether it definitely applies to you, or only somewhat or not at all?				
Certainly antinuclear	19	12	23	11
Somewhat antinuclear	17	14	18	4
Ambivalent (somewhat anti- and somewhat pro-)	14	12	15	3
Neither	24	21	26	5
Somewhat pronuclear	15	19	12	- 7
Definitely pronuclear	13	22	7	-15

Source: Resources for the Future (RFF) Survey for the U.S. Council on Environmental Quality.

Measurement

The model to be estimated consists of several measures of attitudes toward nuclear power, and an array of variables that measure the personal characteristics, knowledge, attitudes/values[8] and beliefs that have been postulated to cause these attitudes. Table 1 gives the wording and distribution of the answers to key nuclear power questions. For example, when given the opportunity to take a position between going ahead with nuclear power or phasing out the existing plants, 47% in the survey chose the middle alternative, which said we should continue to use the 70 plants already in operation and finish those 91 that were then under construction. Approximately equal segments of the sample either favored the national policy of building more plants or the view of the antinuclear movement that nuclear power should be phrased out (23% and 20%, respectively). In answers to another question, 38% said they regard nuclear power plants as "not so safe" or "dangerous."

Sample surveys in the U.S. and elsewhere consistently find strong differences in views about nuclear power for men and women, and the Resources for the Future survey is no exception. As shown in Table 1, twice as many men as women in the RFF survey said "we should continue to build more nuclear power plants as needed," and men were three times as likely to believe nuclear power to be "very safe." Reed and Wilkes (1981:ii) call this difference "one of the most consistent and frequently cited findings in the relevant social science and public opinion literatures" (see also Brody, 1981; Dunlap and Van Liere, 1978). This finding cannot be attributed to a general tendency on the part of women to be risk-averse, since studies of attitudes toward cancer risks find no sex differences that even approach this magnitude (Cambridge Reports, 1977, 1978).

In order to test the first hypothesis it is necessary to measure "exaggerated fears." Because the RFF survey was not originally designed to test the nuclear phobia theory, only a single variable is sufficiently consistent with that approach to merit analysis. This is a knowledge question that asked:

TABLE 2
VARIABLE DEFINITIONS FOR MODEL

Variable	Definition	Range and Direction
Energy knowledge	General energy information; scale consists of four items described in this chapter's Technical Appendix.	1-5 (5 = high knowledge)
Belief that nuclear plants can explode	"Do you think that it is possible for a nuclear power plant to explode and cause a mushroom-shaped cloud like the one at Hiroshima or don't you think that is possible?"	1 = possible 0 = not possible
Children	Do you have any children (under the age of 18)?	1 = yes, 0 = no
Education	Education attained, where 1 = up to grade 8, and 6 = one or more years of post-graduate education.	1-6 (6 = high)
Concern about future scientific research	"Here are a number of statements about different topics on which I would like to ask your opinion. Would you please indicate for each whether you agree strongly, agree, disagree or disagree strongly? . . . (g) Future scientific research is more likely to cause problems than to find solutions to our problems."	1-4 (4 = "Strongly agree")
Concern about technology	Same format as previous variable. "People would be better off if they lived a more simple life without so much technology."	1-4 (4 = "Strongly agree")
Seeing self as environmentalist	"Now I am going to read you some phrases that describe different kinds of interests people have. As I read one, would you please tell me whether it definitely applies to you, or only somewhat or not at all . . . an environmentalist?" This item is also a component of the scale of environmental attitudes (the next variable).	1-3 (3 = "Definitely an environmentalist")
Environmental priority	Index of seven items that measure pro and anti-environmental attitudes, self-definition as an environmentalist, and environmental activism. See Technical Appendix of this chapter for a description.	-5 to +5 (+5 = high)
Concern about national defense	People coded as to whether or not they chose "making sure that this country has strong defense forces" as the first or second most desirable national goal out of twelve. (This question is part of the "post-materialism" value scale of Inglehart, 1977).	1 = defense listed as first or second choice 0 = defense listed third or lower

TABLE 2 (Continued)

Aversion to hazardous waste dump	Question which asks people how close a "disposal site for hazardous waste chemicals (which the) government said...could be done safely and . . . which would be inspected regularly for possible problems" could be built to their house before the respondent would "want to move to another place or to actively protest or whether it wouldn't matter to you one way or another how close it was?" Answers were given in miles and divided by 100.	0.1 - 5.0 (5 = 500 miles)
Concern about poor	"Now, I'd like to find out how worried or concerned you are about a number of problems I am going to mention: a great deal, a fair amount, not very much, or not at all. If you aren't really concerned about some of these matters, don't hesitate to say so . . . . (b) The problems of the poor?"	1-4 (4 = "A great deal")
Affected by air pollution	"People are affected in different ways by the problems our country faces. For each of the problems I am going to mention, please tell me how much you, yourself, are affected in terms of the kind of life you live and your personal enjoyment of your surroundings. Would you say it affects you a great deal, a fair amount, just a little, or not at all? . . . (b) Air pollution?"	1-4 (4 = "A great deal")
Age	"Here is a list of age groups. Would you call off the letter by the age group you happen to be in?"	1-6 (6 = oldest)
Concern about energy	Same question format as concern about poor: "(f) Shortages of oil, gasoline, coal, natural gas,electricity or other fuels?"	1 = Concerned "a great deal" or "Fair amount" 0 = others lowest
Favor renewable energy sources	Those who chose energy conservation, water power or solar energy as their choice for the most desirable energy source when asked to choose from a list of seven energy options which one they think "we should concentrate on" most "looking ahead to the year 2000."	1 = favor renewables 0 = favor others
See nuclear power as lowest priority	Same format as previous variable, except that nuclear power was named as the one source of energy that the respondent "would like to see us spend the <u>least</u> effort to develop."	1 = nuclear power lowest priority 0 = others lowest

> Do you think that it is possible for a nuclear power plant to explode and cause a mushroom-shaped cloud like the one at Hiroshima or don't you think that is possible?

The question directly evokes the link between nuclear power and the destructive potential of nuclear weapons with its references to "mushroom-shaped cloud" and "Hiroshima." An erroneous belief in this possibility was widespread: 52% of the sample said they believed it was possible, while 16% were not sure.

Knowledge about energy and nuclear matters is measured by a four-item scale that is described in the Technical Appendix of this chapter. The value/attitude items on the lay rationality hypotheses consist of the following: an index of environmental concern that is described in the Technical Appendix, measures of two factors that might predispose the person to favor nuclear energy (concerns about energy shortages and about air pollution), two variables that measure attitudes toward science and technology, and one item each on social equity and national security. The respondents' aversiveness to site-specific technological hazards is measured by a question on how close they are willing to live to a regulated and inspected hazardous waste chemical dump site. Table 2 provides more specific information on these variables.

Data Analysis Procedures

The statistical procedure I used, which is called a block recursive simultaneous equation system, is appropriate for the general model described earlier. The model posits a set of relationships in which (a) personal characteristics, knowledge, attitudes/values and beliefs (I will call them "stage one factors" here for convenience) explain people's views about nuclear safety, (b) the stage one factors explain people's views about building more nuclear power plants "indirectly" (i.e., through the effects these variables have on views of nuclear safety) as well as directly, and (c) the stage one factors and the views on nuclear safety explain people's personal positions on the nuclear debate. The statistical analysis, details of which are reported in the Technical Appendix, consists of three equations, one for each of the three stages described above (a, b and c).

In my first efforts to test this model, I included sex as one of the stage one variables. Its effects tended to be statistically meaningful but relatively modest in magnitude. I then tested a number of interactions between sex and other variables, such as education, knowledge, having children and the environmental index. The findings were suggestive, but complex, and led me to hypothesize that the factors influencing men's and women's reactions to nuclear safety and nuclear power were so different that proper specification required separate models for each sex. A statistical test reported in the Technical Appendix of this chapter confirmed this hypothesis. Figures 2 and 3 therefore present separate estimations of the model for women and men.[9]

To permit direct comparisons, the same model or set of variables was used in both Figures, even though some of the variables have a significant effect for only one sex. For the same reason, the coefficients for each relationship (indicated by the number on the arrow between two variables) are presented in their "unstandardized" form. Thus it is not possible to make meaningful comparisons between different pairs of variables, but it is possible to compare the coefficients for the same relationship in the male and female models. For example, the relationship between environmental attitudes and views toward nuclear safety is slightly stronger for women (.11) than for men (.09).

The comparative strength of each relationship is also reflected to a large degree by its level of significance. This is indicated by the thickness of the arrow connecting a pair of variables.[10] The absence of a line between two variables means that the variable on the left does not have a statistically interpretable direct relationship with the variable on the right.

Findings

Hypothesis 1 predicts that the people who believe a nuclear power plant can explode like an atomic bomb will tend to be more concerned about nuclear safety. This hypothesis is upheld both for men and for women at the .01 significance level, although the magnitude of the effect differs somewhat between men and women. The difference is revealed more clearly in a separate analysis, when the explosion item is regressed on nuclear safety by itself. As a *single predictor*,

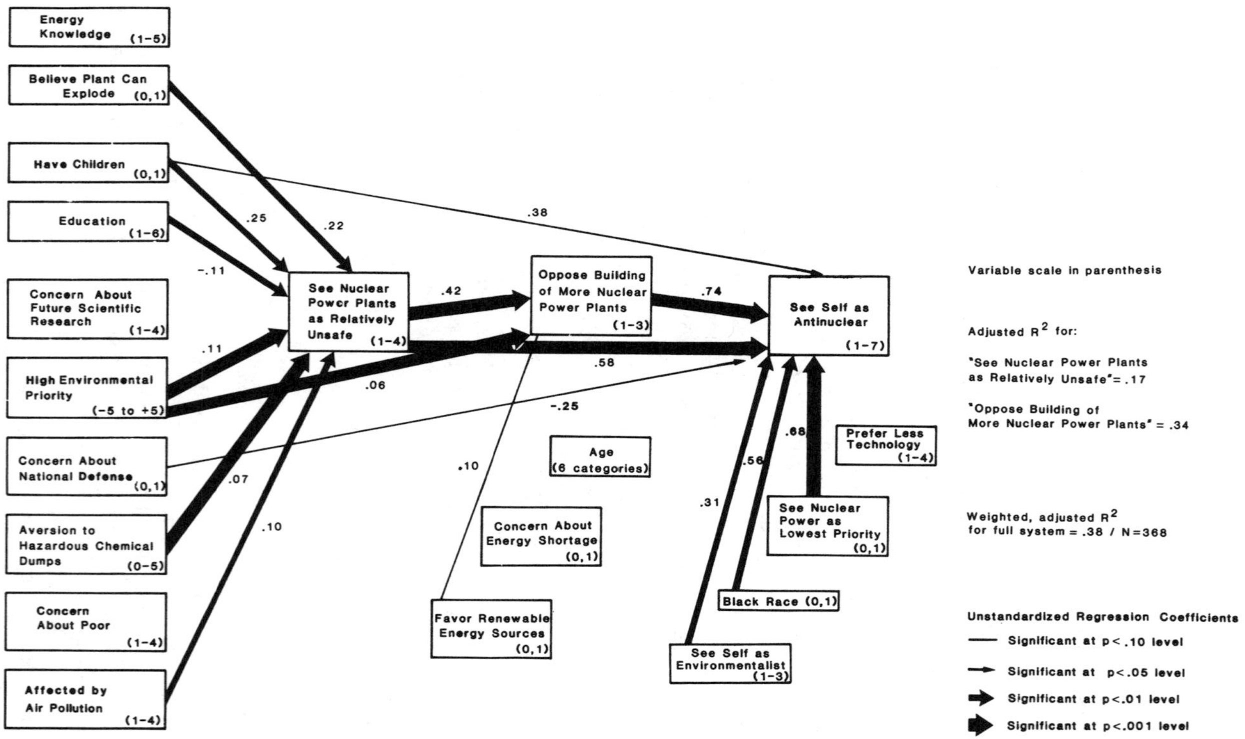
Energy Knowledge (1-5)
Believe Plant Can Explode (0,1)
Have Children (0,1)
Education (1-6)
Concern About Future Scientific Research (1-4)
High Environmental Priority (-5 to +5)
Concern About National Defense (0,1)
Aversion to Hazardous Chemical Dumps (0-5)
Concern About Poor (1-4)
Affected by Air Pollution (1-4)
See Nuclear Power Plants as Relatively Unsafe (1-4)
Oppose Building of More Nuclear Power Plants (1-3)
See Self as Antinuclear (1-7)
Age (6 categories)
Concern About Energy Shortage (0,1)
Favor Renewable Energy Sources (0,1)
Prefer Less Technology (1-4)
See Nuclear Power as Lowest Priority (0,1)
Black Race (0,1)
See Self as Environmentalist (1-3)
.25
.22
-.11
.11
.07
.10
.42
.06
.38
.74
.58
-.25
.10
.68
.56
.31
Variable scale in parenthesis
Adjusted R2 for:
"See Nuclear Power Plants as Relatively Unsafe"= .17
"Oppose Building of More Nuclear Power Plants" = .34
Weighted, adjusted R2 for full system = .38 / N=368
Unstandardized Regression Coefficients
Significant at p< .10 level
Significant at p<.05 level
Significant at p<.01 level
Significant at p<.001 level

Figure 2. Path Model for the Female Position on the Nuclear Debate

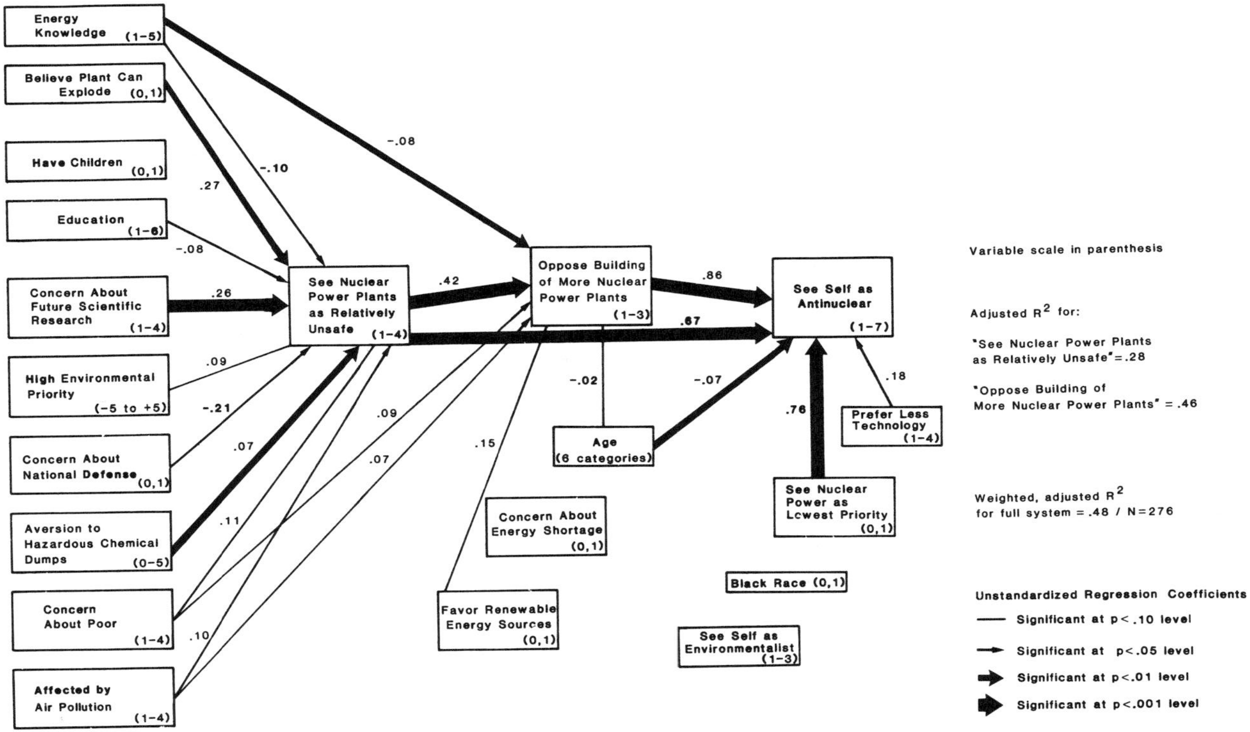

Figure 3. Path Model for the Male Position on the Nuclear Debate

it accounts for 8.9% of the variance in nuclear safety for men, while only accounting for 2.7% of the variance for women.

The male-female difference is even more dramatic in the test of Hypothesis 2, which predicts a negative relationship between knowledge and concern about nuclear safety. Figure 2 shows that the knowledge variable has no relationship with any of the dependent variables for women. Figure 3 shows that lower energy knowledge affects men's acceptance of power plants both indirectly (through safety concerns) and directly, being roughly equal to fears about explosions in the strength of its effects for men. H_2 is therefore rejected for women and confirmed for men.

The third hypothesis predicts that education will be inversely related to safety concerns. This hypothesis is confirmed both for men and for women. Here too the effect is stronger for men, although the relationship is not especially strong for either sex.

To summarize: this test of the nuclear phobia theory shows that factors consistent with it do affect people's acceptance of nuclear power to some extent by increasing their concern about nuclear safety. The magnitude of this effect is very small for women, contrary to the stereotype of women as more irrationally averse to technological risks. For men, however, the effects of such factors are not as small, accounting for about 40% of the variance in safety concerns that can be explained by the model. This finding--that the sexes differ markedly in the degree to which energy knowledge is related to their assessment of nuclear power--may account for the contradictory findings of previous studies on this topic. Unless the sexes are analyzed separately, the relationship is hidden.

According to the lay rationality hypotheses, the variables represented by the lower six boxes along the left sides of Figures 2 and 3 (those that measure attitudes/values, beliefs, and general orientation toward risk) will substantially explain the three dependent variables beginning with nuclear safety concerns. To the extent that these variables explain more of the variance than do education, knowledge and fears of explosions, the lay rationality theory is a superior explanation for people's views about nuclear power.

Turning to Hypotheses 4-6, we find strong support for the lay rationality view, in that the value-risk items have sizable effects for both men and women. The particular attitude/values that appear to influence men's and women's attitudes toward nuclear power differ, however.

- For both sexes the strongest predictor of nuclear safety concern is a value measure, although the values differ for men and women. Environmentalism is associated with concern about nuclear safety for women, but it has only a slight relationship for men. Conversely, the item on skepticism toward the future benefits of scientific research is strongly predictive of nuclear safety concerns for men, while it fails to enter the equation for women.

- Other value measures also enter the model for both men and women, as shown by the two figures, although again the patterns are different for the two sexes. Concerns about the problems of the poor do not have an effect for women, for example, while they have (modest) effects for men on two of the three dependent variables. The item on technological concerns enters the model for men on the final dependent variable, while an environmental variable occupies a parallel position in the women's model.

- Variables associated with risk and concern about air pollution problems also enter the model as predicted. The magnitude of their effects is the same for men and women. Concern about energy shortages does not affect either men's or women's views about nuclear power in these two models.

- Having children under the age of 18 has a strong effect on nuclear safety concerns, but only for women. This variable also has a direct effect on women's positions on the nuclear debate.

To summarize: the results for the hypotheses based on the lay rationality approach are also positive. Attitudes toward technology and the environment, together with other attitudes/values such as concerns for the poor and averseness to technological risk, are associated with the dependent variables in the manner and strength predicted. People's attitudes toward nuclear power are indeed affected by their attitudes/values, although the pattern of effects is different for men and women.

We have now seen that hypotheses derived from both of the approaches are supported by these data. Is one theory better than the other in explaining people's views about nuclear power? Using the amount of the explained variance attributable to each theory as a criterion, the lay rationality theory is clearly more successful in explaining these data. If the model for nuclear safety concerns, the key dependent variable, is estimated without the three measures of the nuclear phobia theory (fears of explosions, knowledge, and education) it still accounts for 14% of the variance for women and 21% for men. A reverse analysis, using just the three independent variables from the nuclear phobia theory, explains much lower proportions of the variance (5% and 10%, respectively, for women and men).

Why are women more opposed to nuclear power than men? We can be more certain about what does *not* cause the difference than what does. Insofar as these data can be used to test the nuclear phobia theory, they clearly show that women's greater opposition to nuclear power is not caused by a greater level of irrational fears. It should be noted here that women do tend to be more likely than men to believe that nuclear power plants can blow up like an atomic bomb, and women's average energy knowledge level is lower than men's. But given the weakness of these variables as determinants of women's attitudes toward nuclear power, they cannot account for the male-female difference. As shown earlier, belief that nuclear plants can blow up accounts for more of the variance in men's than in women's safety concerns, and knowledge is not related to attitudes toward nuclear safety for women when the other variables in the model are taken into account. What about women's commitment to environmentalism? Hensler and Hensler (1979:95) speculate that women are more committed to environmental protection than men are, and that this accounts for their greater opposition to nuclear power. The RFF data do not support this hypothesis, since men and women have the same average scores on the environmental values index. Nor can the difference be explained by a greater optimism on the part of men toward the effects of science and technology, since men and women also share similar mean scores on these variables.

The data patterns in Figures 2 and 3 suggest that women are more opposed to nuclear power than men because of the different perspectives they bring to the issue. First, the parental role apparently makes women more sensitive to the risks presented by nuclear power, while it has little effect on men's views. Second, women appear to regard nuclear power as an environmental problem, while men tend to view it as a technological/scientific problem.[11] Men and women in this sample are equally likely to hold environmental beliefs, but it appears that the environmentally committed man is only slightly more likely to be concerned about nuclear safety than is his less environmentally oriented brother. The implication is that men tend not to bring their environmental views to bear on the issue of nuclear power. Men tend to be affected instead by the degree to which they are optimistic or pessimistic about the future effects of technology--and pessimism about technology is less widespread in American society than is environmentalism.[12]

PART III: CONCLUSIONS AND DISCUSSION

The purpose of the preceding analysis has been to assess the rationality of the public's opposition to nuclear power. Although "rational" and (especially) "irrational" are words used in everyday discourse about the nuclear debate--as when *Time* headlines a story, "The Irrational Fight Against Nuclear Power" (Stoler, 1978:71)--the concepts elude simple definition when they are considered as concepts instead of as stereotypical labels.

In comparing what I call the nuclear phobia approach with the lay rationality approach, I am assessing competing explanations of the ways in which people reach a determination that nuclear power plants may be unsafe. The first posits an emotional response to unconscious fears, and holds that people are too scared to assess the facts properly; the second posits a cognitive response whereby people assess the information available to them by means of the decision criteria they normally use in situations where the outcomes are uncertain and potentially risky.

Nuclear power does have fearsome overtones stemming from its association with nuclear weaponry, and this aspect of the technology contributes to its controversial character. Many persons are indeed misinformed about energy issues, as shown by their responses to knowledge questions. But insofar as I can measure irrational factors with the present data, their effects on public assessments of nuclear safety (and thus of nuclear power) are relatively small for men, and small indeed for women. The notion of a nuclear phobia as the major explanation for opposition to nuclear power simply does not accord with the findings of this study, nor with those of the only other study that has examined this question empirically (Hensler and Hensler, 1979).

My findings are more consistent with the view that lay rationality accounts for the greater part of the public concern about nuclear safety. Most people obtain information about nuclear power from the media, conversations with friends, and other sources such as the groups they belong to. In processing this information to arrive at an opinion about nuclear power, they do not employ expected utility theory and an ambition to optimize in the strict sense of formal or "classical" rationality (cf. Simon, 1976), but appear to use instead a set of lay heuristics or rules of thumb and to seek a solution that is "good enough" or that satisfies. Most people probably do react intuitively to the issue, without much awareness of their cognitive processes, just as business executives do when they are faced with the business situations that arise (Simon, 1976:145). According to studies of these cognitive processes, people draw heavily on past experience to detect the important features of a given problem, using these features to retrieve relevant information from long-term memory (Simon, 1976). The findings of the present study suggest that men and women draw on different aspects of their past experiences when they consider the issue of nuclear safety. For women, their roles as mothers and their perceptions of environmental threats are particularly salient, whereas optimism about the ability of science to solve future problems and perceptions of the net benefits of technology are more influential for men.

How well served is the public by its "subjectively rational" decision process? Research on everyday rationality, as summarized further by Slovic and his colleagues (1984) in Chapter 5 of this volume, demonstrates the rather modest information-processing capability that humans possess, and suggests a propensity toward bias under certain conditions. But neither my research nor theirs can determine, at least at this stage in the Atomic Age, whether the public's concern about nuclear safety is an "exaggerated" or a prudent response to uncertainty, or whether the use of "primitive judgmental heuristics" leads to inferential shortcomings or to healthy folk wisdom. Such determinations must wait for future findings on answers to questions that have not yet been answered: Was the accident at Three Mile Island a fluke or a harbinger of things to come? Will carbon dioxide emissions from the burning of coal lead to significant or irreversible climate change? To what extent will our continued commitment to nuclear power increase the risks of nuclear war through proliferation? Can renewable energy sources account for sufficient energy production to permit us to turn away from the nuclear option? Can nuclear power plants be constructed with adequate attention to quality control, or are we destined to see continuing quality control failures in the future?

Implications

The nation's present policy is to promote the expansion of nuclear power as one of several ways to meet our future energy needs. This open-ended expansion policy is supported by only a minority of the public at present. Relatively few people take the extreme antinuclear position that existing plants should be shut down, as Rankin and his colleagues (1984) note in Chapter 2 of this volume, but a majority are profoundly ambivalent about the technology, as Freudenburg and Rosa (1984b) note in the concluding chapter, and would prefer to phase out our commitment to the peaceful atom. What are the implications of my analysis for those who wish to increase the public acceptance of nuclear power?

In the first place, the rational dimension of public concerns should be acknowledged. To paraphrase Harvey Sapolsky's advice to the proponents of fluoridation (1968:431), the proponents do not enhance their chances when they act as though there is no legitimate opposition to nuclear power.

To attribute public concern about nuclear safety to sensationalist media coverage or to fear-mongering by its opponents is fall into a paternalist trap. To assume that public concerns are obviously erroneous because they differ from the current technological consensus is to ignore the lessons of history, as Mazur's chapter (1984) in this volume clearly points out. The history of nuclear power over the past decade can be interpreted in several ways, but the interpretation offered by the President's Commission on the Accident at Three Mile Island (1979)--to cite just one recent analysis--suggests that those who believe they alone possess the technological truth are imperfect guides to a technological future.

Second, recognition should be given to the larger dimensions of the nuclear debate. David E. Lilienthal, the first chairman of the Atomic Energy Commission, and later its earliest critic, devoted his last book to a defense of nuclear energy. In this book he describes the value issues that underlie the protest against nuclear power:

> To a large extent it has been a protest against the misuse of science, the misdirection of enormous forces that human ingenuity has brought into being. It is a protest against the abuses of industrial technology that poison the land instead of nurturing it . . . . It is a protest against governments . . . that spend billions in an endless, insane atomic arms race that consumes the cream of the world's resources and much of its brightest human talent (Lilienthal, 1980:110).

Sometimes proponents of nuclear power treat these concerns as irrelevant and denigrate those who hold them as "elitists," members of the "new class," or "antigrowth fanatics." They believe the debate should be restricted to technical issues. But every technology has social consequences, and our present choice of energy technologies commits us to a particular path for a long time to come. Perhaps inevitably, the public's awareness of a potentially sinister dimension to the nuclear dream occurred long after nuclear power was given a key place on the nation's energy agenda. At the present time, if given a choice, the vast majority of the public would prefer a different agenda. Rightly or wrongly, they associate conservation and solar technologies with a future society in which environmental limitations are respected and individual autonomy is enhanced. Therefore to give the impression that utilization of these potentially benign sources of energy is not a national priority, as the Reagan Administration has done, can only serve to promote public resentment about continued funding for nuclear power.

Third, the best way to open a genuine dialogue with the concerned public about nuclear safety is to emphasize candor in nuclear information programs. When accidents or problems occur, it is counterproductive to minimize them. The effect of Three Mile Island (TMI) on the public's acceptance of nuclear power would probably have been much worse if it had not been for the prompt and public acknowledgment by the Nuclear Regulatory Commission of the accident's seriousness, and the forthright (and therefore reassuring) behavior of Harold Denton, the President's spokesperson on the scene. The early public statements by the new chairman of the Nuclear Regulatory Commission, Nunzio J. Palladino, about the "inexcusable" failure of the nuclear industry's quality assurance programs, suggest that he may have adopted a similar stance toward the industry's problems. Candor should also characterize the discussion of the possibility of future mishaps. In the first part of the nuclear age, the impression was created by those in charge of nuclear policy and regulation that an accident like TMI was so unlikely as to be impossible (Green, 1980:47). This impression rendered the actual event all the more threatening to the public.

Fourth, every effort should be made to establish credibility. Owing to the legacy of suspicion created by the failures described by H. Peter Metzger in *The Atomic Establishment* (Metzger, 1972), this admits of no quick fixes. Unless the Nuclear Regulatory Commission vigorously enforces quality assurance regulations, Chairman Palladino's candor will have no lasting positive effect. To the extent to which the public believes that efforts to expedite nuclear licensing will compromise safety or reflect a return to the "mindset" identified by the Kemeny Commission (President's Commission on the Accident at Three Mile Island, 1979:8), confidence in nuclear power will erode further.

Perhaps the most troublesome aspect of nuclear power to the analyst of public opinion is its present vulnerability to a potential backlash if a future accident would injure innocent bystanders. It would not take a mammoth disaster of the kind imagined by those who were studied by Paul Slovic to create such a backlash. I conjecture that a breach of a containment that resulted in, say, the death of 100 people and the long-term contamination of ten square miles, might suffice to render the nuclear option politically unacceptable. A lesser amount of incontrovertable physical harm to the public is likely to require expensive modifications of existing plants and future designs. I advance this conjecture because attempts to assess the potential public response to such events are rare (see, however, Slovic et al., 1980). Whether it is rational or irrational to expose ourselves to this risk is yet another unanswered question.

ACKNOWLEDGEMENTS

The author acknowledges, with gratitude, the research assistance of Richard T. Carson, and the helpful comments on earlier drafts provided by Denton R. Morrison and Clifford S. Russell. Partial support for this research was provided by the Ethical and Value Implications of Science and Technology Program of the National Science Foundation. The author alone is responsible for its content.

TECHNICAL APPENDIX

Methods Used

The RFF study used the split-half technique to increase the number of questions that could be asked in a half-hour interview. Roper and Cantril divided the total sample of 1576 respondents into two halves, "X" and "Y," each of which is a national probability sample. Approximately one fourth of the questions were asked only in the X or the Y version, while the others were used in both versions. Because all the energy knowledge and attitude-toward-technology measures appear only in the X version, the present analysis is limited to that version, which was administered to a total of 840 respondents.

The set of attitude/value, knowledge and background variables selected for possible inclusion in the final model were screened by separately regressing them on each of the three dependent variables in turn. This process allowed me to examine the effect of each variable with the effects of the others held constant. Where it appeared to be warranted, I also tested for non-linear and interaction effects. Through this screening process I identified those variables which had no statistically significant effect on the dependent variables. I set the significance level at .10 since variables which are only marginally significant in this data set may, under other circumstances, have more explanatory power and therefore deserve to be considered by other researchers. Variables were dropped from the segment of the model for which they were ineffectual predictors. Education, for example, had no effect on opposition to building more nuclear power plants once perceived nuclear power plant safety was introduced into the regression equation. Because of this, it appears in the model only in relation to perceived safety.

I estimated a block recursive simultaneous equation system using both ordinary least squares (OLS) and the Zellner Seemingly Unrelated Regression Technique (SUR) (Zellner, 1962)--the latter on the assumption that the error structure between the three equations in the model is related. As the Zellner technique showed significant correlation between the error structure of the three equations I report only the unstandardized coefficients from the SUR estimation. I do not report results from the OLS estimations because there are no major differences between them and the SUR results. Since the SUR technique did reduce the standard errors of the parameters, however marginally, it is the better estimation technique.

I use the unstandardized coefficients because standardization, in Duncan's words, "tends to obscure the distinction between the structural coefficients of the model and the several variances and covariances that describe the joint distribution of the variables" (1975:51). Given the different variances in the male and female samples, only the unstandardized coefficients permit direct comparisons between the two models. Each of the equations described below was tested for multicollinearity using the technique described in Belsley et al., 1980. The condition index numbers from these tests indicate that multicollinearity is not a significant problem. I tested for non-linearity primarily by examining the cross-tabulations of key relationships.

To test the hypothesis that nuclear attitudes are best specified by separate models for men and women, I used the Chow F test (Chow, 1960) to test the significance of the difference of the coefficients between the entire sample and the male and female sub-samples. The test confirmed the hypothesis, so I preceded with the separate estimations that are shown in Figures 2 and 3. (The F values and significance levels were as follows: perceived nuclear plant safety, $F = 2.4$, $p < .01$; opposition to further nuclear plant construction, $F = 3.4$, $p < .001$; seeing self as antinuclear, $F = 2.4$, $p < .01$. In each case the sample size is 644. The number of variables in each equation range from 9-11.)

Scale Construction

Energy Knowledge Scale. This knowledge scale is constructed from four items in the questionnaire. One point was given for each correct or partially correct answer, and 0 was given when people were incorrect or not sure. The scores were summed to give a total that ranges from 0-4. The correct answer is in italics. The first two of these items were closed-ended (respondents were given a list of possible responses and asked to choose one of them); the last two items were open-ended.

- Nuclear power plants are built near bodies of water. Do you think that's because the water is used as another source of power, as a disposal place for waste, or is used for cooling purposes?

  11% - Another source of power
  16% - A disposal place for waste
  52% - For cooling purposes
  21% - Not sure

- From what you have heard or read, do you think we produce enough oil in this country to meet our present energy needs or do we have to import some oil from other countries?

  29% - Produce enough oil
  63% - Have to import some oil
  7% - Not sure

I'm going to read you a short list of topics and incidents that have been mentioned in the news media over the past year or so. As I mention one, if you happen to have heard or read about it, would you please tell me what it refers to?

- The accident at Three Mile Island: can you tell me what happened there?

74% - *Correct: nuclear reactor accident; Harrisburg incident; accident that almost caused a meltdown*
19% - Not sure
4% - Incorrect
3% - Partially correct: Presidential Commission; in Pennsylvania; No reference to nuclear power

- Synfuels or synthetic fuels: can you tell me what they are?

37% - *Correct: gas or oil made from coal or oil shale or tar sands; coal gasification; coal liquification or coal liquids*
5% - Partially correct: President Carter's new billion dollar plan; new source of energy recently proposed by President Carter and debated in congress
15% - Incorrect
42% - Not sure

The sample size for these items was 825 persons. The distribution of responses was as follows:

No. of correct answers	Percentage of Respondents
0	10%
1	23
2	24
3	24
4	18

Environmentalism Scale. This second scale, called "ENVINDEX" below, was developed from respondents' answers to seven items in the survey. ENVIDEX was initially set at zero, and then increased or decreased by one point at a time depending on a respondent's answers to the selected items:

If NEITHERD = 1 then ENVINDEX = ENVINDEX - 1
If POLLUTE = 1 then ENVINDEX = ENVINDEX - 1
If ENVMOVT = 4 then ENVINDEX = ENVINDEX - 1
If ENVIST = 3 then ENVINDEX = ENVINDEX - 1
If VPOLCST = 3 then ENVINDEX = ENVINDEX - 1
If AIMCLEAN = 1 then ENVINDEX = ENVINDEX + 1
If ENVMOVT = 1 then ENVINDEX = ENVINDEX + 1
If ENVIST = 1 then ENVINDEX = ENVINDEX + 1
If VPOLCST = 1 then ENVINDEX = ENVINDEX + 1
If LETTERD = 1 then ENVINDEX = ENVINDEX + 1

Where (a) NEITHERD takes the value of 1 if the respondent volunteered a response of preferring not to pay high prices or taxes for environmental quality, and is 0 otherwise.

(b) POLLUTE takes the value of 1 in cases where "protecting nature against pollution" was chosen as the respondent's least favorite goal.

(c) ENVMOVT represents the respondent's attitude toward the environmental movement: 1 = "active participant," 4 = "non-sympathetic."

(d) ENVIST is a question asking for the respondent's self-identification as an environmentalist: 1 = "definitely," 3 = "not at all."

(e) VPOLCST involves the respondent's stand on the tradeoff between environmental standards and cost: 1 = support of extreme environmental standards at any cost; 3 = the position that environmental standards cost more than they are worth.

(f) AIMCLEAN has the value of 1 if "protecting nature from being spoiled and polluted" was chosen as one of the respondent's aims, and O otherwise.

(g) LETTERD has the value of 1 for respondents who reported sending a letter or contacting an official on an environmental matter, and has the value of O for other respondents.

The Range of ENVINDEX is +5 to -5, with distribution as follows:

Range	Percentage of Respondents
5	1%
+4	2%
+3	6%
+2	15%
+1	21%
0	25%
-1	17%
-2	9%
-3	3%
-4	1%
-5	0%

FOOTNOTES

[1]In the language of cognitive psychology what I mean by irrational here is behavior that "represents impulsive response to affective mechanisms without an adequate intervention of thought" (Simon, 1976:131).

[2]The findings of these various studies vary in detail, although not in substance. The study by Otway et al. (1978) of a set of people in Austria is worth describing somewhat more fully. They chose the subsets of their respondents who were the most and the least opposed to nuclear power and compared their beliefs. Those in favor were much more likely than those opposed to believe that nuclear power will "raise the standard of living" and "increase my country's economic development." Conversely, those opposed were more likely to believe the use of nuclear power will "lead to accidents which affect large numbers of people at the same time," "mean exposing myself to risks which I cannot control" and "lead to transporting dangerous substances," to cite three of the strongest differences.

[3]In this regard a letter written in 1973 to the editor of *Not Man Apart*, the biweekly magazine of the antinuclear environmental organization Friends of the Earth, is revealing of the tension within the antinuclear movement over the use of rational argument. The author castigates the editor for going about opposing nuclear power the "wrong way" and complains that:

> [Like] most of your ads . . . the latest [one] that ran in . . . the *Washington Post* adopts the tone of Reasonable Men speaking to Reasonable Men. The dominant impression is that this question is basically scientific in nature. This approach, while it preserves our own self-image as Responsible Spokesmen and Concerned Intellectuals, plays right into the hands of the nuclear proponents . . . we end up having to attack pieces of arrant nonsense like Fault Tree Analyses (one-in-a-billion chance of serious accident) while the public assumes that as long as we're arguing about incomprehensible numbers, nothing terribly serious can be wrong (Navarre, 1974:2).

[4]Robert Lifton's research assistant has described his data gathering effort for Lifton (Carey, 1982:20-21), which partially consisted of 55 in-depth interviews. The data from these interviews are never presented quantitatively in Lifton's

book, but are drawn upon for qualitative inferences. Lifton's conclusion about the relationship between fear of nuclear weapons and opposition to nuclear power is made without reference to any systematic data.

[5]Path analysis is a statistical technique for evaluating complex causal models by using a series of regression equations. For a brief note on regression, see Footnote 1 of Chapter 2 in this volume, by Rankin et al. (1984). For a technical discussion, see Land (1969). See also the discussion of "Data Analysis Procedures" below.

[6]The second study was conducted for Consolidated Edison by the Columbia University Energy Research Center. According to a news item in *Nucleonics Week*, it found "knowledge about energy, nuclear energy in particular, strongly correlated with attitude . . . with people knowledgeable in this area . . . much more likely to favor nuclear energy" (June 25, 1981:11). A paper by Cole and Fiorentine (1983) reporting the results of this study only became available when this chapter was in proof.

[7]"Multivariate techniques" are simply those that allow researchers to use multiple independent or explanatory variables. These techniques can reveal the unique or net effect of a given explanatory variable on the dependent or outcome variable, with the effects of other explanatory variables being "controlled," or held constant statistically. The statistical technique being used in this chapter--path analysis based on multiple regression--is a form of multivariate analysis that is particularly common in the social sciences.

[8]Strictly speaking some of the variables I call "values" are measures of "attitudes," where attitudes are overall judgments about an object in terms of favorableness or unfavorableness (Thomas et al., 1980:3) and values represent more fundamental and enduring judgments about desirable end states (Rokeach, 1973). Thus stated, the distinction seems clear, but in practice it is often difficult to say whether a particular question measures only an attitude or whether it taps a more fundamental value orientation. I use "values" here in the sense of attitudes/values, which measure people's preference structures.

[9]The final sample sizes for these estimations are 276 men and 368 women, for a total of 644. The reduction in sample size is due to the elimination of every person who gave a "don't know" for any of the variables in the model. This

procedure means that the results apply only to those persons who have expressed opinions about nuclear power.

[10]Each coefficient's meaning is interpretable by reference to the variables' value ranges, which are shown in parentheses. For example, in Figure 2 the coefficient of .11 between the environmental priority index and nuclear safety concerns means that each increase of one point along the 11-point environmental index increases the respondent's score on the four-point nuclear safety item by .11. Comparing this relationship for men and women, we see that the magnitude is similar (.09 for men and .11 for women) although its statistical significance is lower for men because of the smaller number of men in the sample. A negative coefficient signifies an inverse relationship between a given pair of variables--indicating that, on average, as a person's score on one variable goes up, that same person's score on the other variable goes down at the magnitude indicated.

[11]I note here that in a recent paper Cole and Fiorentine offer a somewhat different explanation for the male-female difference. Based on their analysis of data from two surveys conducted for Northeastern utilities, they assert that "the reasons why women are more likely than men to oppose nuclear power are their generally lower level of information about nuclear power which increases their fear and their higher value placed on human life" (1983:21). This conclusion is based on their interpretation of the causal chain implied by a pattern of bivariate relationships (women are more opposed to nuclear power than men; women are less knowledgeable about nuclear power than men, etc.). I found a similar pattern of bivariate relationships in the early stages of my analysis of the RFF data. The advantage of using a multivariate model of the type employed in this chapter is that it allows the analyst to choose from among the several causal interpretations that are consistent with this pattern of bivariate relationships.

[12]For example, as Marrett (1984) notes in Chapter 13 of this volume, only about 30% of the persons in recent national surveys agree with the idea that future scientific research is more likely to cause problems than to bring solutions to our problems, and the RFF data are consistent with this average. By comparison, 55% of the people in the RFF survey disagree with the proposition that environmental problems are not as serious as some people would have us believe (Mitchell, 1980b).

REFERENCES

Belsley, D. A., E. Kuh and R. E. Welsch
1980 *Regression Diagnostics.* New York: John Wiley and Sons.

Benedict, Robert, Hugh Bone, Willard Leavel and Ross Rice
1980 "The Voters and Attitudes Toward Nuclear Power: A Comparative Study of Nuclear Moratorium Initiatives." *Western Political Quarterly* 33 (#1, March):7-23.

Bishop, George F.
1976 "The Effect of Education on Ideological Consistency." *Public Opinion Quarterly* 40 (#3):337-348.

Bowman, C. and M. Fishbein
1978 "Understanding Public Reaction to Energy Proposals: An Application of the Fishbein Model." *Journal of Applied Social Psychology* 8 (#4): 319-340.

Brody, Charles J.
1981 "Sex Differences in Attitudes Toward Nuclear Power." Paper presented at the annual meetings of the American Sociological Association, Toronto, August.

Cambridge Reports
1977 *An Analysis of Citizen Attitudes Toward Cancer Risks.* Cambridge, MA: Cambridge Reports, Inc. (Report prepared for Union Carbide Corporation, June.)
1978 *Public and Worker Attitudes Toward Carcinogens and Cancer Risk.* Cambridge, MA: Cambridge Reports, Inc. (Report prepared for Shell Oil, April.)

Carey, Michael J.
1982 "Psychological Fallout." *Bulletin of the Atomic Scientists* 38 (#1, January):20-24.

Chow, Gregory C.
1960 "Test of Equality Between Sets of Coefficients in Two Linear Regressions." *Econometrica* 28 (#3, July):591-605.

Clelland, Donald A. and Michael C. Bremseth
1980 "Explanations of Public Response to a Nuclear Energy Alternative." Paper presented at the annual meetings of the American Association for the Advancement of Science, San Francisco, January.

Cole, Stephen and Robert Fiorentine
1983 "The Formation of Public Opinion on Complex Issues: The Case of Nuclear Power." Paper presented at the annual meetings of the American Association of Public Opinion Researchers, Buck

Hill Falls, PA. May 21. Working Paper Series 830506.

Duncan, Otis Dudley
1975 *Introduction to Structural Equation Models.* New York: Academic Press.

Dunlap, Riley E. and Kent D. Van Liere
1978 "Environmental Concern: A Bibliography of Empirical Studies and Brief Appraisal of the Literature." Monticello, IL: Vance Bibliographies (Public Administration Series Bibliography P-44).

DuPont, Robert
1981a Testimony before Subcommittee on Energy Research and Production. U.S. House of Representatives, Washington, D.C., December 15.
1981b "The Nuclear Power Phobia." *Business Week* (September 7) 14-16.

Fishbein, M. and I. Ajzen
1975 *Belief, Attitude, Intention, and Behavior: An Introduction to Theory and Research.* Reading, MA: Addison-Wesley.

Freudenburg, William R. and Eugene A. Rosa (eds.)
1984a *Public Reactions to Nuclear Power: Are There Critical Masses?* Boulder, CO: Westview Press/ American Association for the Advancement of Science.
1984b "Are the Masses Critical?" Pp. 331-348 in William R. Freudenburg and Eugene A. Rosa (eds.), *Public Reactions to Nuclear Power: Are There Critical Masses?* Boulder, CO: Westview Press/American Association for the Advancement of Science.

Gottlieb, Melvin
1981 Testimony before the Subcommittee on Energy Research and Production. U.S. House of Representatives, Washington, D.C., December 15.

Green, Harold
1980 "On the Kemeny Commission," *Bulletin of the Atomic Scientists* 36 (#3, March):46-48.

Groth, Alexander J. and Howard G. Schutz
1976 *Voter Attitudes on the 1976 Nuclear Initiative in California.* Davis, CA: Institute of Governmental Affairs, University of California. (Environmental Quality Series, No. 25, December).

Gyorgy, Anna
1979 *No Nukes: Everyone's Guide to Nuclear Power.* Boston, MA: South End Press.

Harris, Louis
1978 *Public and Leadership Attitudes Toward Nuclear Power Development in the United States.* New York: Louis Harris and Associates. (Study No. P2846).

Hensler, Deborah R. and Carl P. Hensler
1979 *Evaluating Nuclear Power: Voter Choice on the California Nuclear Energy Initiative.* Santa Monica, CA: RAND Corporation.

Hosmer, Craig
1978 "The Energy-Growth Debate." Pp. 121-134 in Milton R. Copulos (ed.), *Energy Perspective: An Advocate's Guide.* Washington, D.C.: The Heritage Foundation.

Hoyle, Fred
1977 *Energy or Extinction? The Case for Nuclear Energy.* London, England: Heinemann.

Kasperson, Roger E., Gerald Berk, David Pijawka, Alan B. Sharaf and James Wood
1979 "Public Opposition to Nuclear Energy: Retrospect and Prospect." Pp. 259-292 in Charles T. Unseld, Denton E. Morrison, David L. Sills and C. P. Wolf (eds.), *Sociopolitical Effects of Energy Use and Policy, Supporting Paper 5.* Washington, D.C.: National Academy of Sciences.

Land, Kenneth C.
1969 "Principles of Path Analysis." In Edgar F. Borgatta (ed.), *Sociological Methodology 1969.* San Francisco: Jossey-Bass.

Lifton, Robert Jay
1979 *The Broken Connection: On Death and the Continuity of Life.* New York: Simon and Schuster.

Lilienthal, David E.
1980 *Atomic Energy: A New Start.* New York: Harper and Row.

Logan, Rebecca and Dorothy Nelkin
1980 "Labor and Nuclear Power." *Environment* 22 (#2, March):6-13, 34.

Lounsbury, John W., Eric Sundstrom and Robert C. de Vault
1979 "Moderating Effects of Respondent Knowledge in Public Opinion Research." *Journal of Applied Psychology* 64 (#5, May):558-563.

March, James G.
1978 "Bounded Rationality, Ambiguity, and the Engineering of Choice." *The Bell Journal of Economics* 9 (#2, Autumn):587-608.

Marrett, Cora Bagley
1984 "Public Concerns About Nuclear Power and Science." Pp. 307-328 in William R. Freudenburg and Eugene A. Rosa (eds.), *Public Reactions to Nuclear Power: Are There Critical Masses?* Boulder, CO: Westview Press/American Association for the Advancement of Science.

Mazur, Allan
1984 "Media Influences on Public Attitudes Toward Nuclear Power." Pp. 97-114 in William R. Freudenburg and Eugene A. Rosa (eds.), *Public Reactions to Nuclear Power: Are There Critical Masses?* Boulder, CO: Westview Press/American Association for the Advancement of Science.

Metzger, H. Peter
1972 *The Atomic Establishment.* New York: Simon and Schuster.

Mitchell, Robert C.
1980a "How 'Soft,' 'Deep,' or 'Left?' Present Constituencies in the Environmental Movement for Certain World Views." *Natural Resources Journal* 20 (#2, April):345-358.
1980b *Public Opinion on Environmental Issues: Results of a National Opinion Survey.* Washington, D.C.: President's Council on Environmental Quality.

Morrison, Denton E.
1980 "The Soft, Cutting Edge of Environmentalism: Why and How the Appropriate Technology Notion is Changing the Movement." *Natural Resources Journal* 20 (#2, April 1):275-298.

Navarre, Gabriel
1974 "Letter to the Editor." *Not Man Apart* 4 (#3, February):2.

Nealey, Stanley M. and William L. Rankin
1978 *Nuclear Knowledge and Nuclear Attitudes: Is Ignorance Bliss?* Seattle, WA: Battelle.

Nelkin, Dorothy
1981a "Anti-nuclear Connections: Power and Weapons." *Bulletin of the Atomic Scientists* 37 (#4, April):36-40.
1981b "Native Americans and Nuclear Power." *Science, Technology, & Human Values* 6 (#35, Spring): 2-12.
1981c "Nuclear Power as a Feminist Issue." *Environment* 23 (#1, January/February):14-25.

Nisbet, Robert
1979 "The Rape of Progress." *Public Opinion* 2 (#3, June/July):2-6.

Otway, Harry J., Dagmar Maurer and Kerry Thomas
1978 "Nuclear Power: The Question of Public Acceptance." *Futures* 10 (April):109-118.

Pahner, Philip
1976 *A Psychological Perspective of the Nuclear Energy Controversy.* Laxenburg, Austria: International Institute for Applied Systems Analysis.

President's Commission on The Accident at Three Mile Island
1979 *The Need for Change: The Legacy of TMI.*

Washington, D.C., U.S. Government Printing Office.

Rankin, William L. and Stanley M. Nealey
1978 The Relationship of Human Values and Energy *Beliefs to Nuclear Power Attitudes.* Seattle, WA: Battelle.

Rankin, William L., Stanley M. Nealey and Barbara D. Melber
1984 "Overview of National Attitudes Toward Nuclear Energy: A Longitudinal Analysis." Pp. 41-67 in William R. Freudenburg and Eugene A. Rosa (eds.), *Public Reactions to Nuclear Power: Are There Critical Masses?* Boulder, CO: Westview Press/American Association for the Advancement of Science.

Reed, John H. and John M. Wilkes
1981 "Technical Nuclear Knowledge and Attitudes Toward Nuclear Power Before and After TMI." Paper presented at the annual meetings of the Society for the Social Study of Science, Atlanta, November.

Rokeach, Milton
1973 *The Nature of Human Values.* New York: Free Press.

Sapolsky, Harvey M.
1968 "Science, Voters and the Fluoridation Controversy." *Science* 162 (October 25):427-433.

Simon, Herbert
1976 "From Substantive to Procedural Rationality." Pp. 129-148 in Spiro J. Latsis (ed.), *Method and Appraisal in Economics.* Cambridge, England: Cambridge University Press.

Slovic, Paul, Baruch Fischhoff and Sarah Lichtenstein
1980 "Perceived Risk." Pp. 181-214 in Richard C. Schwing and Walter A. Albers, Jr. (eds.), *Societal Risk Assessment: How Safe is Safe Enough?* New York: Plenum Press.
1984 "Perception and Acceptability of Risk from Energy Systems." Pp. 115-135 in William R. Freudenburg and Eugene A. Rosa (eds.), *Public Reactions to Nuclear Power: Are There Critical Masses?* Boulder, CO: Westview Press/American Association for the Advancement of Science.

Slovic, Paul, Sarah Lichtenstein and Baruch Fischhoff
1979 "Images of Disaster: Perception and Acceptance of Risks from Nuclear Power." Pp. 223-245 in Gordon Goodman and William D. Rowe (eds.), *Energy Risk Management.* London, England: Academic Press.

Stoler, Peter
1978 "The Irrational Fight Against Nuclear Power." *Time* (September 25):71-72.

Sundstrom, Eric, Robert C. DeVault and Elizabeth Peele
1981 "Acceptance of A Nuclear Power Plant: Applications of the Expectancy-Value Model." Pp. 171-189 in Andrew Baum and Jerome E. Singer (eds.), *Advances in Environmental Psychology, Vol. 3, Energy: Psychological Perspectives*. Hillsdale, NJ: Erlbaum.

Theberge, Leonard J.
1981 Testimony before the Subcommittee on Energy Research and Production. U.S. House of Representatives, Washington, D.C., December 15.

Thomas, Kerry, E. Swaton, M. Fishbein and H. J. Otway
1980 "Nuclear Energy: The Accuracy of Policy Makers' Perceptions of Public Beliefs." Laxenburg, Austria: International Institute for Applied Systems Analysis.

Zellner, Arnold
1962 "An Efficient Method of Estimating Seemingly Unrelated Regressions and Tests for Aggregation Bias." *Journal of the American Statistical Association* 58:348-368.

Part 3

Whose Back Yard?

Barbara Farhar-Pilgrim,
William R. Freudenburg

7. Nuclear Energy in Perspective: A Comparative Assessment of the Public View

INTRODUCTION

While attitudes toward nuclear power can be interesting even in isolation, they can be interpreted far more clearly when they are seen within a broader context. This chapter is intended to help provide two kinds of comparative contexts. First, we will review studies that allow us to compare attitudes toward nuclear power with attitudes toward other energy supply technologies. Second, we compare relatively abstract attitudes toward nuclear power "in general" with attitudes toward more concrete facilities near respondents' own homes.

Our findings can be summarized briefly at the outset. At least since the days of the 1973-74 oil embargo the U.S. public has shown consistent support--in the abstract--for virtually any energy supply source or technology that holds promise of increasing the availability or reliability of energy supplies, or of decreasing U.S. dependence on imported oil. Nuclear power is clearly one of those technologies. Comparative analysis reveals, however, that the public views nuclear power as being the least desirable of the energy technologies that are available to us for future development.

At a more concrete level, energy facilities in people's own back yards are seen as being less acceptable than are

Pp. 183-203 in William R. Freudenburg and Eugene A. Rosa (eds., 1984) *Public Reactions to Nuclear Power: Are There Critical Masses?*

TABLE 1
COMPARATIVE PREFERENCES FOR ENERGY SUPPLY SOURCES, NATIONAL SAMPLES

Energy Alternatives	Chosen in Top 3		Top 3 minus Least Preferred	
	SERI Data[a]	CEQ Data[b]	SERI Data	CEQ Data
Solar energy	66%	61	+63	+55
Energy conservation	45	35	+41	+32
Synfuels	38	26	+33	+16
Hydropower	34	31	+26	+21
Coal	36	36	+23	+27
Oil and natural gas	34	28	+22	+19
Nuclear energy	27	23	−18	−10

[a]Data from Gallup national survey of home owners conducted for the Solar Energy Research Institute, October-November 1980. Question was: "Here is a list of several energy sources available to us. Please rank the top three energy sources you would prefer to see developed to meet our future energy needs. (1 = most preferred, 2 = next most preferred, 3 = third most preferred.) Now, please indicate the source you least prefer." Response categories: Coal; Nuclear energy; Energy conservation (reducing energy needs by adding more home insulation, driving a fuel-efficient car, etc.); Water power from dams or falls (hydropower); Synfuels (for example, industrial plant converts oil shale or coal into a liquid or gas) (Farhar-Pilgrim and Unseld, 1982).

[b]Data from Resources for the Future Survey of adults 18 and over conducted by Roper and Cantril for the Council on Environmental Quality, January-March 1980. Question was: "Here is a list of several ways to get energy. Looking ahead to the year 2000, and this nation's energy needs, which two or three of these sources of energy do you think we should concentrate on the most? This list includes coal; nuclear energy; energy conservation steps such as more and better home insulation and cars that get good mileage; water power from dams or waterfalls; solar energy including energy from the sun and wind; oil and natural gas; and synfuels which are a new kind of fuel made by industrial plants which convert oil shale into oil or coal to a liquid or gas. Which two or three do you think we should concentrate on the most? Now, looking at the [list] again, which *one* of these sources of energy would you like to see us spend the *least* effort to develop?" (Mitchell, 1980).

hypothetical facilities "somewhere." This pattern holds for virtually any type of centralized energy facility, but the actual level of acceptability depends in large part on the type of facility in question. In particular, the broader U.S. public prefers almost any other type of local facility to a nearby nuclear power plant.

Nuclear host communities--the specific communities where nuclear facilities have actually been built--have tended to be more favorable toward nuclear power than have samples of the general public. Recent evidence, however, suggests that prospective nuclear host communities may be significantly less eager to welcome new nuclear neighbors in the future.

PREFERENCES FOR NUCLEAR ENERGY IN PERSPECTIVE

As several other chapters in this volume show, national poll data over the past several years have reflected majority favorability toward the general idea of using nuclear power, although the strength of that favorability has declined noticeably since the Three Mile Island accident (see especially Chapter 2, by Rankin and his colleagues, 1984; see also Farhar et al., 1980). Respondents tend to be favorable in their answers to relatively abstract items that ask about "your general opinion of nuclear power" or feelings "toward nuclear power plants in general." A closer examination of the available surveys reveals that this pattern may be part of a broader tendency; samples of the general public tend to favor the idea of most energy supply sources, at least in the abstract. Thus we may be likely to learn more about real public acceptability of nuclear facilities by comparing public responses to several energy supply alternatives.

Several studies have asked respondents to choose from among a list of possible energy supply sources (Roper, 1979; Harris, 1975, 1976, 1978, 1979a, 1979b, 1979c; Research Triangle Institute, 1979; Ruttenberg, Friedman, Kilgallon, Geutchess and Associates, Inc., 1975; City of Colorado Springs, 1975; NBC/AP News, 1979). Although the data from these studies are not strictly comparable, they do reveal certain patterns (Farhar et al., 1980). One evident pattern is

TABLE 2
"ABSTRACT" AND "CONCRETE" ATTITUDES
TOWARD NUCLEAR AND SOLAR POWER (PERCENT)

	Favor	Unsure	Oppose
Nuclear Power Facilities[a]			
Abstract: nuclear power in general	57	12	31
Concrete: nuclear power "within five miles"	36	7	55
Residential Solar Use[b]			
Abstract: solar use in general	77	18	5
Concrete: solar use on my home	58	22	20

[a]Data from Louis Harris surveys of August 1978. Questions were: Abstract--"In general, do you favor or oppose the building of more nuclear power plants in the United States?" Concrete--"Do you favor or oppose having a nuclear power plant within five miles of your community?"

[b]Data from Gallup national survey, October-November 1980. Questions were: Abstract--"Based on your understanding of solar energy for homes, how do you feel about it--do you strongly favor, favor, oppose, or strongly oppose its use?" Concrete--"Given what you know about solar energy right now, do you strongly favor, favor, oppose, or strongly oppose the idea of using it on *your* home?" (Farhar-Pilgrim and Unseld, 1982).

public support for virtually any domestic source that is expected to decrease dependence on foreign oil. Another pattern is a majority preference for the development of solar energy in the immediate future, with the expressed hope that it will be a significant energy producer by the year 2000. Nuclear energy was preferred by minorities of one quarter to one third of the samples in these comparative studies. Synfuels and fossil fuels were not found to be strongly preferred future energy sources.

Two 1980 national surveys used virtually identical items to compare preferences for energy supply sources. They also asked about least preferred sources (Farhar-Pilgrim and Unseld, 1982; Mitchell, 1980). Data from the two surveys are presented in Table 1. Solar energy is far and away the most preferred future energy supply source, with energy conservation a somewhat distant second. Nuclear energy is by far the least favored energy source. In short, if given other options, the public would evidently choose no further development of nuclear power.

The "Not In My Back Yard" Problem

Our understanding is likely to be further improved if we consider specific as well as general types of concerns. It may be one thing to ask about an energy technology in a general or relatively abstract way, while being quite another to ask about an actual facility in a specific location. Indeed, as can be seen by Chapter 2 of this volume, by Rankin and his colleagues (1984), respondents tend to be far less favorable toward local siting of nuclear power facilities than toward the idea of nuclear power in the abstract.

In national surveys, respondents now show fairly strong opposition to the idea of having a "local electric company . . . build a nuclear power plant in this area." Several studies have found even greater opposition in cases where questionnaire items have specified actual distances--e.g., "having a nuclear power plant constructed within 20 miles of where you live," or "the construction of a nuclear power plant . . . within 5 miles of here" (Rankin et al., 1981; Farhar et al., 1980; Melber et al., 1977). Note that these items deal more concretely with the actual siting of a nuclear plant, placing the facility in the respondent's own vicinity. The results show that the *general* idea of nuclear energy is

TABLE 3
"TOLERANCE DISTANCE" FOR VARIOUS FACILITIES[a]

Facility	Average (mean) Tolerance Distance, in Miles
A 10-story office building	5.8
A large industrial plant or factory	13.9
A power plant that uses coal for fuel	20.5
A disposal site for hazardous waste chemicals if the government said disposal could be done safely and that the site would be inspected regularly for possible problems	81.4
A nuclear power plant	91.0

[a]Data from Resources for the Future national survey of adults 18 and over, conducted by Roper and Cantril for the U.S. Council on Environmental Quality, January-March 1980. Question was: "Finding new places to build new industrial and power plants is sometimes difficult these days. I'm going to mention five types of buildings or sites. Assuming that they might be built and operated according to government environmental and safety regulations, you might or might not feel strongly about living close to them. For each type of plant please tell me the closest such a plant could be built from your home before you would want to move to another place or to actively protest, or whether it wouldn't matter to you one way or another how close it was?" (Answer in number of miles) (Mitchell, 1980).

more acceptable to the public than the *specific* possibility of having a nuclear power facility built near their own homes.

This pattern is not strictly limited to nuclear power facilities. To some extent, poll data suggest that virtually any energy supply source sounds like a good idea until it is planned for a nearby location. Coal development, for example, may be somewhat more popular as an abstract idea than it is among residents near proposed coal development projects or coal-fired power plants (Farhar et al., 1979). A 1980 national survey on solar energy also found home owners to be more favorable toward the idea of using solar energy for homes in general than toward the idea of using it on their own homes, as shown in Table 2 (Farhar-Pilgrim and Unseld, 1982).

While the general pattern appears to hold for most kinds of energy technologies, however, it is clear that some types of facilities are far more tolerable than others. Some are apparently less tolerable; specifically, nuclear power facilities appear to be less acceptable locally than most other installations. An item in a 1980 national survey measured a "tolerance distance" for five types of facilities: a ten-story office building, a large factory, a coal-fired power plant, a disposal site for hazardous waste chemicals, and a nuclear power plant. The results are summarized in Table 3. Respondents were asked how close each kind of facility could be built to their homes before they would want to move or actively protest. The majority preferred that a nuclear facility be at least 50 miles away, and the mean distance preferred was over 90 miles--the greatest distance for any of the facilities considered. Even a controlled hazardous waste disposal site was slightly more tolerable than a nuclear power plant, at a mean distance of over 80 miles (Mitchell, 1980).

Perhaps partly because of this consistently low popularity of nuclear power, national samples tend to show roughly the same rankings of preferability for "local" facilities as for energy supply technologies more generally. Table 4 shows that when presented with a list of energy supply sources for producing electrical power for local needs, national samples from 1977 through 1980 consistently selected solar energy as the most preferred type of local facility, with nuclear power being the least preferred (and most opposed) type.

TABLE 4
COMPARATIVE PREFERENCES FOR LOCAL ENERGY FACILITIES[a]

Type of Local Power Plant	Approve				Disapprove			
	1977	1978	1979	1980	1977	1978	1979	1980
Solar energy	--	84%	87	86	--	5	8	10
Hydroelectric power	--	87	80	82	--	6	6	6
Natural gas	--	69	68	64	--	24	26	28
Coal	41	65	71	60	47	28	24	33
Oil	--	62	54	44	--	30	40	48
Nuclear energy	47	41	34	28	39	43	60	63

[a] Data from national surveys conducted by Response Analysis Corp. in 1977 and 1978, and conducted in 1979 and 1980 by Associates for Research in Behavior, Inc. Question was: "Here is a list of different ways of producing electrical power. Suppose a new power plant had to be built in this area. For each of these ways of producing electricity please tell me whether it would be all right with you if this method were used in this area, or whether you would be against using it in this area."

In short, comparative data show that nuclear power facilities are consistently singled out as the least popular type of energy facility, whether they are being considered in the abstract or in the concrete.

The Special Case of Nuclear Host Communities

One important point to keep in mind is that energy facilities--if they are to be built--are built in specific locations. This fact gives a particular importance to the specific ("host") communities that are selected as sites for nuclear power plants. At least until the time of the Three Mile Island (TMI) accident, moreover, virtually every known study of nuclear host communities showed strong majority support for proposed or actual facilities (Melber et al., 1977:49-64). Such a pattern would have important and favorable implications for nuclear power plant construction if it were to continue. A recent study, however, has revealed that TMI apparently led to a reversal of the earlier pattern. Only four post-TMI host community surveys could be found, but all four showed clear majority opposition to the local facilities in question. The change was so distinct that the study accounted for over 70% of the variation across the 35 available surveys simply by knowing whether people were interviewed before or after the TMI accident (Freudenburg and Baxter, 1983; Wisniewski and Freudenburg, 1981).

It is necessary to use extreme caution in interpreting such a small number of data points, but at a minimum, this recent evidence clearly shows that it is no longer safe to assume that the economic and other benefits of local facilities will automatically lead to support from local residents. The complexities of finding acceptable sites for future facilities could be greatly multiplied if future nuclear host communities show similar patterns.

Why These Particular Views?

Perhaps the best way to understand the overall picture is to compare the full range of major perceived advantages and disadvantages of the available energy alternatives--with the comparison including sociopolitical as well as engineering factors. Table 5 provides a summary of the perceived advantages of using nuclear energy, coal, and solar energy--both

TABLE 5
PERCEIVED ADVANTAGES OF ENERGY SUPPLY SOURCES

GENERAL			SPECIFIC TO LOCAL COMMUNITY		
Nuclear Energy	Coal	Solar Energy	Nuclear Energy	Coal	Solar Energy
Cheaper power	Abundant domestic availability	Helps consumers save energy costs over the long term	Reduced cost of electricity	More tax money for better schools	Increases self-reliance
Lack of air and water pollution; clean energy	Reduces dependence on foreign oil	Is more reliable	Increased business	More jobs	Increases resale value of homes
Conserves natural resources	Lower cost	Conserves natural resources	More jobs	Reduce out-migration of young people	More jobs
Increase in scientific/technical knowledge		Protects environment	Higher incomes	Higher incomes	Keeps energy costs in local economy
Avoiding future shortages		Increases independence from utilities	Lower taxes		Reduces energy costs
Domestic availability		Reduces need for more large power plants	Meet new people		Improved environment
Reduces dependence on foreign oil		Increases independence from federal policies	Fame for community		Increases public participation in energy supply
Efficient		Domestic availability	Increased land values		Reduces utility bills
Progressive		Reduces dependence on foreign sources	Other industrial development		Protects against rising costs
			More recreation areas, entertainment, tourist attractions		Psychological rewards (innovation, status)
			Better schools		

[a] Refers to decentralized solar applications only.
Sources: Farhar et al., 1979, 1980; Farhar and Unseld, 1982; based on existing survey data.

TABLE 6
PERCEIVED DISADVANTAGES OF ENERGY SUPPLY SOURCES

GENERAL			SPECIFIC TO LOCAL COMMUNITY		
Nuclear Energy	Coal	Solar Energy	Nuclear Energy	Coal	Solar Energy
Radioactivity leakage	Higher costs, increased prices	Warranty coverage	Lowers property values	Adverse effects on groundwater supply	None defined in existing research, although existing studies have not generally included a specific emphasis on large-scale "centralized" solar technologies
Disposal of radioactive wastes	Air pollution, "dirty" air	Initial cost	People could not live nearby	Land would be ruined by strip-mining	
Potential for accidents, explosions, or meltdowns	Acid rain increase	Operating reliability	Fear; controversy	Pollution would harm crops and grazing	
Thermal pollution of water	Negative health effects	Reputability of solar firms	Danger of radiation	Negative health effects	
Threat of sabotage	Global climate effects	Damage to systems	Bad for environment	Air pollution	
Air pollution	Unfair advantage of coal regions over non-coal regions	Safety of systems	Air pollution	Reduces incentives for oil exploration	
Health effects		Insurance coverage	Thermal pollution of water	Large increases in population	
Safety problems, risks		Early obsolescence	Unsightly	No improved community services	
Expensive, high costs		Financing problems	Noise	Loss of control over important decisions that affect community life	
Need stringent controls		Climate concerns	Too expensive	Increases in crime	
Dangers to workers in nuclear plants		Lower resale value of homes	Inefficient, breakdowns	Less community solidarity, (unity, friendliness)	
Shortage of plutonium		Possible problems with utilities	Puts people out of work	Economic depression when mines close in the future	
Sites not available		Aesthetics	Bad for health		
Inefficient		Efficiency	Birth defects		
Public anxiety		Still new, experimental	Increased traffic congestion		
Nuclear proliferation; terrorism			Housing shortages		
			Crowding in schools		
			Increased crime		
			Drugs in schools		

[a] Refers to decentralized solar applications only.
Sources: Farhar et al., 1979, 1980; Farhar and Unseld, 1982; based on existing survey data.

in general and for the local community--as drawn from existing public opinion polls. Table 6 summarizes the perceived disadvantages of the three energy supply sources. The point here is not the degree of accuracy of these perceptions; rather, it is that varying but significant proportions of the public perceive these to be the salient characteristics of the three different energy alternatives.

When the lists are compared, it is relatively easy to see why nuclear power, even with all the advantages it can offer, still comes out the least preferred source of energy. The kinds of disadvantages connected with it represent thorny sociopolitical and technical issues that can be extremely costly to resolve. The disposal of radioactive wastes (discussed at greater length in Chapter 9, by Zinberg, 1984) may be the most obvious example, but fears over nuclear proliferation or the leakage of radioactivity may prove almost equally complex. In comparison, while the coal issues are significant, regulatory procedures and controls appear adequate to handle most of them. Solar energy appears to be more benign, and to have more positive perceived consequences, than either nuclear energy or coal. The greater popularity of new solar energy technologies may be due, in part, to the relatively longer societal experience with both coal and nuclear energy. However, studies and experience to date suggest that solar-related problems may be relatively tractable through sound business and policy action.

Of existing energy sources, then, decentralized solar applications appear to have the greatest chance of social acceptability. Local acceptability for large-scale solar installations such as wind farms or power towers remains largely to be assessed, but would probably be lower.

The question remains whether the public is "correct" or "incorrect" in its perception of the impacts of energy supply alternatives. The fact is, neither the public nor the energy decision makers know--nor do we currently have the information we would need to make such a determination. The necessary comparative assessments of energy supply options have not been conducted at national, regional, or local levels. Nor have existing studies generally considered all the relevant questions. The nation has been relying on engineering solutions to energy supply problems, but recent experiences have made it increasingly clear that "better engineering" can provide only one part of the answer to energy policy questions in the future. Decisions on what facilities to build, and where to build them, have become increasingly complex sociopolitical problems.

A common argument is that the public does not understand the various energy alternatives and their implications, and that ignorance is the main reason people take the positions they do. As can be seen from the chapters by Mitchell (1984) and by Slovic and his colleagues (1984) in this volume, this argument is misleading; it contains part, but not all, of the truth.

In general, the public is not well informed about the more technical aspects of energy technologies and facilities (Farhar et al., 1979). This may not be the relevant point, however; most people also have relatively little understanding of the technical aspects of their automobiles, such as the fluid mechanics of their brake systems. They also have little reason to worry about such details so long as automotive engineers have done their work well enough that the brakes will be able to stop the car reliably. In the nuclear power debate, as in debates over automotive safety, people become concerned if they find reason to believe that the technical details have not been adequately dealt with, or if the social and environmental impacts of the technology are unacceptable even after the engineering problems have been "solved."

An important implication is that public information and education programs, while needed, are not likely to eliminate the sociopolitical problems of nuclear energy development; the problems are not simply matters of public ignorance. For the public to become truly "informed" on relevant issues, a number of "non-technical" questions will require answers:

- Who needs the facility and why?
- Whom will it benefit? Whom will it harm?
- How much will it cost? Who will pay for it?
- How will it affect the national and local economy? Will it help the balance of payments or create more jobs?

TABLE 7
COMPARISON OF CARTER AND REAGAN BUDGET PROPOSALS FOR NUCLEAR ENERGY, SOLAR ENERGY, AND ENERGY CONSERVATION--U.S. DEPARTMENT OF ENERGY, FISCAL YEAR 1982

	Carter ($ Millions)	Reagan ($ Millions)	Change ($ Millions)	(%)
Nuclear fission	813	1100	+287	+35
Nuclear fusion	506	434	- 72	-14
Total nuclear energy:	1319	1534	+215	+16
Solar energy	576	170	-406	-70
Energy conservation	922	104	-818	-89

Sources: Carter figures taken from Jimmy Carter's budget package of January 1981; Reagan figures come from the revised U.S. Department of Energy budget of September 1981. The solar energy figures do not include hydropower or geothermal expenditures, nor do they include funds for construction of a permanent facility for the Solar Energy Research Institute near Denver, Colorado.

- What will its political impact be? How will it affect local political constituencies? Does it have implications for national domestic and foreign policy?

- Will it work reliably? What effects will it have on the physical environment (air, land, water, crops, and so on)?

- Who will pay for the increased community services required, or offset any damages caused by the project?

Even when it comes to the "technical" questions--which in many ways are actually simpler than the "non-technical" ones--we have seen that consumers perceive different advantages and disadvantages for each major energy supply source. These perceptions contribute to the public's ultimate attitudes toward the various energy supply sources and facilities.

PUBLIC OPINION AND PUBLIC POLICY

While some questions remain unanswered, it is clear that one strong answer is beginning to emerge: Whether we focus on the local level or the more abstract level, the general public prefers essentially any energy supply alternative over nuclear power. The final section of our chapter will examine the energy policy priorities of the Reagan Administration in light of this information.

The Reagan Administration's approach to energy policy is summarized in Davis's (1984) contribution to this volume; see also Marshall (1981); Hershey (1981). The approach has two main themes--budget cutting and the reduction of regulatory controls--that will provide the focus for our discussion.

The issue of budget cuts is particularly significant given the fact that the energy research budget can provide a relatively straightforward indicator of an administration's priorities. As can be seen from Table 7, the Reagan Administration has increased federal funding for the one energy supply system--nuclear power--that is shown by the existing data to be the least acceptable to the U.S. public. At the same time, government programs for preferred approaches--

solar energy and energy conservation--have been cut severely in the name of a "balanced" budget. It is clear that something more than budget balancing is involved, however, as can be seen from the actual energy budget data. Just the *increase* in fiscal year 1982 nuclear spending was larger than the *total* funding for the nation's solar program in that same year.

It does not appear that a free market rationale could support this degree of support or subsidy for nuclear energy. The federal subsidies already devoted to nuclear energy far exceed those devoted to solar energy (Cone et al., 1980; see also the discussion by Rosa and Freudenburg, 1984, in Chapter 1 of this volume). The "undistorted" free market cost of nuclear energy would have to reflect the full range of costs, both direct and indirect, that are involved in nuclear production of electricity. If this policy were followed, the economic viability of nuclear energy--forced to survive without subsidies--would be further called into question.

The reduction of the "regulatory burden" on the nuclear industry would also appear to be ill-advised, given our analysis of the public opinion findings. Although citizens were generally not directly asked whether regulations for nuclear power plants should be relaxed, the high degree of opposition to local nuclear facilities may be telling us that most people do not think the local costs of nuclear power facilities or coal development projects are *adequately* regulated and compensated at present. If regulations were seen as being adequate--let alone excessive--there would seem to be little reason to oppose nuclear facilities, even in one's own back yard.

The Administration's efforts to modify existing regulations are in part a response to the desires of the nuclear power industry. The industry's views are summarized by Szalay in Chapter 12 of this volume (1984); in essence, they call for a "streamlining" of existing procedures. If the modifications are indeed perceived by the U.S. public as a case of streamlining, our judgment is that the proposals will be reasonably well received; red tape and bureaucracy may be even less popular in the United States than are local nuclear power plants. On the other hand, if the proposals are perceived as implying or causing any weakening of nuclear safety safeguards, they would seem quite likely to lead to more intense and widespread opposition to nuclear energy--particularly with regard to proposed nuclear facilities at specific local sites. If this were indeed the case, the nuclear power industry's own proposals could inadvertently result in far longer delays and higher costs for nuclear power in the long run.

The opposition to nuclear power does not mean that the public would prefer existing facilities to be dismantled. The investment in these facilities is too great, and certain areas of the country are too dependent on nuclear power to make nuclear abandonment a widely acceptable policy decision. But as can be seen from Chapter 2, by Rankin and his colleagues (1984), there is considerable support for operating only those plants that have been built, and for delaying or foregoing the construction of any new ones.

Our interpretation of the existing data leads us to conclude, in short, that strict and careful regulation may be required if the public is to accept continued nuclear power facility siting and operation. Any perceived weakening of regulatory controls would be accompanied by risks of increased opposition, greater uncertainty, lengthier delays, and higher long-run costs.

ACKNOWLEDGEMENTS

The authors wish to thank Eugene A. Rosa and two anonymous reviewers for helpful comments on an earlier draft. This is Scientific Paper Number 6473, Agricultural Research Center Project 0478, Washington State University.

REFERENCES

Colorado Springs, City of
1975 "Assessment of a Single-Family Residence Solar Heating System in a Suburban Development Setting, Project Phoenix." *Solar Heated Residence Annual Report* (July).

Cone, Bruce, D. L. Benchley, V. L. Brix, M. L. Brown, K. E. Cochran, P. D. Cohn, R. J. Cole, M. G. Curry, R. Davidson, J. Easterling, J. C. Emery, A. G. Fassbinder, J. S. Fattorlini, Jr., B. Gordon, H. Harty, B. Lenerz, A. R. Maurizi, R. Mazzuchi, C. McClain, D. D. More, J. H. Maxwell, N. J. Sheppard, F. Solomon and P. Sommers
1980 *An Analysis of Federal Incentives Used to Stimulate Energy Production.* Richland, WA: Battelle Pacific Northwest Laboratories.

Davis, W. Kenneth
1984 "Nuclear Power under the Reagan Administration." Pp. 257-265 in William R. Freudenburg and Eugene A. Rosa (eds.), *Public Reactions to Nuclear Power: Are There Critical Masses?* Boulder, CO: Westview Press/American Association for the Advancement of Science.

Farhar, Barbara C., Charles T. Unseld, Rebecca Vories and Robin Crews
1980 "Public Opinion about Energy." *Annual Review of Energy* 5:141-172.

Farhar, Barbara C., Patricia Weis, Charles T. Unseld and Barbara Burns
1979 *Public Opinion about Energy: A Literature Review.* Golden, CO: Solar Energy Research Institute (SERI/TR-53-155).

Farhar-Pilgrim, Barbara and Charles T. Unseld
1982 *America's Solar Potential: A National Consumer Study.* New York: Praeger Publishers.

Freudenburg, William R. and Rodney K. Baxter
1983 "Public Attitudes Toward Local Nuclear Power Plants: A Reassessment." Paper presented at the annual meetings of the American Sociological Association, Detroit, September.

Freudenburg, William R. and Eugene A. Rosa (eds.)
1984 *Public Reactions to Nuclear Power: Are There Critical Masses?* Boulder, CO: Westview Press/American Association for the Advancement of Science.

Harris, Louis and Associates
1975 *A Survey of Public and Leadership Attitudes Toward Nuclear Power Development in the United States.* New York: Louis Harris and Associates.

1976 *A Second Survey of Public and Leadership Attitudes Toward Nuclear Power Development in the United States.* New York: Louis Harris and Associates.

1978 *A Study of New York State Voters Attitudes Toward Nuclear Power Plants.* New York: Long Island Farm Bureau and Suffolk County for Safe Energy.

1979a "Americans Favor Synthetic Fuels Bill." *ABC News-Harris Survey* 1 (84, July 11).

1979b "Sharp Increase Seen in Number of Americans Who Consider the Energy Problem in U.S. Very Serious." *ABC News-Harris Survey* 1 (52, April 30).

1979c "Majority of Americans Favor President Carter's Energy Proposals." *ABC News-Harris Survey* 1 (99, August 14).

Hershey, Robert D., Jr.

1981 "President Offers Plans for Revival of Nuclear Power: Reprocessing Ban to End, Faster Licensing Asked: A Breeder Reactor and Waste Storage Pressed." *New York Times* (October 9):A1, A26.

Marshall, Eliot

1981 "Reagan's Plan for Nuclear Power." *Science* 214 (4519, October 23):419.

Melber, Barbara, Stanley Nealey, Joy Hammersla and William Rankin

1977 *Nuclear Power and the Public: Analysis of Collected Survey Research.* Seattle, WA: Battelle Memorial Institute, November.

Mitchell, Robert Cameron

1980 *Public Opinion on Environmental Issues, Results of a National Public Opinion Survey.* Washington, D.C.: U.S. Government Printing Office.

1984 "Rationality and Irrationality in the Public's Perception of Nuclear Power." Pp. 137-179 in William R. Freudenburg and Eugene A. Rosa (eds.), *Public Reactions to Nuclear Power: Are There Critical Masses?* Boulder, CO: Westview Press/American Association for the Advancement of Science.

NBC/AP News

1979 "NBC/Associated Press News Poll." *The Denver Post,* Denver, CO. May 6.

Rankin, William L., Barbara D. Melber, Thomas D. Overcast and Stanley M. Nealey

1981 *Nuclear Power and the Public: An Update of Collected Survey Research on Nuclear Power: Draft Topical Report.* Seattle, WA: Battelle Human Affairs Research Centers.

Rankin, William R., Stanley M. Nealey and Barbara D. Melber
1984 "Overview of National Attitudes Toward Nuclear Energy: A Longitudinal Analysis." Pp. 41-67 in William R. Freudenburg and Eugene A. Rosa (eds.), *Public Reactions to Nuclear Power: Are There Critical Masses?* Boulder, CO: Westview Press/American Association for the Advancement of Science.

Research Triangle Institute
1979 *National Assessment of Educational Progress, Denver, CO: Assessment on Energy Knowledge and Attitudes.* Raleigh, NC: Research Triangle Institute.

Roper Organization, Inc.
1979 *Roper Reports.* New York: Roper Organization, Inc. (79-5, April).

Rosa, Eugene A. and William R. Freudenburg
1984 "Nuclear Power at the Crossroads." Pp. 3-37 in William R. Freudenburg and Eugene A. Rosa (eds.), *Public Reactions to Nuclear Power: Are There Critical Masses?* Boulder, CO: Westview Press/American Association for the Advancement of Science.

Ruttenberg, Friedman, Kilgallon, Geutchess and Associates, Inc.
1975 *Survey of Attitudes and Opinions of Electric Power Consumers in Ohio.* Columbus, OH: Ohio Electric Utility Institute.

Slovic, Paul, Baruch Fischhoff and Sarah Lichtenstein
1984 "Perception and Acceptability of Risk from Energy Systems." Pp. 115-135 in William R. Freudenburg and Eugene A. Rosa (eds.), *Public Reactions to Nuclear Power: Are There Critical Masses?* Boulder, CO: Westview Press/American Association for the Advancement of Science.

Szalay, Robert A.
1984 "A Nuclear Industry View of the Regulatory Climate." Pp. 295-306 in William R. Freudenburg and Eugene A. Rosa (eds.), *Public Reactions to Nuclear Power: Are There Critical Masses?* Boulder, CO: Westview Press/American Association for the Advancement of Science.

Wisniewski, Robert L. and William R. Freudenburg
1981 *The Socio-Environmental Impacts of Energy Development on Local User Groups and Water Resource Planning: Nuclear Energy Development in the Twin Harbors Region.* Pullman, WA: Washington Water Research Center.

Zinberg, Dorothy S.
1984 "Public Participation in Nuclear Waste Management Policy: A Brief Historical Overview." Pp. 233-253 in William R. Freudenburg and Eugene A. Rosa (eds.), *Public Reactions to Nuclear Power: Are There Critical Masses?* Boulder, CO: Westview Press/American Association for the Advancement of Science.

Cynthia B. Flynn

8. The Local Impacts of the Accident at Three Mile Island

As can be seen from Chapter 2 of this volume, by Rankin and his colleagues (1984), the accident at Three Mile Island (TMI) appears to have had significant consequences for the nation's attitudes toward nuclear power. This chapter will summarize what happened at TMI, and will briefly review the accident's effects on 11 other nuclear power plant sites that were being studied under a Nuclear Regulatory Commission contract at the time. The analysis focuses on three areas of importance to the local communities: effects on individuals, on the local economy, and on organizations. A chronology of significant events at TMI is a key part of the presentation; for more detailed reports of the accident itself, readers may wish to consult Rubinstein (1979), Mathews et al. (1979), Marshall (1979), or the President's Commission on the Accident at Three Mile Island (1979).

THE ACCIDENT AT THREE MILE ISLAND

Until fairly recently, Three Mile Island was simply an 814-acre island in the Susquehanna River, about nine miles downstream from Harrisburg, Pennsylvania (see Figure 1). The Metropolitan Edison Company (a subsidiary of General Public Utilities, Inc., of New Jersey) built two Babcock and Wilcox pressurized water reactors on the island during the

Pp. 205-232 in William R. Freudenburg and Eugene A. Rosa (eds., 1984) *Public Reactions to Nuclear Power: Are There Critical Masses?*

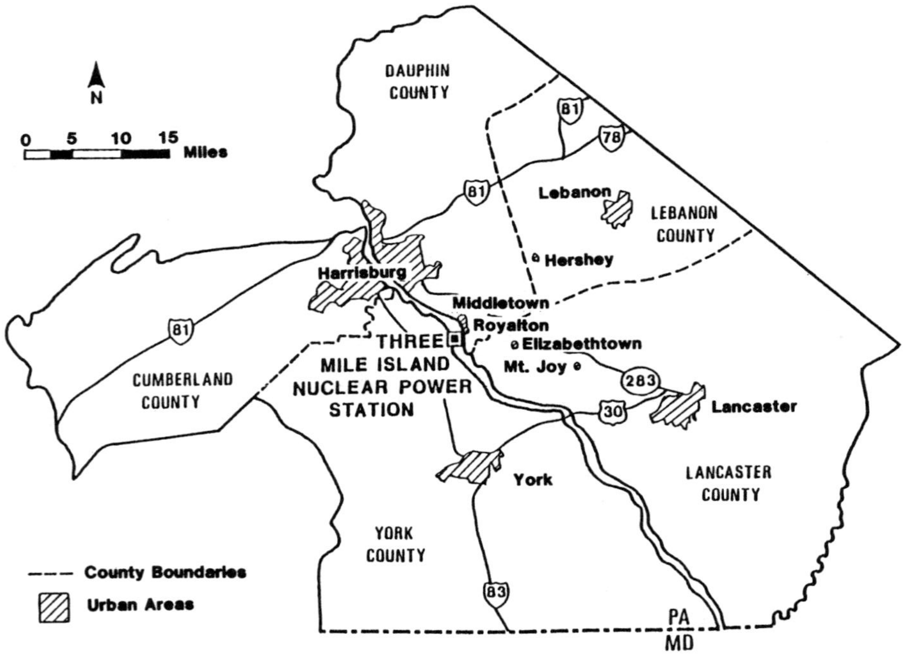

Figure 1. Location of Three Mile Island Nuclear Power Station

Source : Rand McNally Road Atlas

1970s (U.S. Nuclear Regulatory Commission, 1972). Unit 1, also known as TMI-1, went into commercial service in September 1974. Unit 2 went into commercial service in December 1978, and hit national headlines four months later.

At 4:00 a.m. on Wednesday, March 28, 1979, Unit 1 was shut down for refueling; Unit 2 was operating at 97% of its capacity. The situation seemed relatively normal, except for a blockage in one of the plant's lines that had occurred twice before. Just 37 seconds after 4:00 a.m., however, the operators' efforts to clear the line led indirectly to a shutdown of the main feedwater pumps of TMI-2. The shutdown of these pumps meant that the "secondary" or electricity-generating system of the power plant was no longer removing heat from the "primary" system--the heat-producing loop in the reactor's core. It was a potentially serious problem, but one that the reactor was designed to handle. Almost immediately, the electricity-generating turbines shut down, as they were supposed to. Within a single second, all three of the auxiliary feedwater pumps of the plant started up, as they were designed to do. Within 14 seconds, they had reached full pressure, and they should have kept the situation under control.

Unfortunately, the water from these auxiliary pumps never reached the primary loop of the reactor. Unknown to the operators of the plant, two valves between the auxiliary pumps and the primary system were closed, blocking the flow. Two lights on the control panel would have warned the operators about the situation, but it was contrary to normal procedures for the valves to be closed, and one of the warning lights was covered by a yellow maintenance tag.

At 45 seconds after 4:00 a.m.--just eight seconds into the incident--the reactor "scrammed," or shut down, as it had been designed to do. This immediately stopped the chain reaction that had been taking place in the reactor core, although the core continued to release a great deal of heat because of the radioactive materials it contained.

Since the water from the auxiliary feed pumps did not reach the reactor's primary system, the temperature and pressure in that system built up extremely rapidly. Within three to six seconds of the time the main feedwater pumps shut off, pressures reached the point that triggered a "pilot-operated relief valve" or PORV, which opened to let off some of the pressure in the primary system. Some ten seconds later, an indicator in the plant's control room showed that the valve had closed again properly. It hadn't. Instead, it was to stay open for several hours, during which time some thirty thousand gallons of water were to leak from the primary cooling system.

Within less than two minutes the steam generators in the primary loop had boiled dry. Some 17 seconds later, the primary system pressure had dropped to the point that automatically started the high pressure injection pumps of the plant's emergency core cooling system. After approximately two minutes, however, the plant operators--who had scored well above the mean on industry licensing tests--overrode the automatic system, and throttled back the flow. They were worried that the pressure might build up to the point where it could burst the reactor's cooling system. In retrospect, this turned out to have been a mistake.

At about 4:08 a.m. the operators discovered the improperly closed valves and opened them up. The open PORV, however, was not to be discovered and closed for another two hours; unfortunately, by then, the damage would have been done. Meanwhile, the operators were to be subjected to a barrage of alarms and warning lights, all while trying to deal with a situation that was completely outside their training and experience; the President's Commission on the Accident at Three Mile Island (1979:111) was later to refer to "a cascade of alarms that numbered 100" within minutes of the time the accident began.

By about 4:16 a.m., "saturation temperature" had been reached--meaning that boiling could occur anywhere in the system--and "voids," or steam pockets, were forming in the cooling water lines. At about 4:33 a.m., the core temperature went off the scale. By 4:50 a.m., the operators had called in their supervisors.

At 5:41 a.m., being concerned about vibration in the system and the possibility of damaging their pumps because of the voids, the operators shut down two reactor coolant pumps. This apparently sealed the fate of the reactor. "With the pumps turned off, all circulation stopped, and within the next fifty minutes substantial portions of the core became uncovered, damaging the fuel elements" and leading to a release of radioactivity and a buildup of hydrogen (Rubinstein, 1979:40).

At 6:56 a.m. high radiation levels led to the notification of officials from the Nuclear Regulatory Commission (NRC) and the state, and to the declaration of a "site emergency." Some fifty to sixty people were in the control room attempting to resolve the crisis. Half an hour later, the local Babcock and Wilcox representative arrived in the control room, and a "general emergency" was declared, indicating the further-increased seriousness of the situation. Shortly thereafter, roughly three hours after the accident began, personnel at the regional and national offices of the NRC were alerted.

The first wire service story on the accident would not be filed for another two hours. Soon after it was filed, at 9:15 a.m., the NRC notified the White House of the accident. A team from the NRC regional office arrived at the site at about 10:15 a.m., just about the time that the radiation levels in the control room had reached the point that required the evacuation of all but essential personnel. At about 11:30 a.m., controllers attempted to lower the pressure of the primary cooling system to the point that would trigger the activation of the plant's low-pressure decay heat removal system. Some six hours later, after it had proved impossible to lower the pressure that far, officials decided instead to try to increase the pressure in the system. Finally, some thirteen and a half hours after the accident began, operators managed to get one of the reactor coolant pumps to start, and another two and a half hours later they managed to start a second pump. This approach, fortunately, proved to be successful, and the beginning of the end of the crisis was in sight. By about 8:00 o'clock Wednesday evening, the operators were using normal cooling-down procedures, and the incident appeared to be over.

In some ways, the worst of the actual safety hazards probably were over at that point, but the more infamous implications of the accident were just beginning to unfold. *Science* magazine was later to be quite critical of the lack of press coverage on Wednesday:

> The accident at the Three Mile Island nuclear power plant was dangerously out of control for at least 48

> hours, according to a preliminary staff report given to the Nuclear Regulatory Commission . . . . During the first 13½ hours after the accident began, the reactor core overheated and then began to disintegrate . . . . A mistaken move during this early period . . . would have caused serious damage to the control machinery and possibly produced a disaster in Pennsylvania. While this explosive and extremely hazardous situation developed, the people of Harrisburg were given bland assurances that the reactor was under control and that they had nothing to fear (Marshall, 1979:280).

It would be on Friday, two days after the worst of the accident, that the press reports would indicate more reason for alarm. On Thursday, March 29, analyses of some of the primary system cooling water indicated that considerable damage had been done to the core. In addition, it became clear that some form of a hydrogen explosion probably occurred at about 2:00 p.m. on Wednesday afternoon. This discovery, together with the continued presence of voids in the primary system, led to increasing concerns over the probability of a hydrogen bubble in the reactor containment building. It was to take two days to analyze this situation and another three days to get it under control, although news releases continued to state that the situation was largely under control, and that the public had little to fear, until the next day.

It was on Friday morning, more than 50 hours after the accident began, that the NRC Emergency Operations Center discussed the possible need to evacuate residents of nearby communities. After some deliberations, the NRC chairman called Richard Thornburgh, the governor of Pennsylvania, and suggested the governor recommend that people in the vicinity of the plant stay indoors. At about 11:00 a.m. on Friday, President Carter directed that a senior NRC official be sent to the Three Mile Island site to serve as his personal representative on the scene. Harold Denton, the director of the NRC Office of Nuclear Reactor Regulation, was the person so designated; he left for the plant site shortly. Slightly after noon, the NRC chairman contacted the governor and suggested an advisory or recommendation that pregnant women and pre-school age children within five miles of the plant leave the area temporarily. The governor promptly issued just such an advisory, and also advised that all schools within five miles of the plant be closed.

During the day, there was increasing discussion about the hydrogen bubble, and representatives of the Department of Energy, the Environmental Protection Agency, and the Federal Disaster Assistance Administration, among others, joined the NRC personnel and state officials who were already at the site. About 6:00 that evening, the NRC chairman issued a press release declaring that there was "no imminent danger of a meltdown" of the reactor core, and by 8:30 p.m., the governor had lifted his advisory for people within five miles to stay indoors. He continued to recommend, however, that pregnant women and pre-school children remain out of the area.

By Saturday afternoon, various sets of calculations were converging on the conclusion that the hydrogen bubble conditions were not likely to lead to an explosion, and that it would probably be possible to vent the hydrogen if the situation worsened. On Sunday, the first of April, President Carter himself--a former nuclear engineer--arrived at the scene. Further evaluations indicated that an explosion of the hydrogen bubble was highly unlikely or even impossible. Even so, it was not until several days later, on the fourth and fifth of April, that most news reports indicated the situation was increasingly under control, and that experts on the site were beginning to understand what had gone wrong.

THE IMPACTS OF THE ACCIDENT

Background

At the time of the Three Mile Island accident, twelve nuclear power sites were being studied under a Nuclear Regulatory Commission (NRC) contract, and Three Mile Island was one of those sites. The studies had been designed to assess social and economic impacts resulting from the construction and operation of the nuclear power stations, focusing on factors such as the provision of services, changes in local housing markets, population changes, and public responses to the facilities. The general purpose of the "post-licensing studies" was to increase the NRC's ability to understand such impacts, and thus to be able to avoid or lessen the negative impacts of future installations. The cases were selected to

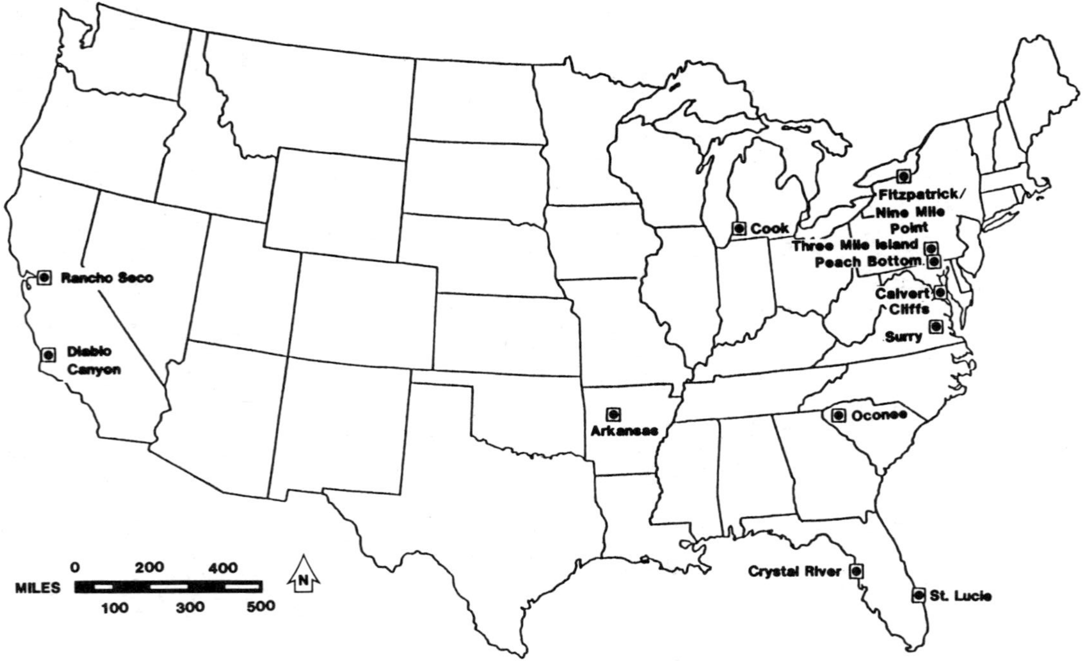

Figure 2. U.S. Nuclear Regulatory Commission Post-Licensing Study: Case Study Sites

include some operating experience; except for the Diablo Canyon site in California, where operations were delayed, the plants were in electrical production (see Figure 2 for a map of the study sites). The contractors for the post-licensing studies were Mountain West Research, Incorporated, and Social Impact Research, Incorporated.

To measure the effects of the accident at Three Mile Island and the communities closest to it, a variety of data sources were used. These included published documents and statistics, data provided by the local utility (Metropolitan Edison Company), household surveys conducted for the NRC and by others, other research about the accident, newspaper files, and interviews with key informants.

The following analysis covers a period of two years following the accident (see Table 1). Because court cases are still pending and because clean-up of Unit 2 and preparation for the restart of Unit 1 are incomplete, the effects of the accident will continue to be felt in the future, and this discussion is necessarily a limited one.

Effects of the Accident on South-Central Pennsylvania

Individual Effects. The most significant effect of the accident on the people in the region was the evacuation experience. From newspaper accounts and interviews, it appears that the general public was not unduly alarmed during the first two days of the accident. But on Friday, March 30, some areas were scenes of chaos, with whole neighborhoods evacuating. At 8:00 Friday morning, there had been an unexpected radiation release, which was reported by the media later in the day. It was also later on Friday that the Governor of Pennsylvania issued his advisories. Finally, Friday was the day on which residents learned that an unexpected hydrogen bubble was building up in the reactor, and that experts on the scene were at a loss to explain where it came from.

Particularly since earlier press reports seemed to indicate that there had been little to fear, many local residents found Friday's events and information to be both threatening and confusing. Individuals felt that they had to take responsibility for deciding who would evacuate, and when, where

TABLE 1
THREE MILE ISLAND UNITS 1 AND 2
CHRONOLOGY

PRECONSTRUCTION PERIOD

November 1966: Public Announcement of Unit 1
February 1967: Public Announcement of Unit 2

CONSTRUCTION PERIOD

May 1968: Construction Permit for Unit 1 issued
November 1969: Construction Permit for Unit 2 issued
April 1974: Operating License for Unit 1 issued

OPERATING PERIOD

September 1974: Unit 1 begins commercial operation
February 1978: Operating License for Unit 2 issued
December 1978: Unit 2 begins commercial operation
17 February 1979: Unit 1 shut down for refueling

EMERGENCY PERIOD

Wednesday, 28 March 1979, 4:00 a.m.: Feedwater pumps supplying Unit 2 shut down.

Wednesday, 28 March 1979, 9:06 a.m.: Associated Press files first wire-service story on the accident.

Thursday, 29 March 1979: News accounts indicate situation increasingly under control.

Friday, 30 March 1979, 8:00 a.m.: Unannounced radiation release.

Friday, 30 March 1979, 10:30 a.m.: Governor Thornburgh recommends that persons near TMI remain indoors and close their windows.

Friday, 30 March 1979, 12:30 p.m.: Governor issues advisory that pregnant women and preschool children leave the region within a 5-mile radius of the plant and that all schools in the area be closed.

Friday, 30 March 1979, 2:00 p.m.: Harold Denton arrives at the plant site.

Saturday, 31 March 1979, 8:23 p.m.: AP reports story from NRC that hydrogen bubble could explode.

Sunday, 1 April 1979, 1:00 p.m.: President Carter arrives at the plant site.

Monday, 2 April 1979, morning: Denton announces decrease in size of bubble and implies danger of explosion is less than originally thought.

TABLE 1 (Continued)

Wednesday, 4 April 1979: Schools outsidc 5-mile radius reopen, but those within a 5-mile radius remain closed and the governor's advisory remains in effect.

Saturday, 7 April 1979: Evacuation shelter at the Hershey Park Arena closed.

Monday, 9 April 1979: Governor's advisory withdrawn.

Wednesday, 11 April 1979: Middletown area schools reopen.

POST EMERGENCY PERIOD

April 1979: "EPICOR-I" process used to begin decontaminating water containing low levels of radioactivity stored in auxiliary building.

June 1979: Pennsylvania Public Utility Commission (PUC) refuses to allow TMI-Unit 2 to be included in Metropolitan Edison rate base.

August 1979: Petitions filed to intervene in federal hearings on start-up of TMI-Unit 1 (hearings scheduled for February 1980).

September 1979: Release of Kemeny Commission Report.

October 1979: EPICOR-II begins processing low-level waste water.

January 1980: Release of the Rogovin Report.

January 1980: Pennsylvania PUC hearings on rate increases begin.

February 1980: Two TMI pumps leak radioactive krypton into the environment.

March 1980: Radioactive krypton gas released from Unit 2 air chamber.

March 1980: TMI accident anniversary rally in Harrisburg.

10 May 1980: PUC grants interim rate increase; Unit 1 removed from rate base.

28 June 1980: Radioactive krypton gas released from Unit 2 containment building.

July 1980: First successful entry into Unit 2 reactor building.

29 October 1980: Unit 1 restart hearings begin.

9 December 1980: GPU files $4 billion suit against the NRC.

June 1981: Unit 1 restart hearings end; submerged demineralizer system begins processing high-level waste water.

and how they would do so. In some ways, the decision was more stressful for parents whose children were in the elementary grades (rather than being preschoolers) or who lived just beyond the recommended five-mile limit. Decisions had to be made about which, if any, of the normal day-to-day responsibilities would be met--and at a time when it was not clear to citizens how serious nor how imminent the threat actually was. The decision about evacuation appears to have been particularly difficult for housewives who were at home alone, were separated from their children at school, and were unable to reach their husbands because of jammed telephone lines.

Surveys show that much of the public was stressed and upset during the accident period. Approximately a third of the population of 370,000 who lived within 15 miles of the plant evacuated. The evacuees traveled an average distance of 100 miles, were gone from home an average of five days, and spent an average of about $300 in additional expenses. Many persons in the area lost work and/or pay. The response closer to the plant was even more dramatic. Although fewer than 6% of the people within five miles of the station fell within the criteria of the governor's advisory, surveys show that about 60% of the approximately 21,000 people left the area. In the 5-10 mile ring, 56,000 (44%) did so (Flynn and Chalmers, 1980).

In a few households, the absence of a clear order to evacuate (the governor had issued only an "advisory") resulted in disagreement over evacuation. About 12% of the respondents in the NRC survey said that members of their families disagreed over the decision, with some disagreeing strongly (Flynn, 1979). Most of these families did not actually evacuate; the family members who had wanted to leave were undoubtedly especially upset, given the general level of tension in the area.

In some cases, women and children were evacuated so that their safety would be ensured, while the men stayed to work and maintain their property, pending an explicit evacuation order. There were concerns about looters, along with a certain fatalism, in this group. About 45% of the persons in such split households later reported they felt that whatever happened was in God's hands (Flynn, 1979).

Finally, some residents appear to have been affected very little by the accident; they remained calm and did not alter their daily routines. One woman told of how surprised she was to find out that anyone had evacuated. She had carried on her normal activities during the weekend after the accident, and wasn't aware of the extent of the evacuation. Similarly, none of her friends had left the area. On the whole, the households where everyone stayed reported a greater confidence in authority than did those households where some or all of the people evacuated. They were aware that there were problems at the plant, but did not consider the problems personally threatening since the authorities had not issued an explicit evacuation order (Flynn and Chalmers, 1980).

For most people, the emotional effects of the accident were short-lived, although the effects were quite intense for a significant minority. The Task Group on Behavioral Effects of the President's Commission on the Accident at Three Mile Island found that over a quarter of the persons living near the plant experienced "severe demoralization" in the period shortly after the accident (Dohrenwend et al., 1981:168). These persons had a level of demoralization that was higher than the mean or average score from a sample of community mental health center clients, "most of whom were suffering from chronic mental disorders" (Dohrenwend et al., 1981: 167). The percentage of nearby persons with such high levels of demoralization dropped to about 15% by the time two months had passed. Unobtrusive measures of stress, such as alcohol consumption, also rose early in the accident period, but quickly returned to normal levels (Mileti et al., 1982; see also Baum et al., 1980; Bromet, 1980; Clemente et al., 1979; Kasl et al., 1981a, 1981b; Sills et al., 1982).

With the passage of time, fewer people are worried about emissions from Three Mile Island, fewer continue to see the station as a serious threat, and fewer show behavioral stress symptoms. As of 1981, studies by the Pennsylvania Department of Health failed to provide evidence of measurable health effects due to the accident (Goldhaber, 1981). A workshop sponsored by the Nuclear Regulatory Commission, however, reported

> There was an increased incidence of somatization [physical symptoms of stress], found more

> frequently and at greater levels among individuals living closer to TMI . . . immediately after the TMI-2 accident. With the passage of time since the accident, symptomatology generally decreased in frequency and extent, although in one study symptom reporting was still elevated above expected levels as much as seventeen months after the accident (Walker et al., 1982:xix).

For some residents, it may be that the accident has caused a permanent change in their day-to-day activities and levels of stress. This is particularly true of those who are active in antinuclear groups. In addition, studies conducted during the first year after the accident showed that a small proportion of the general public continued to experience economic effects or had made definite plans to move or to change jobs. These represent significant personal effects (Flynn and Chalmers, 1980; see also Baum et al., 1983).

Opposition to the TMI station remains high; surveys indicate that about 50% of the people in the local area oppose the restart of Unit 1. They list several reasons for their opposition, including mistrust of Metropolitan Edison and the NRC, concern about the stress effects of the restart, and continuing concern about the health effects of the accident (Houts et al., 1980; Kraybill, 1980).

Immediately following the emergency period, the credibility of the NRC was very high, due largely to the efforts of Dr. Harold Denton during that period. However, this trust was eroded substantially during the next year. The findings of the Kemeny and the Rogovin Commissions, for example, indicated how serious the accident had been. Many local residents were also upset about the venting of radioactive krypton gases from the reactor during the clean-up process (the NRC itself eventually agreed that the release should have been delayed). Finally, the public also came increasingly to realize that because of technical problems, regulatory requirements, financial considerations and legal challenges, the clean-up of Unit 2 would not be accomplished quickly.

While the most immediate effects of the accident have clearly been transitory, residents of the area recognize the potential for continuing effects as decisions are made about the future of the generating facility. Their continuing feelings of vulnerability cause them both concern and resentment.

The extent of their future anxiety will depend on the actual progress of repairs and operation at the plant site, on the extent of public participation in the decision-making process, on their perceptions of the logic and fairness of the decisions that are made, and on the credibility of the decision-making bodies (see also Sills et al., 1982).

Economic Effects. The accident's short-term economic effects on area households included both income losses and extraordinary expenses. Households in which at least some members evacuated incurred substantially greater costs than did the others. For instance, in the 15-mile ring, costs per household with evacuees averaged $296, while costs for non-evacuating households averaged $41. Assuming that the average annual family income in the area was about $17,000, these costs amount to an average of 1.75% of the total annual incomes for evacuating households, and to 0.24% for non-evacuating households (Flynn, 1979). Long-term economic effects are not discernable for the average household.

After an initial impact on the real estate market, the accident's effects appear to have become negligible (Gamble and Downing, 1981). Migration into and out of the five-mile ring around the station can be explained by standard demographic predictors, such as marital status, age, sex, income and so forth. It is possible to "explain" a small additional proportion of the moves, in a statistical sense, by knowing whether or not the household evacuated at the time of the accident. But although those migrating into the five-mile ring around the station express somewhat more pronuclear opinions than those moving out, the attitudinal factors do not improve the prediction of who moves (for further discussion, see Goldhaber et al., 1981). There is currently no evidence of a higher housing vacancy rate nearer the plant. A more salient issue than proximity seems to be the cost of electrical power; real estate ads have used the fact that a house is not located in the Metropolitan Edison service area as a selling point.

During the emergency period following the accident the direct economic effects included interrupted local production and reduced local employment and income. The losses were conspicuous during the first week of April, but very minor after that time. For instance, a large grocer in Middletown told the following story, which is indicative of the more seriously affected businesses:

> Business was a bit slow, about 75% of normal, the day after the accident, but on Friday it dropped off to only 30% of normal. The store remained open, but during the course of the day, 60 of the store's 80 employees went home. On Friday evening, only four employees out of a usual night shift of 15 showed up. On Saturday the store remained open despite the fact that only 20-25 of the normal crew of 70 were on hand. Business on Saturday was about 40% of normal. The store closed as usual on Sunday and then opened on Monday with only 25% of its workers present. The situation remained much the same on Tuesday; business was only 20% of what it usually was. On Wednesday, a week after the accident, the situation changed markedly. Many employees were back, and business was about 80% of its usual level. The situation continued to improve until Saturday, when business was essentially back to normal, and all but three or four employees had returned (Flynn and Chalmers, 1980).

The best measure of total short-term economic disruption is probably the estimate of residents' accident-related income losses (and gains) derived from the NRC Telephone Survey, a sample of 1504 households that were contacted through random-digit dialing techniques (Flynn, 1979). One of the advantages of these estimates is that they include short-term income gains (including insurance payments) and account for proprietors' income as well as wage and salary income. Net losses within 15 miles of the site are estimated to have been about $9 million, or about 0.25% of annual personal income. Employment losses were estimated to have been of the same order of magnitude. Unreimbursed losses to individuals are being considered in a class-action lawsuit.

Accident-related economic losses to businesses are also the subject of a class-action lawsuit. The total amount of such claims is not known at this time. The agriculture and tourism sectors of the economy were particularly vulnerable to the accident. In a television documentary, an area resident reported:

> It is very difficult to walk away from 75 head of cattle, and five goats, and seven ducks, and thirty cats and two dogs, and leave these animals at the

> mercy of whatever. We couldn't bring ourselves to shoot them, and we couldn't bring ourselves to leave them, and we just didn't know what to do (WITF-TV, 1979).

Following the accident, one large dairy serving Harrisburg reported that sales dropped 18% during the first week and 15% during the second week.

Telephone contacts with the ten major lodging and convention centers in the area revealed initial losses of nearly $2 million in gross sales directly attributable to the TMI accident. A major trade show scheduled for the Pennsylvania Farm Show Building in Harrisburg was cancelled, as were other conferences and meetings. On the other hand, a substantial number of transients, including media representatives, technicians and government personnel, came into the area during the emergency period. In short, both negative and positive economic effects were visible in the tourism sector (Flynn and Chalmers, 1980).

Other sectors were also significantly affected during the emergency period, but continuing effects were not apparent; in fact, continuing disruption of economic activity due to the accident is conspicuous by its absence (Commonwealth of Pennsylvania, 1979, 1980). Retail trade, for example, was estimated to have lost over $39 million in business during the first week following the accident (Flynn and Chalmers, 1980) and to have lost perhaps 5-10% of this amount in income. It is possible, however, that the local economic effects may eventually become strongly positive if significant expenditures are made to rehabilitate Unit 2 and/or to modify and upgrade Unit 1.

Against this apparent backdrop of "return to normalcy," there is concern within the business community about the effect of the accident on the continued growth and development of the area--particularly the Metropolitan Edison Company's service area. Upon investigation, it appears that the concern is based not so much on abstract dimensions of the area's image, but rather on the potential effect of the accident on the cost of power. There is presently much confusion about the extent to which recent increases in the price of electricity are due to the accident. A study of the Metropolitan Edison service area conducted by Weston, Inc., showed that the cost of keeping the undamaged Unit 1 idle is $95 million per year (Lebanon Valley Chamber of Commerce, 1981). The study also showed that the average residential customer has experienced a 50% increase in electricity costs over March 1979 levels, an increase that is at least twice as great as increases in residential electricity costs in nearby areas over the same period. The rates for industrial users have increased even faster.

There is a clear appreciation that future prices depend on a complex set of political/regulatory decisions. This is coupled with concern that the uncertainty of future electricity prices may significantly affect relocation and expansion plans, even if the prices eventually prove to be no higher than they would have been without the accident. Some local studies indicate that the accident will not deter expansion of manufacturing establishments, but others disagree (Flynn, 1982).

Organizational Effects. The accident at Three Mile Island strained existing governmental organizations in several respects. The most obvious strains were those that were created for organizations having responsibility for emergency preparedness. First, because a formal emergency was never declared, the role of the Civil Defense coordinators was ambiguous. Given the already fragmented responsibility for public safety in most of the municipalities, this ambiguity was quite difficult to handle in some cases. Even where structural problems were handled smoothly, this was often due to the flexibility of the individuals involved. Some progress has been made since the accident in clarifying roles at the state and local levels.

Second, it is clear that the lack of a specific evacuation plan prior to the accident complicated the work of local emergency agencies. Besides having responsibility for pre-operations planning and for handling requests for information from the public, personnel at the emergency operations centers had to develop *ad hoc* plans that would normally require months of input. In fact, more than two years after the accident, even though all of the local municipalities had invested considerable time in their efforts, many local people believed local authorities still had not completed satisfactory, integrated plans. In most instances, further refinements to the plans were ongoing.

Third, institutions other than emergency agencies were equally unprepared for the accident. The agencies with responsibility for special populations, such as prisoners and hospital patients, had no plans for evacuating them prior to the accident. There were also no procedures for identifying and moving the institutions' essential records and equipment.

There was considerable expansion in the antinuclear movement in the TMI area (see the discussion in Walsh, 1981). This expansion has affected federal, state, and local decision makers, and it will continue to affect them. At the local level, antinuclear groups were instrumental in the passage of resolutions that opposed the reopening of TMI. The various groups have learned to work together, and have intervened in NRC and other regulatory hearings regarding the restart of TMI Unit 1, the recovery of Unit 2, and the issue of psychological stress. They have also provided information to the public on the class-action suits.

Relationships among and within agencies at the federal level have been clarified or changed because of the accident. For instance, the NRC is now responsible for assessing on-site hazards, while the Federal Emergency Management Administration (FEMA) is responsible for coordinating all other federal agencies having support roles. The NRC itself has undergone a series of reorganizations in response to the accident and the findings of the various investigatory commissions.

Finally, the nuclear industry has funded three new organizations in response to the accident. The industry's responses are described by Szalay (1984) in Chapter 12 of this volume. Briefly, however, the three new organizations deal with training programs, analysis of incident reports from the plants and dissemination of their findings, and an insurance pool to cover the cost of replacement power in the event of an accident. Some of the accident's other effects on the nuclear industry can be seen from the experiences at the 11 other case study sites, which will be discussed in the next section.

Effects of the Accident on the Other Case Study Sites

When the accident occurred at Three Mile Island, it was immediately apparent that the effects of the accident would not be confined to the TMI site. Given the national significance of the accident, and the revision of NRC regulations that followed the accident, every nuclear station in the country was affected in some way or another. This section of the present chapter provides a brief review of the accident's effects on the 11 other sites that were included in the NRC post-licensing studies. Peach Bottom Nuclear Generating Station, one of the twelve case study sites, is located just 35 miles downstream from TMI on the Susquehanna River. Furthermore, four of the eleven other study sites have Babcock and Wilcox units that are similar in design to the damaged unit at Three Mile Island.

Direct Economic Effects. In the aftermath of the accident, the NRC revised several of its regulations (U.S. Nuclear Regulatory Commission, 1980b, 1980c). In order to comply with the new standards, most operating reactors required substantial modifications. For instance, the NRC ordered all Babcock and Wilcox reactors to be shut down for a brief time while additional safety modifications were made. In addition, the new regulations required all stations to have an off-site technical center capable of monitoring the reactor core at all times.

In most cases, the required retrofitting or reactor modification was not complete by summer 1981. Some utilities estimated that it would take as long as two additional years to reach full compliance. The cost of the retrofitting varied depending on the design of the plant, but generally exceeded \$15 million; costs were considerably higher at some sites, reaching \$40 million at Calvert Cliffs. The plants had averaged some 1000 person-months of effort through 1981 to make the required changes (Chalmers et al., 1982).

Training Programs. The new NRC regulations require that each control room operator spend at least one week per year training with a simulator. Many utilities already had such a program, but some did not. At one extreme, Calvert Cliffs bought its own simulator, at a cost of about \$10 million, for the use of its operators. At a minimum, the utilities in the post-licensing studies held one special training session for their operators to communicate the new NRC requirements. Several utilities added personnel to their training staffs, increased the training period for new operators, or otherwise made major modifications in their training programs.

Emergency Planning. Evacuation plans were modified at all sites. Prior to the accident, the planning radius for evacuation at most sites was two to five miles; most utilities increased this radius to at least ten miles after the accident. Another change common to most sites was the installation of additional sirens and/or communications equipment in the local communities. Some utilities have instituted ongoing public information programs. These programs use public meetings, the press, and leaflets to describe the new emergency plans. The costs through 1981 for these programs range from about $400,000 to $10 million, with a median cost of $4 million.

Additional Issues Raised at Other Locations. Residents of the Peach Bottom Study Area, living 35 miles from TMI, were not far removed from the uncertainty and trauma of the two-week emergency period. A telephone survey of 250 households in the Peach Bottom area five months after the accident showed that a majority of households prepared for a possible evacuation, although none of those interviewed actually left (Pijawka, 1980). The survey showed that the TMI accident had minimal impact on the individual household's economic situation. The major consequence of the TMI accident on the Peach Bottom area was its effect on local institutions. It led to the emergence of public controversy over the safety of the Peach Bottom plant, the emergence of an antinuclear interest group, and the initiation of independent planning efforts to mitigate the potential hazards of the Peach Bottom station. The latter included a set of rules to govern the shipment of low-level wastes from the power plant.

During and immediately following the accident, all of the utilities involved in the post-licensing studies issued statements to the press. Nearly all the plants that had a design different from TMI emphasized this fact. The good operating histories of the plants were cited, and the safety modifications that were made to the plant were described. At the Oconee site, new training programs for operators were also highlighted. Given these factors, the owners of ten of the eleven other case study stations (Diablo Canyon was not in operation) stated that their facilities had much lower risks of accidents than did TMI.

After the accident the NRC required a review, and in most cases a revision, of the utilities' evacuation plans. Modification of the plans usually took several months, and many are not yet complete. At most sites evacuation planning was a public concern, and improvements in the plans were lead stories in the press. In some locations there was public participation in the process of plan revision.

At most sites there was evidence of heightened and increased concern over existing nuclear stations. Public concern appears to have been short lived and minimal at some sites (Cook, Oconee, Surry, St. Lucie, Crystal River) and serious at others. For instance, at the Diablo Canyon site, there was evidence to associate heightened public concern to the Three Mile Island event (see also the discussion by Farhar-Pilgrim and Freudenburg, 1984, in Chapter 7 of this volume). Interviews with antinuclear activists indicated renewed efforts because of TMI and a growing antinuclear constituency. Regional antinuclear organizations grew in size and commitment after TMI, and those that opposed Diablo Canyon also opposed Rancho Seco. While local public opposition at the Arkansas Nuclear One plant remained consistently low throughout that facility's history, a small antinuclear group surfaced as a result of TMI. Although the group did not receive much public support, it was noteworthy that an opposition group had even surfaced in Pope County, Arkansas (Chalmers et al., 1982).

CONCLUSIONS

The residents of south-central Pennsylvania were affected by both immediate and long-term impacts from the TMI accident. The short-term impacts included economic, social and psychological costs for individuals and groups; at the same time, local institutions also were seriously affected. The longer-term impacts appear to be smaller in magnitude to date, but in many respects, the accident is not "over" (Sills et al., 1982; U.S. Nuclear Regulatory Commission, 1980a, 1980b, 1980c).

The economic impacts of the Three Mile Island accident were significant in the short run, but appear to have been less significant since then--except for Metropolitan Edison Company, and hence for its customers. The effects of the restart of Unit 1 (the undamaged reactor) and the continuing effects of the cleanup at Unit 2 are not measurable as yet, and they remain potentially large. At the time this was being written, the employment and income of people directly employed on the island was larger than would be the case with two normally operating units. Various proposals for Unit 2 could result in effects that would be directly comparable to a major new construction program.

Major impacts were also incurred by utilities operating and constructing nuclear generating stations throughout the country. These impacts were the result of modifications to the structure of the facilities and to the preparations for the possibility of emergencies. The 11 other utilities in our study have already incurred very large costs as a result of the accident, ranging as high as $100 million. These utilities all expect to incur continuing costs as a direct result of the accident. Presumably, these costs would eventually be reflected in consumers' rates.

Local institutions really were not prepared for "the unthinkable," and for the most part they are still not adequately prepared today, although some progress has been made. While social and political life has largely returned to normal, there have been significant changes. The question of the psychological stress of the TMI-1 restart was argued in the courts for four years after the accident. The issue was--and still is--important to antinuclear groups in the area of TMI, and it demonstrates a significant change in the views of local communities toward the TMI facility. However, in spite of the seriousness of the accident, and the concern it has raised, measures of social and economic change suggest that the impacts were relatively small in percentage terms. The resilience and flexibility of the community social systems have been demonstrated through the rapid return to normal social life.

IMPLICATIONS FOR THE FUTURE

At the time of the accident at Three Mile Island, there were 72 operating nuclear reactors in the United States. An additional six dozen plants were in various stages of planning, licensing and/or construction. However, there had been no new orders for plants in the year immediately preceding the accident; the demand for nuclear plants had declined noticeably in the late 1970s.

After the accident, much of the attention of the NRC was focused on the safety of the operating plants, on revising its regulations, and on restructuring the NRC itself. The already-lengthy licensing process all but ceased for several months. In addition to these regulatory delays, utilities have been faced with: (1) a demand for electricity that has fallen well below earlier projections, (2) a recessionary economy where interest rates have soared, and (3) a public that has become increasingly wary of nuclear power. In addition, the undamaged reactor at Three Mile Island is still not back on line; if a unit meeting NRC safety standards can be prevented from producing electricity, and can be excluded from the rate base, the implications for the financing of future plants would be quite serious.

As a consequence, several utilities have tabled their plans for nuclear projects--perhaps doing so indefinitely. The first new construction permit application since the accident was not filed until December 31, 1982, by Puget Sound Power and Light Company. Even this application was not technically "new," because the NRC docket had been opened some eight years previously, when the intention was to build the plant at an alternative site.

On the other hand, there continues to be considerable pressure, both within the NRC and in the nuclear industry as a whole, to resume licensing of nuclear plants. President Reagan has voiced his support for nuclear power and his preference for streamlining the licensing process. The ability of the nuclear industry and the NRC to license proposed plants (and those already under construction) will largely determine the future viability of the nuclear option in the United States. The public response to the accident at Three Mile

Island continues to have a major influence on the viability of that option.

REFERENCES

Ad Hoc Population Dose Assessment Group
1979 *Population Dose and Health Impact of the Accident at The Three Mile Island Nuclear Station.* Washington, D.C.: U.S. Nuclear Regulatory Commission (NUREG-0558).

Baum, Andrew, Raymond Fleming and Laura M. Davidson
1983 "Natural Disaster and Technological Catastrophe." *Environment and Behavior* 15 (#3, May): 333-354.

Baum, Andrew, R. Gatchel, S. Streufert, Charlene S. Baum, Raymond Fleming and Jerome E. Singer
1980 *Psychological Stress for Alternatives of Decontamination of TMI-2 Reactor Building Atmosphere.* Washington, D.C.: U.S. Nuclear Regulatory Commission (NUREG/CR-1584).

Bromet, Evelyn
1980 *Three Mile Island: Mental Health Findings.* Western Psychiatric Institute and Clinic.

Chalmers, James, David Pijawka, Kristi Branch, Pam Bergmann, Cynthia Flynn and James Flynn.
1982 *Socio-economic Impacts of Nuclear Generating Stations: Summary Report on the NRC Post-Licensing Studies.* Washington, D.C.: U.S. Nuclear Regulatory Commission (NUREG/CR-2750).

Clemente, Frank, Idee Winfield, Margaret E. Cawley and Matthew Hastings.
1979 *Community Leaders' Reaction to the Three Mile Island Accident.* State College, PA: Center for the Study of Environmental Policy, The Pennsylvania State University.

Commonwealth of Pennsylvania
1979 *Three Mile Island Socio-Economic Impact Study.* Harrisburg, PA: Governor's Office of Policy and Planning.
1980 *The Socio-Economic Impacts of the Three Mile Island Accident: Final Report.* Harrisburg, PA: Governor's Office of Policy and Planning.

Dohrenwend, Bruce P., Barbara S. Dohrenwend, George J. Warheit, Glen S. Bartlett, Raymond L. Goldsteen, Karen Goldsteen and John L. Martin
1981 "Stress in the Community: A Report to the President's Commission on the Accident at Three Mile Island." Pp. 159-174 in Thomas H. Moss and David L. Sills (eds.), *The Three Mile Island*

Nuclear Accident: Lessons and Implications. New York: New York Academy of Sciences.

Farhar-Pilgrim, Barbara and William Freudenburg
1984 "Nuclear Energy in Perspective: A Comparative Assessment of the Public View." Pp. 183-203 in William R. Freudenburg and Eugene A. Rosa (eds.), *Public Reactions to Nuclear Power: Are There Critical Masses?* Boulder, CO: Westview Press/American Association for the Advancement of Science.

Flynn, Cynthia B.
1979 *Three Mile Island Telephone Survey.* Washington, D.C.: U.S. Nuclear Regulatory Commission (NUREG/CR-1093).
1982 *Socioeconomic Impacts of Nuclear Generating Stations: Three Mile Island Case Study. Volume 12.* Washington, D.C.: U.S. Nuclear Regulatory Commission (NUREG/CR-2749).

Flynn, Cynthia B. and James A. Chalmers
1980 *The Social and Economic Effects of the Accident at Three Mile Island: Findings to Date.* Washington, D.C.: U.S. Nuclear Regulatory Commission (NUREG/CR-1215).

Freudenburg, William R. and Eugene A. Rosa (eds.)
1984 *Public Reactions to Nuclear Power: Are There Critical Masses?* Boulder, CO: Westview Press/American Association for the Advancement of Science.

Gamble, H. B. and R. H. Downing
1981 *Effects of the Accident at Three Mile Island on Residential Property Values and Sales.* State College, PA: Institute for Research on Land and Water Resources.

Goldhaber, Marilyn K.
1981 Personal communication regarding studies by the Pennsylvania Department of Health.

Goldhaber, Marilyn K., Peter S. Houts and Renee DiSabella
1981 *Mobility of the Population Within 5 Miles of Three Mile Island During the Period From August, 1979 Through July, 1980.* Harrisburg, PA: Pennsylvania Department of Health.

Houts, Peter S., Robert W. Miller, George K. Tokuhata and Kum Shik Ham
1980 *Health Related Behavioral Impact of the Three Mile Island Nuclear Incident.* Harrisburg, PA: Pennsylvania Department of Health.

Kasl, Stanislav V., Rupert F. Chisholm and Brenda Eskenazi
1981a "The Impact of the Accident at the Three Mile Island on the Behavior and Well-Being of Nuclear Workers. Part I: Perceptions and Evaluations,

Behavioral Responses, and Work-Related Attitudes and Feelings." *American Journal of Public Health* 71 (#5, May):472-483.

1981b "The Impact of the Accident at the Three Mile Island on the Behavior and Well-Being of Nuclear Workers. Part II: Job Tension, Psychophysiological Symptoms, and Indices of Distress." *American Journal of Public Health,* 71 (#5, May):484-495.

Kraybill, Donald

1980 *Three Mile Island: Local Residents Speak Out Twice. A Public Opinion Poll, 1979-1980.* Elizabethtown, PA: Elizabethtown College.

Lebanon Valley Chamber of Commerce

1981 *What Makes Your Electric Bill so High in Lebanon?* Lebanon, PA: Lebanon Valley Chamber of Commerce.

Marshall, Elliot

1979 "A Preliminary Report on Three Mile Island: The NRC Learns of Negligence, Mechanical Failure, and 48 Hours of Confusion in the Control Room." *Science* 204 (April 20):280-281.

Mathews, Tom, Susan Agrest, Gloria Borger, Mary Lord, William D. Marbach and William J. Cook

1979 "Nuclear Accident." *Newsweek* (April 9):24-33.

Mileti, Dennis S., Donald Hartsoush and Patti Madson

1982 *The Three Mile Island Incident: A Study of Behavioral Indicators of Human Stress.* Fort Collins, CO: Colorado State University.

Pijawka, K. David

1980 *Survey of Public Attitudes Toward the Peach Bottom Plant.* Unpublished draft manuscript. Tempe, AZ: Mountain West Research, Inc.

President's Commission on the Accident at Three Mile Island

1979 *The Need for Change: The Legacy of Three Mile Island.* Washington, D.C.: U.S. Government Printing Office.

Rankin, William L., Stanley M. Nealey and Barbara D. Melber

1984 "Overview of National Attitudes Toward Nuclear Energy: A Longitudinal Analysis." Pp. 41-67 in William R. Freudenburg and Eugene A. Rosa (eds.), *Public Reactions to Nuclear Power: Are There Critical Masses?* Boulder, CO: Westview Press/American Association for the Advancement of Science.

Rubinstein, Ellis

1979 "The Accident That Shouldn't Have Happened: A Narrative Account of What is Believed to Have Occurred, Based on Reports From Many

Experts." *IEEE Spectrum* 16 (#11, November): 33-42.

Sills, David L., C. P. Wolf and Vivien B. Shelanski
1982 *Accident at Three Mile Island: The Human Dimensions*. Boulder, CO: Westview Press.

Szalay, Robert A.
1984 "A Nuclear Industry View of the Regulatory Climate." Pp. 295-306 in William R. Freudenburg and Eugene A. Rosa (eds.), *Public Reactions to Nuclear Power: Are There Critical Masses?* Boulder, CO: Westview Press/American Association for the Advancement of Science.

U.S. Nuclear Regulatory Commission
1972 *Final Environmental Statement Related to Operation of Three Mile Island Nuclear Station Units 1 and 2.* Washington, D.C.: U.S. Nuclear Regulatory Commission.
1980a *Final Environmental Assessment for Decontamination of the Three Mile Island Unit 2 Reactor Building Atmosphere*. Washington, D.C.: U.S. Nuclear Regulatory Commission.
1980b *NRC Action Plan Developed as a Result of the TMI-2 Accident.* Washington, D.C.: U.S. Nuclear Regulatory Commission (NUREG/0660).
1980c *Clarification of the TMI Accident Plan Requirements*. Washington, D.C.: U.S. Nuclear Regulatory Commission (NUREG/0737).

Walker, P., W. E. Fraise, J. J. Gordon and R. C. Johnson
1982 *Proceedings of the Workshop on Psychological Stress Associated With the Proposed Restart of Three Mile Island, Unit 1.* Washington, D.C.: U.S. Nuclear Regulatory Commission.

Walsh, Edward J.
1981 "Resource Mobilization and Citizen Protest in Communities Around Three Mile Island." *Social Problems* 29 (#1, October):1-21.

Dorothy S. Zinberg

9. Public Participation in Nuclear Waste Management Policy: A Brief Historical Overview

Public participation during the short history of nuclear waste management has been as controversial, and for many critics of nuclear energy, as unsatisfactory as the still fiercely contested, fragmented policies that have yet to be implemented. Unlike other significant problems of nuclear power plants, such as safety and siting, that could be dealt with if necessary by shutting plants down until the problems were resolved, nuclear wastes afford no such option. Like Mt. Everest, they are there.

At first ignored as an insignificant problem, they have now assumed major proportions. Nuclear waste issues include a technical uncertainty so unresolved as to divide the experts, a political and environmental impact so uncertain as to impede government action, and a human concern so integral to domestic practice that quite disparate groups--both pro- and antinuclear--perceive the nuclear issue as a challenge to citizens' basic rights to be informed and participate in decision-making processes.

By 1981-82 the American public was ambivalent toward nuclear power; roughly half thought it was safe and the other half did not. But 80% said that the country had not progressed far enough on both disposal and transportation problems, and as a consequence, were "worried" (Yankelovich and

Pp. 233-253 in William R. Freudenburg and Eugene A. Rosa (eds., 1984) *Public Reactions to Nuclear Power: Are There Critical Masses?*

Kaagan, 1981; see also Chapters 2 and 6 of this volume, by Rankin et al., 1984, and by Mitchell, 1984). The public has also shown increasing skepticism about the government's ability to deal with the problems of society. As the percentage of the public voting in national elections has decreased in the past two decades, increasing percentages have been voting on referendum questions. Emotionally charged questions--gun control, busing, abortion, gay rights, the Equal Rights Amendment, the environment and nuclear energy--have elicited passionate responses from otherwise apolitical individuals and groups. Ticket-splitting has increased by 25% in 20 years, as has the percentage of independent voters who will vote for candidates based on their positions on one specific issue (Janowitz, 1978).

It is in this context of increasing public suspicion toward nuclear technology and the federal government that the nuclear waste issue is to be played out. These three elements--government, scientists and technologists, and the public--now exist in a state of considerable tension. For progress to be made, this tension must somehow be resolved--perhaps through the intermediary organizations of state and local governments, through advocacy groups, and through direct participation. As Freudenburg and Rosa (1984) point out in the final chapter of this volume, unless workable policies are adopted, the country may face a de facto moratorium on nuclear power development in the future.

The tension between technologists and citizens is nowhere more evident than in the continuing controversy surrounding nuclear waste disposal. As the Achilles heel of the nuclear fuel cycle, nuclear waste symbolizes the vulnerability of the entire fuel cycle to public antipathy. In the United States, public-initiated legislation has imposed restrictions on nuclear waste storage in at least twelve states. In several European countries the courts have decreed that no new nuclear power plants can be built until the management of nuclear waste has been resolved, and the U.S. Supreme Court has now upheld the constitutionality of a California state law that imposes similar restrictions. Indeed, since 1974, radioactive waste management has increasingly been identified in both the United States and Europe as the one problem that will have to be solved if nuclear energy is ultimately to be acceptable (Zinberg, 1979).

Because the present stalemate is widely believed to stem in large part from years of inadequate planning, poor management and a lack of sensitivity to the concerns of the public, it is useful to examine the history of nuclear waste management as a perspective from which to view current attitudes and practices. The issue may be conceptualized in a triangular form, in which the three points of the triangle consist of scientific and technical information, government policies, and public attitudes, each influencing and being influenced by the other two in varying degrees. This relationship is further complicated by the fact that the information each of the three presents (or conceals) tends to reflect a particular viewpoint--a choice among competing values. This shifting and complex interrelationship has shaped the history of nuclear waste management.[1]

THE HISTORICAL CONTEXT

Although military and civilian nuclear wastes have been accumulating for some 35 and 20 years, respectively, only in the past few years has serious attention been given to the development of a waste management policy. To understand this seeming negligence, we must view the problem of nuclear waste and spent fuel management as having originated with the production of bomb-grade material in 1945. Military wastes caused little concern at first because the producers naturally recognized the overriding urgency of developing weapons for the war. The volume of waste was small, and its disposal appeared to be a minor problem relative to the enormous task of bringing a major war to an end. Furthermore, the rapid success in building nuclear weapons contributed to a state of technological euphoria. Those responsible for harnessing nuclear energy were quite certain that appropriate waste disposal technologies would be developed when needed. But they were unduly optimistic. In the intervening years, technical experts have continued to disagree as to whether the methods for disposal of high-level wastes are in place, almost perfected, or still out of reach--while ever-growing political controversies have further compounded the problem.

It was not until the passage of the Atomic Energy Act in 1954 that the Atomic Energy Commission, or AEC--which had been established to deal with both military and civilian nuclear power--undertook a serious examination of waste disposal. At the AEC's request, the National Academy of Sciences (NAS) began a study of the feasibility of disposal in underground formations. The NAS committee recognized the potential health hazards, the technical problems, and even the political questions associated with this issue. Their report included an important prediction: "Disposal is the major problem in the future growth of the atomic industry . . . . Radioactive wastes are a greater potential danger than the fallout of atomic bomb tests" (National Academy of Sciences, 1957).

The Academy's concern was not shared by the AEC, which wrote optimistically in its 1959 Annual Report, "Waste problems have proved completely manageable in the operation of the Commission . . . . There is no reason to believe that the proliferation of wastes will become a limiting factor in future development of atomic energy for peaceful purposes" (as quoted in Kasperson, 1980). Not surprisingly, no coherent policy emerged at that time--and very little progress was made in the decade that followed.

As recently as the early 1970s, many experts still believed that the scientific and technological problems associated with the disposal of high-level radioactive wastes were largely solved. The only remaining obstacles appeared to be social and political, or as expressed in Washington energese, "nontechnological necessities in the implementation of systems" (Bishop, 1978:57, as quoted in Kasperson, 1980:133).

These "nontechnological necessities" included questions about public participation in and acceptance of policy decisions, and political questions related to the relationship among federal, state and local governments. In the former instance, debates raged about questions such as: Who would take the wastes? How would they be compensated? In the latter, the debate focused on questions of states' rights versus federal pre-emption in the siting of waste repositories. Could a state veto a federal decision? Could a local or county government resist both the state and the federal government? Central to both social and political questions was the increasingly articulated public concern about equity--how might the risks associated with all forms of nuclear waste disposal be fairly distributed?

Equity, however, has remained an elusive quality. In the years since equity considerations moved to center stage in policy planning--and some would argue they are still in the wings--other related obstacles have begun to assume major roles in an ever-growing drama. What had begun as an apparently tractable problem, a scientific-technological one, was to become enmeshed with numerous related social, political and technical issues. Each time one appeared to be solved, several others cropped up in its place, and in recent years the obstacles to implementing waste disposal policies have grown exponentially.

Even the presumably straightforward technical problems have proved to be far less tractable than they once seemed to be. During the years of apparent technical consensus, burial in a stable underground formation was an agreed-upon method for high-level radioactive waste disposal. In 1971, the first site chosen was a salt mine in Lyons, Kansas. Much to the surprise of the AEC, serious objections to this decision were raised by a Kansas state congressman, who brought the issue directly to the public and generated opposition in the Kansas house and senate. He argued that the selection of waste disposal sites had to take into account more than technical feasibility. Any decision, it was argued, had to reflect the views of the people. The federal government alone could not decide whether the salt mine should be used for nuclear waste disposal. In addition, two local scientists from the Kansas Geological Survey maintained that government calculations about the safety of the proposed repository were hasty and inadequate.

The AEC, undeterred and still convinced that the public in Kansas would accept their decision, proceeded to carry out the confirmatory tests. In the summer of 1971, however, the AEC learned that a local salt mining company had started digging two or three miles from the proposed site--and to make matters worse, some 175,000 gallons of water had mysteriously disappeared during a solution mining operation in a nearby mine. It did not require extensive calculations to predict that the Lyons site might easily become Lake Lyons.

In February of 1972 the AEC withdrew its plans to develop the Lyons site, but by then the public had been awakened to the fallibility of AEC procedures. Resentments generated by this encounter between the AEC and the state helped to create the climate of distrust that has clouded most subsequent attempts to deal with nuclear wastes.

Despite the Lyons experience, public resistance to the AEC siting decisions did not unduly concern the Commission. While some notice was paid to non-technical issues--the AEC reports published at the time carried the usual acknowledgement of the necessity to consider the social and political factors in the decision-making process--the AEC generally ignored these considerations in practice.

By the 1970s, however, the AEC was dealing with a situation which had changed markedly from that of the 1950s. During the 1950s, an era marked by an optimism that corresponded to the growth of the economy, little public discussion occurred either about the environment or about nuclear energy. A greater faith in the government marked that earlier period as well; the general who symbolized victory in World War II was elected President. During his tenure, Dwight D. Eisenhower launched the Atoms for Peace program, which was seen as the beginning of a new era when radioactive isotopes would be used in medicine, agriculture and engineering. Visions of an unlimited, cheap energy source abounded.

But particularly with the publication of Rachel Carson's *Silent Spring* in 1962, concern with environmental issues had begun to grow. A *New York Times* book review exhorted the public to action: "It is high time for people to know about these rapid changes in their environment, and to take an effective part in the battle that may shape the future of all life on earth" (Milne and Milne, 1962:1).

This new mood and interest of the public were reflected in the rapid succession of laws that began with passage of the National Environmental Policy Act (NEPA) in 1970. Until that time, agency analysis and decision making were open neither to the public nor even to specialists outside the agency. As a result of NEPA, decisions on radioactive waste management were subject to review by independent committees, and Environmental Impact Statements were mandated. The passage in 1974 of the amended Freedom of Information Act (P.L. 93-502) allowed and stimulated increased scrutiny of government actions by citizens and advocacy groups, who now had access to papers and proceedings previously closed to them. At the same time, judicial action made it possible for citizens and public interest groups to take legal action in opposition to decisions that represented dangers to the environment. Thc landmark Calvert Cliffs court decision, which gave a monumental boost to the morale of nuclear opposition groups in the United States, concluded that "NEPA was not a vague testament of pious generalities but an unambiguous demand for reordering of priorities in specific decisionmaking procedures, including, very particularly, those of the AEC" (Patterson, 1976:193).

As the 1970s progressed, moreover, the persistence of problems began to crack the consensus of the technical experts. In the aftermath of the Lyons experience, for example, an increasing number of observers began to raise questions about the strategy of storing wastes irretrievably underground. Some of the questions were by no means simple ones:

- What would be the consequences if it were found subsequently that safety, health or environmental hazards resulted from this disposal method?

- What should be the ethical considerations? For example, in view of the possibility that advanced technologies might cause nuclear wastes to become new sources of energy, did the society that had consumed so much of the world's energy resources have an obligation to leave the wastes in retrievable form?

If the answer to this second question were affirmative, and the wastes were to be stored in a retrievable mode, then another set of questions was posed:

- Who would guard these wastes, which in some cases would remain hazardous for thousands of years?

- What kind of society would be required to maintain perpetual surveillance over radioactive material?

- Would retrievability increase the likelihood of terrorism and nuclear threats?

The AEC subsequently did opt for retrievable storage and in 1974 attempted to develop a Retrievable Surface

Storage Facility. Its Environmental Impact Statement on the facility received poor ratings from environmentalists, state and local governments, and eventually the Environmental Protection Agency (EPA). The project was abandoned.

By 1975 the AEC (reorganized as ERDA, the Energy Research and Development Administration) began to explore another site, this one in Carlsbad, New Mexico. Although the site was originally proposed for permanent storage of transuranic wastes[2] from military programs, the Department of Energy during the early part of the Carter Administration also favored adding retrievable storage for 1000 spent fuel rods from commercial nuclear power plants. In addition, this project, known as WIPP (Waste Isolation Pilot Plant), would have housed a facility for experiments with high-level defense wastes.

During the lengthy technical preparations for implementing the project, public concerns began to mount locally and nationally. By May of 1978, 33 states had passed laws aimed at controlling some aspect of radioactive waste management (Kasperson, 1980). Superimposed on the growing concern about waste storage sites was the issue of transportation, which increased the uneasiness as plans for WIPP took shape. Carlsbad citizens became alarmed by the publication of reports estimating that 65 truck and train loads of waste would be transported across the state each week. Furthermore, during the preliminary excavations, substantial deposits of potash, natural gas and oil were discovered, thereby arousing the indignation of local workers who protested interference with future employment opportunities--particularly since existing federal legislation prohibited waste disposal sites in areas with potential commercial assets. More recently, Native Americans protested that development of the proposed site would destroy their religious grounds.

In February 1980, five years and $90 million after the project was first sketched out, then-President Carter cancelled WIPP, leaving open the option of further investigations for possible future use. The Carter Administration had decided that it would be necessary to test four or five other sites with differing geological characteristics before agreeing to the construction of a pilot test disposal facility. Three days after the Reagan Administration took office, the Department of Energy announced that it would proceed expeditiously with WIPP, and that nothing more was needed from the state, legally or officially. In the case of WIPP, the federal agencies appear to have neglected once again to take serious account of the concerned public in the early stages of policy planning and to provide an adequate technical basis for the decisions that are announced.

NUCLEAR INFORMATION AND PUBLIC FEARS

The information the public has received about nuclear waste management--and the methods by which the information has been transmitted--have led to fears of deception and exacerbated fears of nuclear power in general. The growing public distrust of scientific and government information is an integral aspect of the immediate problem.

Especially in recent years, public concerns may have come to have almost as much to do with the characteristics of the nuclear power *industry* as with the characteristics of nuclear *power*. As more of the history of nuclear waste management has become public knowledge, there has been a growing awareness that bad judgment and incompetence have often been masked by military and industrial secrecy. Necessary in wartime, secrecy has also characterized nuclear energy production in peacetime, and it has proved to be harmful because of the distrust it has engendered. Open debate after World War II would have resulted in--if not better decisions--at least more acceptable ones.

In practice, the nuclear power industry has tended to be anything but open, striving instead to convey an impression of technical unanimity. This impression eventually became impossible to maintain, particularly in light of the increasing levels of disagreement among technical experts noted above. The desirability of vitrification--immobilizing liquid high-level wastes in glass--was challenged in a 1978 study by the National Academy of Sciences (Holden, 1978:599). By the early 1980s many scientists were involved in arguments about the reliability of salt versus other geological media such as basalt, granite and tuff. As a result of these and related disputes, the public became aware that the technical and political questions had proliferated rather than diminished as more became known about the geology and hydrology (see also the discussions by Burnham, 1979 and Carter, 1983).

Scientists who have traditionally been looked to as experts--authorities beyond the bickering and ignorance that characterize much debate among politicians and non-experts--have found themselves unable to resolve many technical uncertainties. Differing opinions are put forward as to the possibility of accidents if radioactive materials are stored in various geological formations. Competent scientists testify on both sides of the question of whether the levels set for radiation controls are adequate. As recently as May 1979, a group of scientists meeting under the aegis of the National Academy of Sciences could not state with much precision how safe is safe. Their report noted the considerable difference of opinion among experts about the human response to a low dose of radiation. It also raised questions about the risks associated with nuclear proliferation and terrorism. The report concluded that these risks cannot be calculated accurately by technological analysis alone. The NAS report, written in the spring of 1979, was not widely circulated because

> some members of the committee believed the report emphasized one interpretation of the available scientific data to the virtual exclusion of other possible interpretations that had been discussed by the committee (Schatz, 1980:1, 4).

Not until a year later, and then with two members still dissenting and with qualifying reservations from others, was it possible to release the report (National Academy of Sciences, 1980), which incorporated the two conflicting views of the model to be used in calculating cancer risks. The president of the NAS at the time, Philip Handler, being forced to play Solomon, wrote that one model could be used "if social values dictate a conservative approach," while the other should be employed "if one wishes to accept scientists' best judgment while recognizing that the data simply will not permit definitive conclusions" (as quoted in Schatz, 1980:5).

Public Values and Technical Decisions

These uncertainties--and Handler's ultimate way of handling them--demonstrate that the values of a society will influence the policy it ultimately chooses to solve a controversial technical issue. Values will also reflect a society's moral and ethical priorities. If, for example, there is less concern in years to come about leaving energy resources for future generations than there is today, one set of decisions about nuclear waste retrievability can be made. If a certain percentage of fatalities is acceptable for workers, other decisions regarding exposure limits can be made. However, each assumption must be made as explicit as possible, so that both the risks and the equity of those risks are fully understood, and so that a program of economic or other incentives can be developed to compensate those individuals and communities that are asked to assume some of the risks. Fairness, a value often neglected in the rush to industrialization and affluence, will have to be given new attention.

History suggests that nuclear power and nuclear wastes are unique in the fears that they arouse. Pronuclear scientists often do not understand this concern; indeed, they express surprise that the public is so obsessed with safety when so few people have been killed in nuclear accidents. They point out that although more than 100,000 miners have been killed in coal-mining accidents since the turn of the century, this record has provoked little outcry. In part, this difference results from the recognition that mining has killed only miners, whereas the release of radiation from improperly stored wastes could conceivably harm many others who are not directly involved in nuclear power generation. The same argument applies to airplane and automobile fatalities: the majority involve individuals who have chosen the risk, whereas radiation is socially imposed, and is perceived as a restriction on individual freedom by those who oppose it.

In addition, although radioactivity is an accepted part of medical treatment, it is popularly associated with destruction, as Slovic and his colleagues (1984) note in Chapter 5 of this volume. The nuclear holocausts of Hiroshima and Nagasaki, the secrecy of AEC activities, and the deceptions about radioactive fallout during the above-ground nuclear tests in the 1950s--all of these factors taint nuclear power's present image. The continued escalation of nuclear weapons manufacturing maintains for nuclear power its lethal reputation. And not insignificantly, fears about that which is invisible but capable of penetrating people, buildings and the ecosphere continue to contribute to the public's wariness of nuclear power (see also Nelkin, 1981, and the discussion by Mitchell, 1984, in Chapter 6 of this volume). It is interesting to note, however, that after many years of virtual public indifference to nuclear weapons, the rapid growth of the Nuclear Freeze Movement has changed the meaning of "antinuclear" within a short period of time. Only a few years ago, an "antinuclear demonstration" needed no further description; it meant a demonstration against nuclear power. By early 1983, the antinuclear demonstrations being reported in the press--again without modifiers--meant protests against nuclear weapons.

Among scientists, engineers and policy experts, the links between commercial nuclear power and nuclear weapons proliferation have been debated at length. Equally reputable scientists argue that "the connection is dangerous" or that "the connection is tenuous," (Holdren, 1983; Spinrad, 1983) and the controversy continues unresolved. Meanwhile, societal experiences with other technologies have also led to concern. As public misgivings about nuclear wastes were continuing to grow, the generic problems of toxic and hazardous waste disposal, long overlooked, burst into public view. A once-complacent public was shaken by dramatic revelations of contaminated water supplies, uninhabitable houses and communities, sick children, harrowing reports of genetic defects and a rising incidence of cancer. Love Canal, ironically named, came to symbolize the dangers of industrial wastes, as Three Mile Island later came to symbolize the vulnerability of nuclear power plants. Non-biodegradable chemicals such as dioxin and polychlorinated biphenyls (PCBs) continue to pose a threat to public health, and the awareness of the problem is fast taking hold in public consciousness. Consequently, while American faith in technology is still strong (see the discussion by Marrett, 1984, in Chapter 13 of this volume), it is being challenged by those who question society's capacity to control the industrial by-products it has created.

Finally, as the Three Mile Island (TMI) accident demonstrated in 1979, nuclear power problems are always newsworthy, and dissemination of information about them through the media has national and international repercussions. When TMI occurred, for example, a recommendation regarding high-level waste was just about to be introduced in Sweden. TMI forced a parliamentary decision to proceed with a national referendum rather than any further plan for nuclear energy. The hearings also resulted in the dismantling of plans for a major reprocessing and waste disposal center.

The 1980 referendum was presented to a Swedish public that had been bombarded by information for more than a decade, and was undoubtedly the most well-informed public in the world about nuclear energy. Approximately 75% of the public voted; even school children voted on mock ballots in their classrooms. The long-range political results, however, are unclear; none of the three choices on the ballot (pronuclear, antinuclear and a "moderate" approach combining conservation and some nuclear energy) received a majority of the public's consent. The interpretations by the international press of these results provide an interesting example of the difficulty faced by a public in acquiring "objective" information. A sampling of headlines reveals the disparity.

> "Swedish Vote Encourages Other Pronuclear European Efforts"
>
> -- *New York Times,* 3/3/80
>
> "An Overwhelming Majority of Swedes Voted Against Any Further Extension of Nuclear Power in a Special Advisory Referendum Last Sunday"
>
> -- *Nature,* 3/27/80
>
> "Sweden Appears to Endorse Nuclear Energy"
>
> -- *International Herald Tribune,* 3/24/80
>
> "Sweden's Nuclear Referendum Wound Up With Everyone Claiming a Victory"
>
> -- *Nucleonics Week,* 3/27/80

A Swedish nuclear authority who stated that Sweden had voted to phase out nuclear power was surprised indeed when presented with the above headlines.[3] American citizens, if not able to share his surprise, have been equally confounded by differing views put forward by their own government, industry and critics on nuclear waste management "facts."

Public Interest Groups

As the public has become better informed about the technical and political aspects of nuclear power and nuclear waste management, grass-roots organizations and national public interest groups have been formed. In both kinds of organizations, citizens have turned to experts outside the government and industry to initiate appropriate actions. The actions are not limited to antinuclear groups. As the antinuclear Clamshell Alliance can look to the Union of Concerned Scientists for expert advice, so the pronuclear Americans for Energy Independence can rely on their experts, Scientists and Engineers for Secure Energy. Both sides boast their citizens and Nobel Prize winners.

Environmentalists have also begun to have a marked political effect, although their organizations are often not as well funded as many other single-interest groups. As the Reagan Administration cut funds for environmental protection, membership soared in organizations such as the Sierra Club, the Audubon Society and the Environmental Defense Fund. Increasingly, environmentalists' views are taken into account by candidates who perceive them as an influential force, better educated and more likely to vote than the average citizen. Although the groups are not necessarily antinuclear, a majority of them have been active in initiating legal proceedings where nuclear-related issues appear to threaten the environment. Nuclear wastes that have the potential to pollute the ground-water supply, arable soil and the ecosphere are perceived as a lethal threat.

In addition, a new cadre of "public" experts that arose out of nuclear-related problems has been drawn into the nuclear-waste-management fray as advisors and consultants. By and large, this "public" grew from an informal network of scientists, engineers, social scientists, lawyers and policy planners working outside of government and industry. A number of them, acting on behalf of intervenor organizations or as "informed" citizens, participated in the Nuclear Regulatory Commission Goals Task Force, an exercise that attempted to incorporate social and institutional factors into its study of technical problems. This was followed by the Chicago Conference in 1976, which involved five relevant government agencies that specifically sought public participation. A later effort spearheaded by the American Physical Society made two distinct contributions: it clarified the issues, and it demonstrated that it was possible to identify within the scientific community a group of disinterested, technically competent professionals who would be able to comprehend the technical problems and produce an unbiased report (see Metlay and Rochlin, 1979).

Since 1978, the Keystone Center in Colorado (a non-profit education organization interested in environmental issues) has sponsored a series of workshops on national radioactive waste management issues, two of which attempted to design new models for public participation. Several members of the group were veterans of earlier nuclear waste studies and have since joined other workshops--among them the Harvard-Aspen Energy Committees, the Radioactive Waste Management Workshop (1979), the RESOLVE Center for Environmental Conflict Resolution in California (1979-81), and the League of Women Voters' Advisory Board (1980). Several members of the Keystone group took an active part in deliberations during the Carter Administration by meeting with Department of Energy officials (a number of whom attended their meetings), presenting their views to policy planners in Washington, and most recently serving as advisors and observers for a Planning Council that was designed to coordinate federal activities with those of state and local governments.

The League of Women Voters (whose members chaired DOE public hearings) was actively involved in the Keystone, Aspen and Planning Council meetings. In addition, during the past several years the League has launched a vigorous campaign for public education and public participation in nuclear waste management energy issues (see, e.g., League of Women Voters Education Fund, 1982).

Few other groups attempt such an evenhanded approach as the League does. Increasing polarization marks nuclear discussions as the numbers of avowedly pro- and antinuclear groups grow rapidly. In 1975, the *Directory of Nuclear Activists* recorded 149 antinuclear organizations; by 1980, the number exceeded 1500. The pronuclear groups that are catalogued by the Atomic Industrial Forum (AIF) have more than doubled during the same period, to approximately 200 at present, if regional chapters of national organizations are included.

It is evident from these data that the past decade in the United States has been marked by the rapid growth of volunteer and professional organizations that deal with controversial issues at local, state and federal levels; nuclear energy and (particularly) nuclear waste management have been for many their major concern. As the number of activities and the public awareness of the problem have increased, the interrelationship of the issues forming the three points of the nuclear waste management triangle has become more complex. An informed public is demanding that it be included in the political and technical resolutions of the problem.

CONCLUSIONS

In the final days of its lame-duck session, the 97th Congress passed legislation establishing a national policy on the burial of high-level nuclear waste. On January 7, 1983, President Reagan signed into law the "Nuclear Waste Policy Act of 1982," a bill that *initiates* a solution to the problem. It also gives states (or tribal councils, if the site is on an Indian reservation) the right to veto within 60 days the selection of a site within their borders. The veto can be overridden only by a majority of both houses of Congress. Public hearings must be held at each step of the way, and a full environmental impact statement must be prepared before the Department of Energy can make a recommendation to the president.

Clearly, public participation and public interest groups have had an impact on this legislation. Virtually all of the forms of legitimate public participation have played a role in the development of the most recent policy. The public has employed referenda, membership on advisory councils and committees, interventions in public hearings, interactions with regulatory agencies, administrative and judicial appeals boards, citizen-initiated litigation, lobbying, public protests and demonstrations to make itself heard (Organization for Economic Cooperation and Development, 1979).

Now what remains uncertain is the relative role of federal, state and local governments. If their points of view differ and the lines of authority are blurred, the decade-long stalemate will continue. Only the courts will thrive. The "not in my back yard" philosophy of waste disposal continues to intensify as states reject the option of being "host" even to low-level radioactive wastes. High-level waste disposal will elicit even stronger reactions. Much remains to be accomplished in order to achieve the equity and fairness that will provide the underpinnings for consensus.

Despite these obstacles, much has been accomplished, but as we have seen, the history of nuclear waste management policy is not a happy one. Secrecy and even deception on the part of the Atomic Energy Commission have not worked to reduce the public's skepticism about the government's ability to deal with technology-generated problems. Increasing polarization within the scientific and technical community has diminished its credibility.

The public has learned that scientific and technical data, although ultimately crucial for the resolution of nuclear waste problems, are only one point of the triangle, the other points being human and political problems. A satisfactory solution will need to take all of these concerns into account.

In the long run, it is the elected representative who must implement policy. Only by demonstrating willingness to consider public interests in decision making can governments reduce the fears and tensions caused by their past indiscretions.

If the scientists dominate the triangle, technocracy results; if public interest groups are intractable, then the most promising policies cannot be implemented. Surmounting the obstacles in nuclear waste management problems requires, then, a delicate balance among the three groups.

By now it should be obvious that no one group holds title to all knowledge and wisdom. As the public will have to gain much of its information to make decisions about resources and risks from the experts, so will the experts have to listen more carefully to the questions being raised by an increasingly sophisticated public--a public that has learned to take seriously its rights and responsibilities in a participatory democracy.

ACKNOWLEDGEMENTS

Sections of this paper appeared in the chapter "Public Participation: U.S. and European Perspectives," in *The Politics of Nuclear Waste,* edited by E. William Colglazier, Jr. (New York: Pergamon Press, 1982).

FOOTNOTES

[1]For a detailed history of radioactive waste management policy on which this section is based, see the unpublished paper by the former Chief Historian of the U.S. Department of Energy (Hewlett, 1978).

[2]"Transuranic wastes" contain elements with atomic numbers greater than that of uranium. They are artificially produced, coming mainly from the reprocessing of spent fuel and the production of plutonium for nuclear weapons. Transuranics present special difficulties for disposal because some of them take far longer to decay to relatively safe or "background" levels of radioactivity than do naturally occurring materials (for further discussion, see League of Women Voters Education Fund, 1982).

[3]For a lengthy discussion of nuclear waste in Sweden, see Lonnroth (1979). Other Swedish authorities also believed that the vote was to end nuclear power. See especially Ragnarson (1980).

REFERENCES

Bishop, W. P.
1978 "1978 Observations and Impressions on the Nature of Radioactive Waste Management Problems" In W. P. Bishop, N. Hilberry, I. R. Hoos, D. S. Metlay and R. A. Watson (eds.), *Essays on Issues Relevant to the Regulation of Radioactive Waste Management.* Washington, D.C.: U.S. Nuclear Regulatory Commission.

Burnham, David
1979 "Growing Waste Problem Threatens Nuclear Future." *New York Times* (July 9):1.

Carter, Luther
1983 "The Radwaste Paradox: Political Pressures Push for a Speeding up of the Geologic Dispoal Program, but Technical Considerations May Call for a Slowing Down." *Science* 219 (#4580, January 7):33.

Colglazier, E. William
1972 *The Politics of Nuclear Waste.* New York: Pergamon Press.

Freudenburg, William R. and Eugene A. Rosa
1984 "Are the Masses Critical?" Pp. 331-348 in William R. Freudenburg and Eugene A. Rosa (eds.), *Public Reactions to Nuclear Power: Are There Critical Masses?* Boulder, CO: Westview Press/American Association for the Advancement of Science.

Hewlett, Richard G.
1978 "Federal Policy for the Disposal of Highly Radioactive Wastes From Commercial Nuclear Power Plants: An Historical Analysis." Unpublished manuscript.

Holden, Constance
1978 "Panel Throws Doubt on Vitrification." *Science* 201:599.

Holdren, John P.
1983 "Nuclear Power and Nuclear Weapons: The Connection is Dangerous." *Bulletin of the Atomic Scientists* 39 (#1, January):40-45.

Janowitz, Morris
1978 *The Last Half-Century: Societal Change and Politics in America.* Chicago: University of Chicago Press

Kasperson, Roger E.
1980 "The Dark Side of the Radioactive Waste Problem." Pp. 133-162 in Timothy O'Riordan and Ralph d'Arge (eds.), *Progress in Resource Management and Environmental Planning,* Vol. II. New York: John Wiley and Sons.

League of Women Voters Education Fund
1982 *Nuclear Power Primer: Issues for Citizens.* Washington, D.C.: League of Women Voters.

Lonnroth, Mans
1979 "The Back-end of the Nuclear Fuel Cycle in Sweden." Paper presented at the Keystone Conference on Nuclear Waste Management, Keystone, CO, June.

Marrett, Cora Bagley
1984 "Public Concerns About Nuclear Power and Science." Pp. 307-328 in William R. Freudenburg and Eugene A. Rosa (eds.), *Public*

Reactions to Nuclear Power: Are There Critical Masses? Boulder, CO: Westview Press/American Association for the Advancement of Science.

Metlay, Daniel S. and Gene I. Rochlin
1979 "Radioactive Waste Management in the United States: An Interpretive History of Efforts to Gain Wider Social Consensus." Paper delivered at RESOLVE Nuclear Waste Management Process Review Workshop, Palo Alto, CA, December.

Milne, Lorus and Margery Milne
1962 "There's Poison All Around Us Now." *New York Times* Book Review (Sept. 23, Sect. 7):1.

Mitchell, Robert C.
1984 "Rationality and Irrationality in the Public's Perception of Nuclear Power." Pp. 137-179 in William R. Freudenburg and Eugene A. Rosa (eds.), *Public Reactions to Nuclear Power: Are There Critical Masses?* Boulder, CO: Westview Press/American Association for the Advancement of Science.

National Academy of Sciences
1957 *The Disposal of Radioactive Wastes on Land.* Washington, D.C.: National Academy of Sciences, National Research Council, Pub. No. 519.
1980 *The Effects on Populations of Exposure to Low Levels of Ionizing Radiations.* Washington, D.C.: National Academy of Sciences, National Research Council.

Nelkin, Dorothy
1981 "Anti-nuclear Connections: Power and Weapons." *The Bulletin of the Atomic Scientists* 37 (4):36-40.

Organization for Economic Cooperation and Development
1979 *Technology on Trial: Public Participation in Decision-Making Related to Science and Technology.* Paris, France: Organization for Economic Cooperation and Development.

Patterson, Walter C.
1976 *Nuclear Power.* London, England: Penguin Books.

Ragnarson, Per
1980 "Before and After: The Swedish Referendum on Nuclear Power." *Political Life in Sweden,* No. 5. New York: Swedish Information Service, September.

Rankin, William L., Stanley M. Nealey and Barbara D. Melber
1984 "Overview of National Attitudes Toward Nuclear Energy: A Longitudinal Analysis." Pp. 41-67 in William R. Freudenburg and Eugene A. Rosa (eds.), *Public Reactions to Nuclear Power: Are*

There Critical Masses? Boulder, CO: Westview Press/American Association for the Advancement of Science.

Schatz, Gerald S.
1980 "Uncertainties in Estimating Effects of Radiation at Low Doses." National Academy of Sciences *News Report* 30 (#10, October):1, 4-5.

Slovic, Paul, Baruch Fischhoff and Sarah Lichtenstein
1984 "Perception and Acceptability of Risk From Energy Systems." Pp. 115-135 in William R. Freudenburg and Eugene A. Rosa (eds.), *Public Reactions to Nuclear Power: Are There Critical Masses?* Boulder, CO: Westview Press/American Association for the Advancement of Science.

Spinrad, Bernard
1983 "Nuclear Power and Nuclear Weapons: The Connection is Tenuous." *Bulletin of the Atomic Scientists* 39 (2):44-49.

Yankelovich, Daniel and Larry Kaagan
1981 "The American Public Looks at Nuclear: Vaguely in Favor, Clearly Worried." Pittsburg, PA: Aluminum Company of America.

Zinberg, Dorothy S.
1979 "The Public and Nuclear Waste Management." *Bulletin of the Atomic Scientists* January, pp. 134-139.

Part 4

Speaking on Behalf of the Public

W. Kenneth Davis

10. Nuclear Power Under the Reagan Administration

INTRODUCTION

This chapter deals with policies toward nuclear power in the Reagan Administration. Certainly the use of nuclear power is one key to future energy growth in the United States. One should not forget that one third of all energy produced in the United States is used for electric power (U.S. Energy Information Administration, 1983:20). This proportion will become a growing fraction; in fact, the expectation is that it will reach 40% to 50% by the year 2000.[1]

With the high cost of oil and gas, the prospects are dim for economical use of these fuels for new electricity production. In my opinion, solar energy is also not going to be economical for central station electricity generation in the foreseeable future; therefore we are left with coal and nuclear energy as our only options. Both of these are highly capital-intensive, but their costs are about the same if all facilities are included (U.S. Energy Information Administration, 1982c).

The United States has significant coal reserves, probably enough for one or two hundred years. Nuclear energy (including the breeder) can last thousands of years, with fusion energy being an essentially infinite source.

Pp. 257-265 in William R. Freudenburg and Eugene A. Rosa (eds., 1984)
Public Reactions to Nuclear Power: Are There Critical Masses?

There may be some in the press who are peddling the idea that the U.S. Department of Energy is promoting or subsidizing nuclear power. This is a misunderstanding of our goals. This Administration wants to make nuclear power a fully viable and reliable alternative to coal or oil. We want to create situations where utilities can make normal decisions based on economics and reliability. This also means utilities would be unhampered by uncertainties, unpredictable regulatry schedules, and unneeded licensing or other constraints.

This Administration believes nuclear power must be used to meet future electric power requirements. Therefore part of our job is to present facts to the public on the safety, the reliability, and the environmental acceptability of nuclear power. The individual decision, however, is up to the utilities; the government will not intervene, nor do we plan to subsidize the use of nuclear power in any way.

THE NEED FOR NUCLEAR ENERGY

Most credible technical data suggest that nuclear power plants can be built on a comparable basis with coal-fired plants (U.S. Energy Information Administration, 1982c). In fact, it is about 20% cheaper on the average. There are geographical areas, however, where coal is cheaper, and there are other instances where coal would be much less expensive than nuclear power if scrubbers were not needed on low-sulfur coal. Regardless, the reliability and availability of nuclear power is at least comparable to coal. The safety of nuclear power is still undiminished, and in fact was reinforced by the Three Mile Island incident. The whole fuel cycle of nuclear power is environmentally acceptable if properly engineered safeguards are incorporated into the design and operation of the various facilities.

By the year 2000, less than two decades from now, we will need about 1000 gigawatts (gw) of electrical power even at low energy consumption growth rates of 3% to 3.5% per year.[2] Of this, about one half of the 220 gw of capacity that needs to be ordered and constructed could come from nuclear power plants. If this new nuclear-generating capacity is added to the 140 gw that is already operating or being built, we could have 250 gw of nuclear power by 2020. Can we do it? I think it is quite feasible, but only if we restore confidence and reason in nuclear power decision making so that nuclear power can compete freely in the marketplace.

Reagan Administration Policies

The Administration's nuclear policies were outlined in the Presidential statements published on July 16, 1981, and October 8, 1981. The first statement (Reagan, 1981a) dealt with the international nuclear situation. We do not want any misunderstandings on the U.S. non-proliferation policy. The proliferation of nuclear weapons has been a constant concern of the United States for 35 years, and it continues to be a concern, despite some claims to the contrary by some antinuclear elements. There is no backing off at all in our non-proliferation policies. What is different, however, is the Reagan Administration's approach to the issue, which is in contrast to the approach of previous administrations. Some of the earlier policies and programs were unrealistic and probably counterproductive, as when the United States tried to convince other countries with civilian nuclear power programs to reorient their programs, sometimes in ways that I feel would have been contrary to those countries' best interests. We are returning to historic, long-term U.S. government policies on this important subject--regardless of politics.

The President's second nuclear policy statement, announced on October 8, 1981 (Reagan, 1981b), dealt with domestic nuclear power issues. While the statement dealt with the unique problem of nuclear power, it also recognized the financial problems of utilities. These interrelated problems have been addressed in two ways.

First, the Economic Recovery Program is aimed at bringing the economy under control--stimulating productive investments, reducing federal expenditures, reducing personal and corporate taxes, reducing unnecessary regulatory requirements, reducing the inflation rate, and reducing interest rates. By these actions we hope to increase capital investments, increase energy production rates, and increase our standard of living.

Second, in addition to all the aforementioned goals, we believe in the need for increasing utilities' revenues, which are largely under the control of state regulatory agencies.

These regulatory bodies have allowed a rate of return for utilities of 14% to 15% when it has been necessary to borrow money at 17% to 19%. Utility stocks are at 70% to 80% of book value. Utility revenue per kilowatt in constant value dollars increased only 14% for residential rates and 22% overall between 1973 and 1980.[3]

According to the *Statistical Abstract of the United States* (U.S. Department of Commerce, 1981a:424, 591), residential expenditures for electricity totalled $35.5 billion in 1980--less than 2% of the nation's total disposable income of $1827.7 billion. By contrast, alcohol and tobacco consumed $63.2 billion, or 3.5% of our net disposable income.

The new tax laws help utilities by allowing dividend reinvestment and accelerated depreciation rates. The Federal Energy Regulatory Commission hearings on the Construction Work in Progress concept really illustrate the financial problems for utilities. This concept would allow the construction costs of a plant to be included in a utility's rate base while the plant is being built--as opposed to the common practice at present, which is to require utilities to wait until a plant is complete before its costs can be taken into account in the computation of customer rates. The current practice can be a problem for any utility, but it tends to be especially troublesome for those utilities that are building nuclear power plants.

Licensing Reforms. There are also other institutional problems confronting nuclear power. For example, if one accepts the demand or need for nuclear power, and if financing is not a problem, nuclear licensing schedules are still an obstacle. The President directed the U.S. Department of Energy to study the licensing process to determine what changes were needed, and to propose legislation for any changes that could not be dealt with on an administrative basis (Reagan, 1981b). We developed legislative proposals for introduction in the 98th Congress.

The point is that the licensing process must be simplified so that we can focus on the real safety issues, and above all, make the process an orderly one, so that a utility can count on answers on a specific schedule. The Nuclear Regulatory Commission, under Chairman Nunzio Palladino, has also responded to this problem, establishing its own Regulatory Reform Task Force.

Reprocessing. In another vein, the President has revoked the previous unrealistic ban on reprocessing of spent nuclear fuel. He has also stated that private industry should take the lead in establishing nuclear fuel reprocessing facilities. Studies are now underway, particularly with regard to the Barnwell reprocessing plant in South Carolina, which was under construction in 1977 when President Carter announced that reprocessing was not to be the preferred way of handling spent nuclear fuel. Why should industry be interested in this idea? By 1990, existing nuclear plants, as well as those under construction, will be discharging 3300 metric tons of spent fuel per year, which is twice the capacity of Barnwell (U.S. Department of Energy, 1983). Thus a market for reprocessing facilities will exist.

The investment in nuclear power plants is now approximately $100 billion, and the total is rising each year. Thus if nuclear power is a viable option, a few hundred million dollars to put Barnwell into use is not an unreasonable course to consider. There is also a recognized need for plutonium for the Clinch River Breeder Reactor, and for the nation's ongoing breeder reactor development program.

Radioactive Waste Management. As Rosa and Freudenburg (1984) note in the introductory chapter of this volume, and as Zinberg (1984) discusses at greater length in Chapter 9, the disposal of high-level radioactive wastes has been one of the most intractable public and political problems in the entire nuclear power debate. The selection of sites for waste disposal generates intense public interest. No governor appears to want a nuclear waste repository in his or her state. Public hearings on the subject are well attended.

As a way of dealing with this issue, the President directed the U.S. Department of Energy to move swiftly in deploying a system that demonstrates the safe emplacement of high-level nuclear wastes (Reagan, 1981b). Disposal of high-level radioactive wastes has been and continues to be the sole and unique responsibility of the federal government--and we intend to carry it out. We are undertaking a firm program to establish permanent repositories, and to demonstrate emplacement of waste on a retrievable basis in a test facility. We will base the program on waste from reprocessing, but provision will also be made for spent fuel storage.

For the past few years, the waste management program had been diverted to "paralysis by analysis," complete with endless studies, the search for perfect solutions, and the feeling that we could not do anything until we know everything. The Reagan Administration has decided to quit looking for the "holy grail," and to adopt well-known, exhaustively researched, and quite adequate solutions to do the job. The nuclear waste storage legislation passed by the 97th Congress is based on the Reagan Administration's economic philosophy. The users of nuclear-generated electricity will pay the costs for storing the waste, based on a surcharge such as one mill per kilowatt hour. The basic principle is the full recovery of costs. Given recent improvements in the technology for waste disposal, the public acceptability of nuclear waste disposal is likely to increase as the program is implemented. The parallel military waste disposal program should also help with public perception and technology development.

CONCLUSION

In sum, I hope I have demonstrated that the Reagan Administration has the dedication and a positive program to change nuclear power from the "option of last resort." But along with other programs, it is one that relies on the free market, industrial responsibility and initiatives, and a proper partnership between government and the private sector. The Administration is seeking to put the economy back in shape, with budgetary, tax, and regulatory relief programs. Much more should be forthcoming on licensing, regulation, and reversal of legislative constraints pertaining to nuclear power.

FOOTNOTES

[1]The U.S. Energy Information Administration (1982b:174) projects that in the year 2000, total energy consumption will be 103.9 quadrillion BTUs, or quads, with energy consumption by electric utilities being 41.1 quads, or 39.6% of the total. The Office of Policy, Planning, and Analysis of the U.S. Department of Energy (1982:1-17) projects that total consumption will be 97.0 quads in the year 2000, and that electric consumption will be 41.1 quads, or 42.4% of the total. For purposes of comparison, total U.S. energy consumption was 75.91 quads in 1980 (U.S. Energy Information Administration, 1982a:9).

[2]A gigawatt is one billion watts, which is approximately the output of one large nuclear power plant. The North American Electric Reliability Council (1982:10) reports that non-coincident summer peak demand for the contiguous United States was 428.295 gigawatts in 1981. Thus if peak demand grows by 3% per year, it would reach 751.018 gigawatts in the year 2000; if it grows 3.5% per year, it would reach 823.398 gigawatts in the year 2000.

[3]The figures for return on equity and market-to-book ratio are from Edison Electric Institute (1982). Data for yields on new bonds were provided by Moody's Investors Service. Statistics for revenues per kilowatt hour of sales are from Edison Electric Institute (1982:63) and the Bureau of Economic Analysis (BEA) of the U.S. Department of Commerce (1981b). The BEA reports Gross National Product deflators of 1.0575 and 1.7864 to convert 1973 dollars and 1980 dollars, respectively, into constant 1972 dollars. Without correcting for inflation, average revenues per kilowatt hour in the residential sector increased from 2.38 cents in 1973 to 4.93 cents in 1980. This is equivalent to a "real" or inflation-corrected increase, in 1972 dollars, of 2.25 cents in 1973 to 2.76 cents in 1980, or an increase of 23%. Overall, average revenues per kilowatt hour increased from 1.86 cents in 1973 to 4.37 cents in 1980 before correcting for inflation; this is equivalent to a "real" increase, in 1972 dollars, from 1.76 cents in 1973 to 2.45 cents in 1980, or an increase of 39%.

REFERENCES

Edison Electric Institute

1982 *Statistical Yearbook of the Electric Utility Industry/1980*. Washington, D.C.: Edison Electric Institute.

Freudenburg, William R. and Eugene A. Rosa (eds.)

1984 *Public Reactions to Nuclear Power: Are There Critical Masses?* Boulder, CO: Westview Press/American Association for the Advancement of Science.

North American Electric Reliability Council

1982 *Electric Power Supply and Demand, 1982-1991*. Princeton, NJ: North American Reliability Council.

Reagan, Ronald

1981a "Statement on Nonproliferation." Washington, D.C.: Office of the White House Press Secretary, July 16.

1981b "Domestic Nuclear Policy Statement." Washington, D.C.: Office of the White House Press Secretary, October 8.

Rosa, Eugene A. and William R. Freudenburg

1984 "Nuclear Power at the Crossroads." Pp. 3-37 in William R. Freudenburg and Eugene A. Rosa (eds.), *Public Reactions to Nuclear Power: Are There Critical Masses?* Boulder, CO: Westview Press/American Association for the Advancement of Science.

U.S. Department of Commerce

1981a *Statistical Abstract of the United States, 1981*. Washington, D.C.: U.S. Government Printing Office.

1981b *Survey of Current Business* 61 (#7, July).

U.S. Department of Energy

1982 *Energy Projections to the Year 2000: July 1982 Update*. Washington, D.C.: Office of Policy, Planning, and Analysis, U.S. Department of Energy (DOE/PE-0029/1).

1983 *Spent Fuels Storage Requirement*. Richland, WA: Richland Operations Office, U.S. Department of Energy (DOE/RL-83-1; UC-85).

U.S. Energy Information Administration

1982a *1981 Annual Report to Congress, Volume 2: Energy Statistics*. Washington, D.C.: U.S. Department of Energy (DOE/EIA-0173[81]/2).

1982b *1981 Annual Report to Congress, Volume 3: Energy Projections*. Washington, D.C.: U.S. Department of Energy (DOE/EIA-0173[81]/3).

1982c *Projected Costs of Electricity from Nuclear and Coal-Fired Power Plants, Volume 1.* Washington, D.C.: U.S. Department of Energy (DOE/EIA-0356/1).

1983 *Monthly Energy Review, January 1983.* Washington, D.C.: U.S. Department of Energy (DOE/EIA-0035 [83/01]).

Zinberg, Dorothy S.

1984 "Public Participation in Nuclear Waste Management Policy: A Brief Historical Overview." Pp. 233-253 in William R. Freudenburg and Eugene A. Rosa (eds.), *Public Reactions to Nuclear Power: Are There Critical Masses?* Boulder, CO: Westview Press/American Association for the Advancement of Science.

Barry Commoner

11. The Public Interest in Nuclear Power

INTRODUCTION

This is a particularly crucial time to consider the public interest in nuclear power. The U.S. government's policies toward nuclear power and toward energy more generally--policies that are supposed to be conducted in the public interest--are contradictory and disorganized. In the name of the Reagan Administration's belief in the "magic of the marketplace," government efforts to develop alternatives to the expansion of nuclear power, such as photovoltaic cells and more effective energy conservation measures, have been summarily abandoned. Yet the Administration proposes a government takeover of nuclear fuel reprocessing--a crucial part of the industry which, after three expensive fiascos, private enterprise has abandoned.[1] With respect to nuclear power the magic of the marketplace has apparently given way to political sleight-of-hand. And in a gesture that appropriately symbolizes the Administration's abandonment of any pretense of developing a cogent energy policy, the U.S. Department of Energy is still expected to be sacrificed in order to validate Mr. Reagan's campaign rhetoric--a goal seemingly more important to the Administration than a national energy policy.

Different sectors of society--government, business, the public--have their own differing interests in nuclear power. The government is concerned--or should be--with developing

---

Pp. 267-294 in William R. Freudenburg and Eugene A. Rosa (eds., 1984) *Public Reactions to Nuclear Power: Are There Critical Masses?*

an effective national energy program, and therefore with the possible role of nuclear power in it. The government is uniquely concerned with military matters as well, and therefore with the close connection between nuclear power and nuclear weapons. In the U.S. economic system, business is uniquely concerned with governing the use of capital, and therefore with the viability of nuclear power as an investment. The general public is concerned with nuclear power plants' safety, with the price of their electricity and with their impact on the quality of the environment. But more generally, the public is also concerned with the issues that motivate government and business.

In brief, the public interest in nuclear power includes the following concerns: that the nuclear power system should produce electricity at the least possible cost; that it should do so without creating undue environmental hazards; that it should play a positive role in the development of an effective national energy program; that it should strengthen rather than weaken the economy; and that it should foster peace rather than war.

Since the purpose of nuclear power is to produce electricity, and since there are other readily available means of achieving this purpose, the judgment as to how well nuclear power meets the criteria of public interest must be made in comparison with these alternatives. In other words, in order to meet the public interest thus defined, nuclear power should achieve the several aims stated above at least as well as do other means of producing electricity.

It is the thesis of this paper that, on the evidence provided by its recent history, the nuclear power industry in the United States has failed to meet the public interest. I shall also suggest that the appropriate response to this failure is not the imposition of further economic and environmental constraints on the nuclear power industry, but rather the determination by the American people to replace it with better, alternative means of producing electricity.

ECONOMIC CONSIDERATIONS

As background to these considerations, it is useful to delineate the basic relation between a source of energy, such as nuclear power, and the economic system as shown in Figure 1. This diagram asserts that (1) the output of the economic system arises from the production of goods and services; (2) production always requires that thermodynamic work be done (i.e., production is a non-spontaneous, work-requiring process); (3) work must be derived from a suitable source of energy; and (4) the output of the economic system is divided among consumption (by the general public and by military programs), investment of capital in general production and investment of capital in the production of energy. The main outcome of these relationships is that the efficiency of any source of energy must be judged economically, especially with respect to capital. In effect, the overall efficiency of an energy source is determined by the ratio of its economically useful output to the capital needed to generate that output.

The public is most directly concerned with nuclear power's influence on the cost of an essential item of consumption: electricity. Komanoff (1981) has analyzed the relative costs of electricity produced by nuclear and coal-burning plants. He reports that between 1971 and 1978, the capital costs for building nuclear power plants increased twice as fast as did those for coal-fired plants. Nuclear capital costs in real dollars (discounting for general inflation) increased at an average annual rate of 13.5% per year. In contrast, capital costs for coal-fired plants, including scrubbers, increased 7.2% per year; the increase was 4.2% per year if scrubbers are excluded. For plants completed in 1978, nuclear capital costs were 52% greater than coal-fired capital costs (including scrubbers). Komanoff concludes that the capital costs of new nuclear plants (i.e., those now under construction) will exceed those of new coal-fired plants by about 75%. As a result, new nuclear plants are expected to generate electricity at a lifetime cost that is 20% to 25% greater than the cost of electricity generated by new coal-fired plants.

Although the nuclear power industry has claimed that nuclear power costs are consistently lower than the cost of power from other fuels,[2] records of the utility industry show otherwise. *Electrical World,* a utility industry trade journal, has published a series of surveys of the operating characteristics of new power plants that have come on line in the preceding two-year period. The results of these surveys

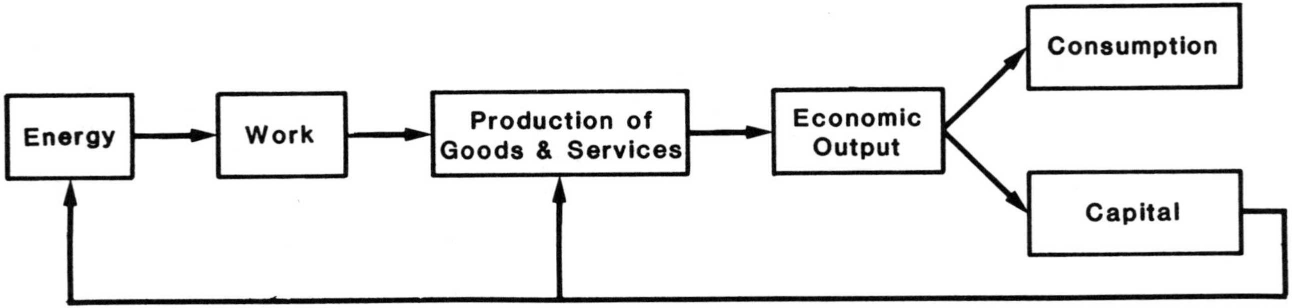

Figure 1. The Role of Energy in an Economic System

with respect to the actual cost of producing electricity by nuclear and coal-fired plants (Friedlander, 1979:55) are summarized in Figure 2. In 1969 the average costs for new nuclear plants were 70% above those of new coal-fired plants. In 1971 no new nuclear plants were reported. In 1973 the average costs for new coal-fired plants were 13% above those of new nuclear plants. In 1975 the nuclear costs exceeded coal-fired costs by 30%; in 1977 coal-fired costs were 8% above nuclear power costs; in 1979 costs at new nuclear plants exceeded costs at new coal-fired plants by 6%. No comparison is possible in the 1981 survey, because power cost figures are not reported for the two nuclear plants that came on line during that period.

These utility data certainly fail to support the nuclear power industry's claim that their plants produce the least costly electricity. It should be kept in mind that the foregoing figures are national averages; depending on regional costs of coal and other factors, the relationship between nuclear and coal-fired costs at a particular location may depart significantly from the average. Nevertheless, these data together with Komanoff's indicate that, on the average, coal-fired plants can be expected to produce electricity at a lower cost than nuclear power plants.

Apart from the relatively narrow (but intense) interest of the public as consumers in the cost of electricity, they have a broader interest in the impact of nuclear power on our troubled economy. One of the most difficult problems relates to the use of capital. Nuclear and fossil-fueled plants differ considerably in their economic characteristics, especially with respect to capital, and these differences strongly influence their overall economic impact. First, nuclear plants are much larger than fossil-fueled plants, and therefore require a greater commitment of capital when a decision is made to build a plant. The 94 nuclear plants once on order for operating dates between 1981 and 2000 averaged 1060 megawatts (mw) in capacity; the 238 fossil plants on order over that period of time averaged 463 mw in capacity (Berman, 1981:72). In addition, nuclear plants require larger capital expenditures than do fossil-fueled plants for equal capacities. For example, Komanoff (1981) estimates that the capital cost of nuclear plants completed in 1978 averaged $887 per kilowatt (kw) in 1979 dollars, while coal plants averaged $583/kw.

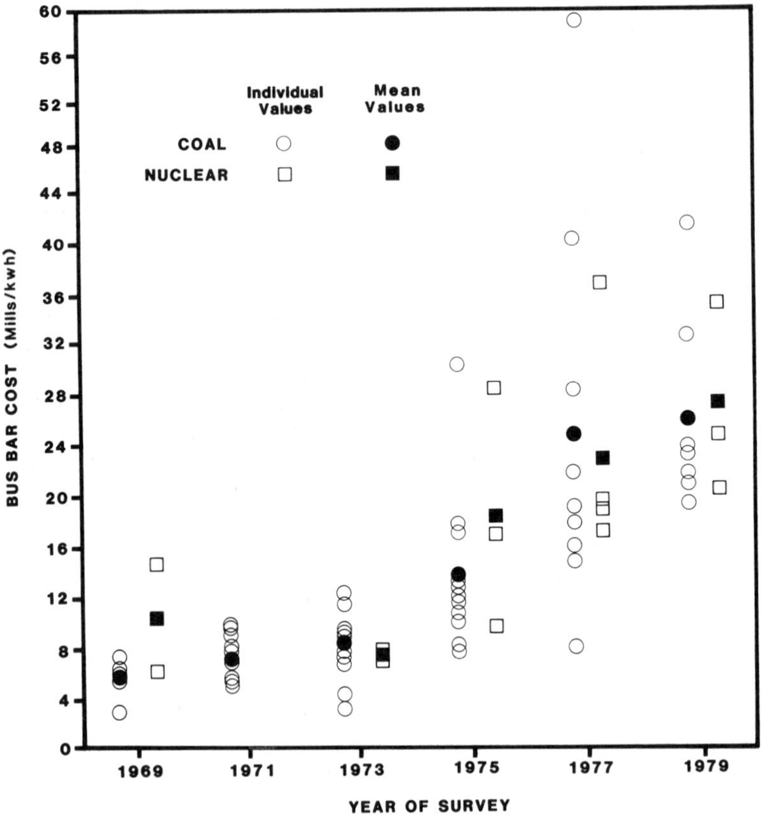

Figure 2. Electric World Steam Station Cost Surveys of New Nuclear and Coal Power Plants

For projected plants in 1988, the values are even more disparate: \$1374/kw and \$794/kw, respectively.

These relationships strongly influence the economic risk involved when a utility orders a power plant. Based on the above figures for recently committed plants (i.e., those to be completed over the next 10 years or so), a typical nuclear plant involves a commitment of \$1.46 billion, while a fossil-fueled plant commits only \$0.37 billion in capital (Komanoff, 1981). This estimate is conservative relative to nuclear plants, since their costs are currently escalating much faster than the costs of coal-fired plants.

There is thus nearly a four-fold difference in the amount of capital placed at risk when a utility orders a nuclear versus a coal-fired plant, and this difference can have a considerable effect on the efficiency of the overall investment. This consequence arises from factors that influence the *time-dependence* of the effective use of the investment. These factors include the following: (1) the time required to design, license and build the plant (since during this time the invested capital brings no return in electrical output); (2) periodic fluctuations in demand (since a plant used below its capacity represents a sunk, temporarily unproductive investment); (3) the fact that there is an instananeous increase in capacity when a new plant begins to operate, while the increase in demand is always gradual (so that the utility will have excess, less productive capacity until demand catches up with the capacity); and (4) the frequency and duration of shutdowns due to technical failures.

The risk associated with the invested capital is largely determined by the effect of these time-dependent factors. The larger the amount of capital invested in a plant, the greater the losses that can be incurred as a result of factors which extend the time before the investment begins to yield a return. Such time-dependent factors tend to reduce the economic efficiency of nuclear plants more than that of coal-fired ones.

According to a survey reported by Olds (1981:70), nuclear plants required lead times (for design, licensing, construction, and testing) of 119-141 months as of June 1980, while the lead times for coal-fired plants were 87-93 months.

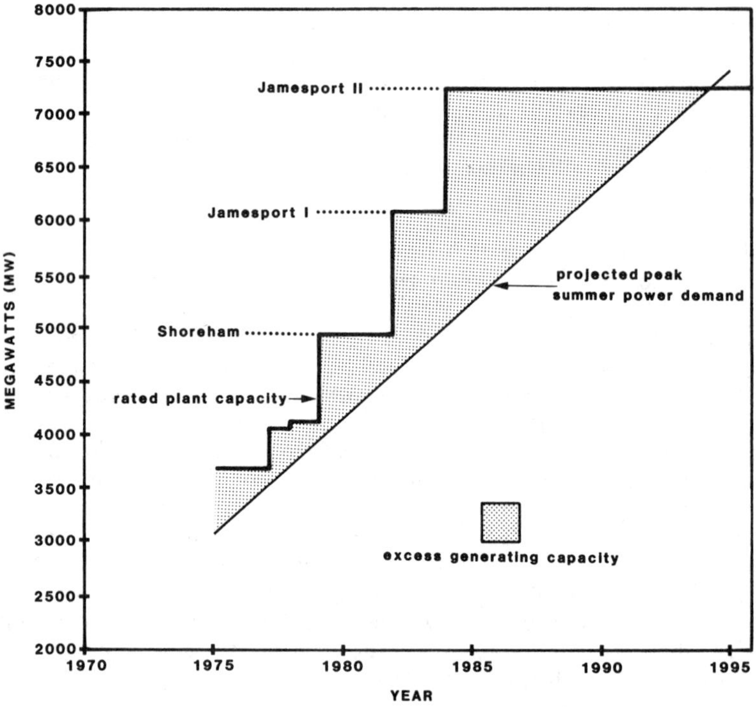

Figure 3 . Projected Peak Summer Power Demand and Installed Generating Capacity - Long Island Lighting Company , 1975-1995

Source: Dubin-Mindell-Bloom Associates, 1975

This means that the four-fold larger sum that a utility invests in a nuclear plant (as compared with a coal plant) is also unproductive for about 40 months longer than is the capital invested in the coal plant.

Variations in daily and seasonal demand are, of course, typical of the electric utility industry; any generating plant closely following the demand will necessarily incur losses, as it will often operate under capacity. The size of such losses depends on the relative balance between the plant's fixed capital (i.e., the cost of building the plant) and its variable capital (i.e., fuel, labor and other operating costs), since the main component of the variable capital (fuel) is expended in direct proportion to output. Here too, nuclear plants are at a disadvantage. For plants expected to operate in 1988, Komanoff (1981) estimates that the cost of the power generated by nuclear plants will be 23% due to fuel, 13% due to other operating expenses and 64% due to construction capital. The comparable figures for a coal-fired plant are: fuel, 50%; other operating expenses, 16%; construction capital, 34%.

Utilities accommodate to this difference by using nuclear plants for baseload (i.e., continuous) operation, and by using coal-fired plants to meet added, temporary demand. This approach is effective so long as there is no unexpected fall in baseload demand. But a decline in baseload demand can occur, for example, with a decline in the economy. Thus a utility that commits capital to a nuclear plant and then part of the way through construction suspends the project because anticipated demand has failed to materialize will suffer much more economic damage than it would have incurred with a coal-fired plant. Recently, such cancellations have been frequent, as Rosa and Freudenburg (1984) show in Figure 1 of their introduction to this volume.

Large plants also incur losses in capital productivity simply because of the very different time constants that govern growth in capacity and growth in demand. In any given power grid, demand grows by small increments over time, as new homes or enterprises are built or new appliances and equipment are added. In contrast, the system's capacity grows by large instantaneous increments, as successive power plants are brought on line. Inevitably, as illustrated in Figure 3, this relationship creates a substantial temporary overcapacity, which represents the inefficient use of capital invested in the plant. The larger the plant, the larger the temporary overcapacity, so that once more, nuclear power plants are at a disadvantage relative to the smaller coal-fired plants. (Note that the initial increments in Figure 3--which are due to the fossil-fueled plants that preceded Shoreham, the utility's first nuclear plant--result in a relatively small overcapacity. Thereafter, when all of the added plants are large nuclear ones, the excess is much larger.) Utilities can of course sell excess power to neighboring systems, but given the high cost of transmission (both economically and energetically), this expedient is not very effective. Since about 55% of the capital cost of a power system is represented by transmission lines,[3] the intensified centralization due to nuclear plants leads to the inefficient use of capital.

Finally, there is the effect of technical breakdowns in reducing the efficiency of the capital invested in a power plant. This effect is measured by the *capacity factor*--the plant's actual electrical output, expressed as a percentage of its designed capacity. Although there has been a continuing debate about the relative capacity factors of nuclear and coal-fired plants, it now appears that coal plants have an advantage over nuclear plants in this respect. In part this is related to size; larger plants, whether nuclear or coal, have had lower capacity factors than smaller ones--an advantage to coal plants because they tend to be smaller than nuclear plants. According to Komanoff (1981), however, coal plant performance is somewhat better than nuclear plant performance even for approximately equal-sized plants. For reasons that are discussed below, this difference is likely to become accentuated with time.

The net result of the foregoing considerations is that because fixed capital dominates the investment in nuclear plants much more than in coal-fired plants, nuclear plants are more likely to suffer losses in economic efficiency arising from time-dependent factors. Since economic efficiency--i.e., the net return on the investment of fixed and variable capital--presumably determines a utility's investment decisions, it is of interest to examine the recent history of these decisions.

From the start of the nuclear power program (in the mid-1950s) to 1973, the utilities ordered more than 150 nuclear power plants. However, between 1973 and 1977, annual orders dropped from a peak of about 38,000 megawatts to about 5000 megawatts. Since 1974, more than 80 orders have been cancelled; no new plants have been ordered since 1978 (Olds, 1981:70; *Electric Power Monthly,* 1982:xii). Some utilities are actively considering the conversion of partially completed nuclear plants to coal. Clearly, utilities have become less interested in building nuclear power plants than they once were. It has been argued that this reflects the recent decline in the demand for power. However, the sharp drop in orders for nuclear plants occurred in the mid-to-late 1970s, well before there were indications of a decreased demand for electricity.

It is also evident that utilities have shifted their relative preference for coal and nuclear plants. This is shown by Figure 4, which records the commitments made by utilities for generating plants (Berman, 1981:73). Nuclear capacity consistently exceeded coal-fired capacity in the annual commitments for plants to be operative between 1982 and 1986. Thereafter, the situation is reversed, and for all commitments made for subsequent dates of operation, coal-fired capacity considerably exceeds nuclear capacity. Since 10 to 12 years elapse between the placing of an order and the expected year of operation, it is evident that utility decisions made after the mid-1970s strongly favored the coal option (see also the discussion by Rosa and Freudenburg, 1984, in the introduction to this volume).

It would appear that since the mid-1970s, the utilities have learned that nuclear power is *not* the most economically efficient way to provide electricity--but not before inflicting on themselves what may prove to be fatal economic wounds. This is evident in the response of investors to the electric utilities. Between 1970 and 1980, there was a sharp decline in the ratings of utility bonds, and between 1965 and 1979 the average market-to-book values of electric utilities (i.e., the relationship between the market price of stock and the value of the utility, as indicated by its assets and liabilities) declined by 72%, while that of all industries declined by only 29% (Olds, 1981:70).

In sum, in its brief history nuclear power has managed to demonstrate that it fails to meet the public interest as an economically efficient means of producing electricity. Nuclear power has failed to meet the initial claim that it would be "too

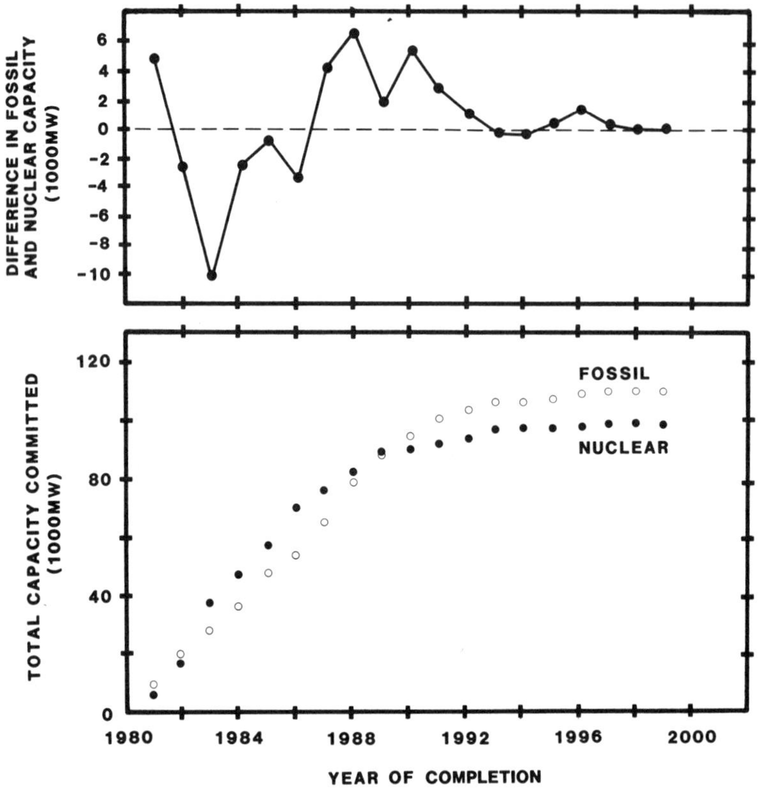

Figure 4. Utility Commitments for Generating Capacity - Coal and Nuclear Power

cheap to meter" (Strauss, 1954); it has been no cheaper than coal-fired power and now appears to be, on the average, more expensive. More broadly, despite a federal subsidy of nearly $40 billion,[4] nuclear power has seriously degraded the economic position of electric utilities, which have become one of the weakest sectors of a shaky economy. The economic failure of the nuclear power industry has clearly surprised the government and industry officials who have fostered it. This curious lapse in the nation's vaunted mastery of modern technology is explained by the industry's environmental problems.

ENVIRONMENTAL QUALITY CONSIDERATIONS

The public interest in environmental quality is usually regarded as the main factor in the debate over nuclear power. The argument is usually structured around the intensity of the environmental and health hazards associated with nuclear power in comparison with those associated with alternative sources of electricity, especially coal. This involves the broad, complex issue of evaluating the relative risks and benefits associated with alternative technologies. It would appear, however, that in the present instance a large part of the issue can be subsumed under the economic evaluation of nuclear power and the coal alternative.

This is largely the outcome of the extensive environmental legislation enacted during the 1970s, which in effect has become a means of translating public judgment about environmental hazards into the economic cost of the required controls. The new legislative machinery--environmental impact statements, regulatory hearings, judicial proceedings--enables public judgments about safety and health hazards to influence the regulatory requirements that are imposed on builders of power plants. The final regulations therefore represent to some degree a public judgment of the appropriate balance between the severity of the risks and the stringency of the countermeasures. In turn, the regulations require new expenditures for revised plant structures and control systems, raising costs and thereby reducing the economic efficiency of power plants.

The response to the environmental hazards of coal-fired plants, which are largely due to stack emissions, is the requirement that such plants install smokestack scrubbers. The response to the environmental hazards of nuclear power plants, which are largely due to emissions of radiation and heat during operation and to the much more extensive radiation hazards in an accident, is the elaboration of regulations regarding the design, testing and operation of the reactor and the handling of waste.

In effect, then, both the nuclear power plant and its most important competitor, the coal-fired plant, have already been required to conform to public judgments regarding the seriousness of their environmental hazards and the importance of reducing them. Evaluations of the impact of environmental concerns on the construction costs of nuclear and coal-fired plants show that these concerns represent the main reason for the disparity between the costs.

An illuminating example is provided by the problem of protecting nuclear plants against earthquakes. The earthquake regulations require that nuclear plants remain operable during the worst earthquake that could "reasonably" be expected to occur during the lifetime of the plant, and to shut down safely during the worst earthquake that could possibly occur at the site (Komanoff, 1981). In order to achieve these goals, plant designers are required to compute, according to procedures defined by Nuclear Regulatory Commission (NRC) regulations, how postulated earthquakes would affect various plant structures. Plants must install seismic instruments to measure the structural response to actual earthquakes, so that the actual responses can be compared with the responses that were assumed in designing the structure. Finally, a long list of specified plant structures must meet stress standards that ensure their stability under projected earthquake conditions. These include major components such as the reactor vessel and cooling loops, but also electrical devices, electronic control equipment, containment and pipe supports, pumps, valves, access parts, structure beams, trusses and columns. Repeated tests are required to determine the response of key items to earthquake-induced motions, in different directions and with different frequencies (Komanoff, 1981).

Szalay's chapter in this volume (1984) complains of the expense of safety regulations, and indeed, Komanoff's survey of the requirements (1981) shows that most of them have been more stringent with time. But the trend appears reasonable. The earliest NRC guides for computing earthquake forces used static models in computing the effect of forces on plant structures, but these were replaced by much more complex regulations based on dynamic models. Prior to 1973, plant designs were governed by the standard code of the American Society of Mechanical Engineers for boiler and pressure vessels. After 1973, the Atomic Energy Commission promulgated an elaborate series of more rigorous, specific standards for various plant components. In the same way, the standards for resistance to earthquake-induced forces were increased. When Unit 1 was built at San Onofre, California, the force expected from the worst potential earthquake at the site was given as .50 g; later, when Units 2 and 3 were built, the value was set at .67 g.

The idle nuclear reactors at Diablo Canyon, California, stand as a monument to the economic impact of these requirements. Originally the reactors were designed to resist the expected force of an earthquake that might be propagated from what then seemed to be the nearest fault. Shortly before the plants were completed, however, a much closer offshore fault was discovered. Accordingly, the expected earthquake force was increased from .40 g to .75 g. This required a reanalysis of the reactor structure, which delayed the opening of the reactors for several years. Finally, late in 1981 it was discovered that the blueprints governing some of the earthquake-proofing structures were faulty; the opening of the plants was delayed once more while the entire problem was analyzed again. In all this time, structural revisions (and the continuing cost of financing the inoperative facility) progressively increased the plants' final cost. No such problems have arisen with coal-fired power plants, which are only required to be twice as resistant to earthquake damage as ordinary buildings.

Besides the direct increases in cost due to progressively added safety measures, delays in licensing and construction also raise capital expenditures by leading to additional financing costs. Again, environmental and safety problems are a major contributor to such delays. For example, an analysis by the Congressional Budget Office of delays in the licensing of 24 nuclear power plant projects between July 1, 1975, and December 31, 1977 (U.S. Congressional Budget Office, 1979) showed that of 49 specific delays, 28 involved reconsideration of safety and environmental issues. An additional six delays were due to public participation in the proceedings, which are always related to such issues. Only five instances of delay were attributed to bureaucratic inefficiency.

The environmental and safety regulations applied to coal-fired plants are far less complex--and costly--than are those applied to nuclear plants. Coal regulations are largely designed to limit stack emissions of sulfur dioxide, particulates and nitrogen oxides. According to Komanoff (1981), coal-fired plants achieved an average reduction of 64% in these emissions between 1971 and 1978, and projections for plants to be completed in 1988 indicate that their emissions will be 91% below the average for 1971 plants. These improvements account for about 90% of the increase in the real costs of constructing coal-fired plants. It is estimated that environmental regulations will add between $120/kw to $230/kw to the cost of a coal-fired plant completed in 1988. This includes costs of about $60/kw to $80/kw for non-emission controls (noise controls and the handling of scrubber sludge, ash and other solid waste).

In contrast, environmental and safety concerns have vastly increased the complexity of nuclear power plants in the last 15 years. As already indicated, measures to resist the force of earthquakes have been increased. In addition, performance standards for valves, pumps, piping and control systems have been increased; testing and documentation procedures have been made more elaborate; protection against internal failure of pipe systems and turbines has been intensified; fire protection measures have been made more stringent; the reactor cooling system has been redesigned, using more costly materials; and many materials and equipment quality requirements have been upgraded (Komanoff, 1981). These changes have played a major role in raising the capital costs of nuclear power plants. Thus while construction costs represented only 50% of the cost of electricity produced by plants that began operating in 1966, this figure reached 77% by 1975 (Scott, 1975), and has declined only slightly since then.

And as new problems arise, new and more costly requirements are added. The accident at Three Mile Island required major revisions in equipment and training procedures. Yet major problems remain unresolved, threatening to add future costs: the embrittlement of reactor containment shells by radiation, steam generator corrosion, the disposition of radioactive waste, and the decommissioning of plants.

The relative simplicity and low cost of environmental regulation of coal-fired plants, as compared with the regulation of nuclear power plants, is the natural consequence of their relative levels of technological maturity. The burning of coal is a mature, well-established technology; its environmental hazards originate in the rather well-understood effects of elevated temperatures on the chemical reactions of carbon, sulfur and nitrogen compounds. These hazards are controllable by equally well-known chemical or physical means. Nuclear reactors represent a relatively new, immature technology; they are based on processes that have far more disruptive effects on matter than do the elevated temperatures encountered in coal burning. The resultant hazards are correspondingly far more intense and complex and the means of controlling them are more difficult, and in many cases, not well developed.

In sum, nuclear power stands out as an inappropriately difficult way of generating electricity. The effort to control the resulting hazards has already raised the cost of nuclear power well beyond that of its immediate competitor, coal, thereby severely limiting its service to the public interest. And the control of as-yet-unresolved hazards will increase this disparity.

NUCLEAR ENERGY'S CONTRIBUTION TO THE NATIONAL ENERGY PROGRAM

It has been argued on occasion that regardless of the cost and the associated hazards, nuclear power *must* be developed in order to avert the dire consequences of a near-total dependence on energy sources which are nonrenewable, and which will therefore become progressively more expensive to harness. Certainly, any rational energy program ought to be based on the gradual replacement of the

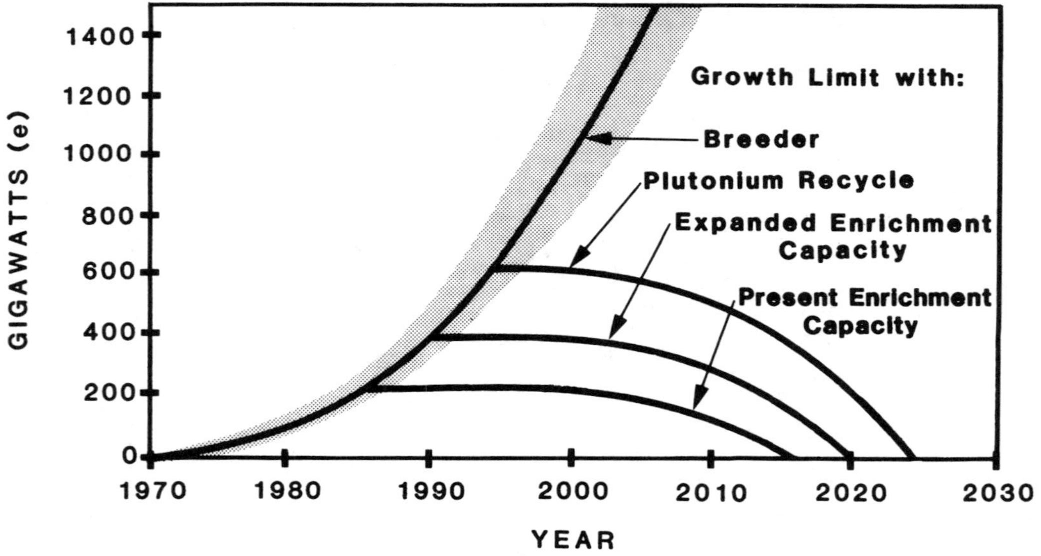

Figure 5. Nuclear Power Growth – Limiting Factors

Source: U.S. Energy Research and Development Administration, 1975.

present non-renewable sources with renewable ones. Nuclear power could conceivably play a role in such a process. A nuclear power system based on breeder reactors--which, properly operating, can produce more fuel than they use--could supply the United States with an appreciable source of electricity for perhaps 1500 to 2000 years. This period is sufficiently long, in comparison with the expected 200-400 year duration of domestic fossil fuel supplies, to allow breeder technology to be regarded, charitably, as renewable. On the other hand, as shown in Figure 5, the present reactor system would run out of fuel in 25 to 30 years (U.S. Energy Research and Development Administration, 1975), and is therefore incapable of contributing to the solution of the nation's long-term energy problem.

Accordingly, the present nuclear power system is relevant to the national energy program only insofar as it is a necessary source of electricity *in the short term*. This issue has been examined by Carlson et al., who concluded:

> Of the 72 nuclear plants now licensed to operate, 64 could be shut down immediately with no loss in electric output or reliability. The remaining eight plants could be phased out over the next few years; and the 94 additional nuclear plants for which construction permits have been issued and which are expected to come on line by 1987 (the current utility planning horizon) or shortly thereafter could be cancelled, also with no shortage in needed power (Carlson et al., 1979:6).

This can be done by running underused coal plants closer to capacity. The few nuclear plants that were essential were those in power districts that lacked sufficient capacity in non-nuclear plants, and/or were not suitably linked to other regions with excess capacity. These observations remain relevant, since the actual nuclear power output declined by about 8% between 1978 and 1980 (U.S. Department of Energy, 1980). Carlson et al. (1979) also showed that the power to be provided by the nuclear plants under construction could be replaced by several alternative sources, such as small-scale hydroelectric installations and decentralized co-generators. Given these considerations, it would appear that the present nuclear power system is not needed to meet the demand for electricity over the next 20 years or so.

There remains the possible argument that the present system must be continued and expanded as a basis for later introducing a system of breeder reactors, because the latter are essential as long-term, renewable sources of energy. In one sense, this argument can be readily countered by observing even the most avid proponents of nuclear power who acknowledge that it would be impossible to develop and perfect--let alone install--the necessary number of breeder reactors in less than 25 to 50 years. I believe this fact is sufficient to dismiss the option, since the continued exponential increase in the cost of producing non-renewable sources of energy is likely to undermine the stability of the economic system much sooner. It would appear, therefore, that no persuasive reasons for continuing the present nuclear power system, or for developing a breeder-based one, can be derived from considerations based on the needs of a national energy program that is capable of resolving the energy crisis. Nuclear plants are not needed to meet present demand; because of inadequate fuel supplies, they cannot meet long-term demand; and a breeder-based system would be too late to prevent the economic collapse threatened by the exponentially rising cost of energy.

While properly regulated coal-burning power plants are a tolerable short-term alternative to nuclear power, they are not suitable in the long term. Coal is non-renewable, and is therefore subject to cost escalation as the more accessible deposits are exhausted. In the long run, it therefore cannot solve the economic problem that is the true dimension of the energy crisis--progressively escalating costs of production. Coal burning also contributes to the serious climatic problems that may be associated with the long-term buildup of atmospheric carbon dioxide concentrations (the greenhouse effect). There appears to be no solution to this problem, other than an eventual halt to the combustion of fossil fuels, including coal.

Thus a rational energy policy would involve, in the short term, the replacement of nuclear power, and in the long term, the replacement of coal-fired power plants as well. The long-term need is for sources of electricity that are renewable and therefore stable in price. Without going into detail here, it is pertinent to note that such sources of renewable solar energy are available. The applicability of photovoltaic cells is limited only by their present price. However, there is considerable evidence that, offered perhaps $500 million in orders over a five-year period, the industry could reduce the price enough to begin to compete with other methods for generating residential electricity in the United States, and to enter several smaller markets even before then (Commoner, 1979). Low-head hydroelectric power installations could probably produce more power than the present nuclear power system--renewably, and at lower, stable costs. Wind generators are already cost-effective in some places, and they will become competitive more widely as the price of electricity continues to escalate (Commoner, 1979).

Such a transition would involve a very considerable *decentralization* of the national power system. This means that one of the criteria for judging present fossil-fueled sources of electricity ought to be their capability of facilitating this transition. Fossil-fueled electric generators that minimize dependence on costly long-line power grids will facilitate the transition; generators that increase dependence on them will do the reverse. On the other hand, small decentralized power plants must be environmentally compatible with the communities in which they will necessarily be located. This requirement effectively restricts the fuel to natural gas, which is non-polluting and can be used to drive cost-effective small-scale generators, especially in the form of cogenerators that provide both heat and electricity. Thus, an enhanced natural gas distributing system, supplying cogenerators sized to match the local demand, is a far better way than nuclear power to facilitate the transition to a renewable, solar power system. As methane becomes available from solar sources (e.g., sewage, garbage or biomass deliberately produced for the purpose), it can gradually replace natural gas.

RELATION TO NUCLEAR WEAPONS

For the purpose of this paper, this complex and grave issue can be summarized in the observation that the proliferation of nuclear power plants increases the potential for the proliferation of nuclear weapons. And again encapsulating an elaborate series of considerations, it is evident that the proliferation of nuclear weapons is not in the public interest. On these grounds, it therefore follows that the further development of the nuclear power system is not in the public interest. This is particularly true of the establishment of a breeder-based plutonium economy, which would considerably exacerbate the problem of preventing the manufacture of clandestine weapons. In this connection, it is regrettable that President Reagan has seen fit to reverse the decision, made by Presidents Ford and Carter, to forego the development of nuclear reprocessing operations in order to avert the dangers inherent in the resultant availability of plutonium.

The close link between nuclear power and the proliferation of nuclear weapons was recognized soon after World War II, and has now been substantiated by events. A detailed review of the technological links between nuclear power and the production of nuclear weapons is available in the report of the Nuclear Energy Policy Study Group (1977). Plutonium is generated in the fuel elements of a number of different types of nuclear power plant reactors. The separation of plutonium from the spent fuel is a well-known process, and is relatively simple compared with uranium enrichment, the alternative means of producing a nuclear explosive. There have been stringent efforts to prevent this approach to the production of nuclear weapons: the Treaty on the Non-Proliferation of Nuclear Weapons and the International Atomic Energy Agency provide incentives for countries to obtain access to nuclear power if they agree not to produce nuclear weapons. Nevertheless, in India and possibly Argentina and elsewhere, nuclear explosives have been produced from material generated from the spent fuel of the country's nuclear power plants.

As an indication of the difficulties involved in preventing diversion of nuclear material, and of the largely unexamined consequences of a plutonium economy for the domestic tranquility that is also an essential feature of the public interest, we might note the following passage from a report prepared for the Nuclear Regulatory Commission by Stanford University professor John H. Barton on the problem of safeguarding plutonium from "terrorists":

> Finally, dissidents might be seized and detained after a plutonium theft. Detention might be justified as a way to isolate and immobilize persons capable of fashioning the material into an explosive device. Conceivably--although the interrogation issue has not been researched for this paper--detention could

> also be used as a step in a very troubling interrogation scheme--perhaps employing lie detectors or even torture. The normal deterrent to such practices--inadmissibility of evidence in court--would be ineffective under the conditions of a nuclear emergency (Barton, 1975:27).

In my view, the catastrophic consequences of nuclear war are such an overriding public concern as to mandate the abolition of nuclear weapons and of any enterprise, such as nuclear power, that threatens this goal. Fortunately, as I have shown, economic considerations need not stand in the way of ending this dangerous and inglorious experiment.

CONCLUSION

It seems evident from the foregoing considerations that when nuclear power is judged against alternative means of producing electricity, its record of serving the public interest is a poor one. Nuclear power plants appear to be economically less efficient than coal-burning plants when both are equipped with safety and environmental control devices sufficient to meet the standards embodied, by public demand, in current regulations. This process is a continuing one, and largely accounts for the progressive escalation of the cost of building nuclear power plants. As Zener (1976) pointed out, actual costs consistently have been 2.2 to 2.5 times higher than the costs originally announced by the utilities; this is indicative of the impact of new safety and health issues that arise during construction. Zener also shows that the utilities' announced costs have themselves consistently been 1.8 times higher than the actual cost of nuclear plants coming on line during the year, indicating that the utilities expect the escalation process to continue.

Indeed, the process of correcting the inherent hazards of the nuclear power system is far from complete; several major sources of these hazards--fuel reprocessing, waste disposal and plant decommissioning--are still inoperative. Past experience with fuel reprocessing suggests that it will remain an environmentally hazardous operation at any cost. Both of the nation's two reprocessing plants designed to handle spent fuel from commercial reactors have failed technologically, leaving in their wake highly radioactive residues that have not yet been cleaned up. A third, incomplete plant has also been abandoned (*New York Times,* 1981). Nor have the hazards associated with the transport of recovered fissionable fuel (especially plutonium) and with the ultimate disposal of high-level wastes been satisfactorily evaluated, let alone solved. The effort to resolve these problems is bound to increase the disparity between the costs of nuclear and coal-fired electricity.

It is sometimes argued that public opposition to nuclear power based on a perceived impression of the attendant hazards is "unreasonable." Such a judgment implies that this public attitude fails to reflect some objective evaluation of the existing hazard. However, one reason for public concern is that nuclear power technology is so new that knowledge about the hazards is increasing fairly rapidly. Several important new issues have surfaced in only the last few years: excessive rusting in steam generator tubes; radiation-induced embrittlement of steel reactor shells; and the inadequacy of evacuation plans. It is likely that public evaluation of nuclear plant hazards reflects, to some degree, the perception that a technology which is still revealing such obvious faults is too worrisome to be tolerated, at least without further efforts to make it safer.

A more basic observation is that the public attitude is founded, quite properly I believe, on a value judgment which is inherently subjective. For example, in choosing between a coal-burning and a nuclear power plant, the public can be expected to consider the relative hazards of the chief environmental effects--let us say, acid rain in comparison with some incidence of radiation-induced cancer. Acid rain from coal-burning plants involves a larger current environmental impact than does cancer induced by radiation escaping from nuclear power plants, if these impacts are measured against background levels. However, there is no "objective" way to compare a given impact on the ecology of Adirondack lakes with a given increment in the incidence of cancer. We can expect most people to be so fearful of the fatal outcome of cancer and the likelihood that this hazard of nuclear power plants will turn out to be worse than presently believed (given the continuing discovery of new hazards) as to regard even a slight increment as being more undesirable than an increase in the acidity of rain.

Elsewhere in this volume, Davis (1984) and Szalay (1984) have argued that the regulatory response to the inherent hazards of nuclear power ought to be weakened for the sake of the future development of the industry. This argument misconstrues the relationship among the hazards, the regulatory response to them, and the consequent effects on the viability of the nuclear power industry. There are alternative ways of producing electricity, and it is up to society to decide what hazards it will tolerate from these sources; the point is that it is within the right of the public to impose requirements on any given source, even if those requirements are so stringent as to destroy the source's economic viability. That is what has happened to nuclear power.

In sum, when nuclear power is tested against the several measures of the public interest--cost, economic impact, environmental hazard, contribution to a national energy program and to the furtherance of peace--it fails. The proper response is not more stringent control of the hazards of the nuclear power system, for this would only increase its present economic deficiencies. Rather, having failed to meet the test of public interest, the industry ought to be retired expeditiously from its participation in the national energy system.

This points to the importance of bringing the public interest to bear on the issue of nuclear power in a *timely* manner. Simply stated, the issues considered in this and similar volumes should have been matters of intensive public discussion and debate 30 years ago, when the decisions that committed the nation to this unfortunate course were first made. There is of course a powerful reason why this rational process did not take place. The United States is thus far committed to a particular manner of governing such decisions, which is in fact enshrined in the opening page of the Atomic Energy Act: "free competition in private enterprise" (Dean, 1953:25). Behind this euphemism is its blunt meaning: The maximization of private profit takes the place of the national interest as the guide to the decisions that determine how we produce and use energy.

The failure of nuclear power, at great cost, may yet serve a useful purpose. It can stand as a signal that the American people now need to govern the energy system--and the system of production that it supports--in the public interest.

FOOTNOTES

[1]Three attempts have been made to establish reprocessing plants to handle spent wastes from nuclear power plants. The first of these, Getty Oil Company's facility at West Valley, New York, was opened in 1966 and closed in 1976, leaving behind radioactive wastes that the state will need to deal with at a cost of close to $1 billion. The second plant was built by General Electric at Morris, Illinois. It broke down soon after opening and has been abandoned. The third facility was under construction at Barnwell, South Carolina, by the Allied Corporation, but in December 1981, after spending about $362 million, the company decided to abandon the project (see New York Times, 1981).

[2]See for example chapters by Kenneth Davis (1984) and Robert Szalay (1984) in this volume. See also the statements made by three representatives of the nuclear power industry in "The Nuclear Marketplace," MacNeil/Lehrer Report, November 25, 1980 (transcript available from the Public Broadcasting System).

[3]Hass et al. (1974:57) provide data regarding the relative cost of transmission and distribution facilities. The figure is not constant with time; in the 1950s and 1960s, it approximated 70%, but more recently, it has been lower.

[4]This is an approximation based on the federal contributions to research and development enrichment and insurance costs, which are estimated at about 28% of the cost of nuclear electricity (for further discussion, see Abott and Nader, 1977).

REFERENCES

Abott, John and Ralph Nader
1977 *The Menace of Atomic Energy.* New York: W. W. Norton.

Barton, John H.
1975 *Intensified Nuclear Safeguards and Civil Liberties.* Washington, D.C.: Nuclear Regulatory Commission.
Berman, Ira M.
1981 "New Generating Capacity: When, Where, and By Whom?" *Power Engineering* (April):72.
Carlson, Richard, David Freedman and Robert Scott
1979 "A Strategy for a Non-Nuclear Future." *Environment* (July/August):6-38.
Commoner, Barry
1979 *The Politics of Energy.* New York: Knopf.
Davis, W. Kenneth
1984 "Nuclear Power Under the Reagan Administration." Pp. 257-265 in William R. Freudenburg and Eugene A. Rosa (eds.), *Public Reactions to Nuclear Power: Are There Critical Masses?* Boulder, CO: Westview Press/American Association for the Advancement of Science.
Dean, Gordon
1953 *Report on the Atom.* New York: Knopf.
Electric Power Monthly
1982 "Prologue: Nuclear Power Development." *Electric Power Monthly* (#2, February):xi-xvi.
Friedlander, Gordon D.
1979 "21st Steam Station Cost Survey." *Electric World* (November 15):55.
Freudenburg, William R. and Eugene A. Rosa (eds.)
1984 *Public Reactions to Nuclear Power: Are There Critical Masses?* Boulder, CO: Westview Press/American Association for the Advancement of Science.
Hass, J. E., E. J. Mitchell and B. K. Stone
1974 *Financing the Energy Industry.* Cambridge, MA: Ballinger.
Komanoff, Charles
1981 *Power Plant Cost Escalation.* New York: Komanoff Energy Associates.
MacNeil/Lehrer Report
1980 "The Nuclear Marketplace." New York: Public Broadcasting System. (Transcript of November 15.)
New York Times
1981 "Allied to Write Off Nuclear Fuel Plant." *New York Times* (December 1):D.1.
Nuclear Energy Policy Study Group
1977 *Nuclear Power Issues and Choices.* Cambridge, MA: Ballinger.

Olds, F. C.
1981 "Outlook for Nuclear Power." *Power Engineering* (November):70.

Rosa, Eugene A. and William R. Freudenburg
1984 "Nuclear Power at the Crossroads." Pp. 3-37 in William R. Freudenburg and Eugene A. Rosa (eds.), *Public Reactions to Nuclear Power: Are There Critical Masses?* Boulder, CO: Westview Press/American Association for the Advancement of Science.

Scott, Robert E.
1975 "Projections of the Cost of Generating Electricity in Nuclear and Coal-Fired Plants." St. Louis, MO: Washington University.

Strauss, Lewis
1954 Speech presented at the meeting of the Association of Science Writers.

Szalay, Robert
1984 "A Nuclear Industry View of the Regulatory Climate." Pp. 295-306 in William R. Freudenburg and Eugene A. Rosa (eds.), *Public Reactions to Nuclear Power: Are There Critical Masses?* Boulder, CO: Westview Press/American Association for the Advancement of Science.

U.S. Congressional Budget Office
1979 *Delays in Nuclear Reactor Licensing and Construction: The Possibilities for Reform.* Washington, D.C.: U.S. Congress.

U.S. Department of Energy
1980 *Annual Report to Congress.* Washington, D.C.: U.S. Government Printing Office.

U.S. Energy Research and Development Administration
1975 *Nuclear Fuel Cycle.* Washington, D.C.: U.S. Government Printing Office (Document ERDA-33).

Zener, C.
1976 "Estimation of Nuclear Power Plant Costs." Pittsburgh: Carnegie Mellon University.

Robert A. Szalay

12. A Nuclear Industry View of the Regulatory Climate

INTRODUCTION

The other chapters in this book have concentrated on public perceptions of nuclear power and its risks, on the need for and the future of nuclear power, and on the public's role in deciding that future. This chapter will focus on the regulatory climate under which nuclear power plants must be built and operated, and on the impact this climate can have on nuclear power's success.

Stated simply, the success of nuclear power--in terms of costs and schedules, in terms of waste disposal solutions, and even in terms of actual plant reliability and risk--is tied to the actions of government regulators and decision makers. In terms of public perception, nothing can sell the benefits of nuclear power to the public more forcefully than a sustained record of success. This success depends to a large extent on government leadership in providing a climate in which the nuclear industry can perform effectively. Industry has its part to do, of course, but contrary to what is projected in the now popular "free market" phrase, the industry is highly regulated, and its self-help initiatives are constrained by the framework within which it must operate.

Burgeoning regulatory requirements have contributed significantly to cost increases, both through additional design

Pp. 295-306 in William R. Freudenburg and Eugene A. Rosa (eds., 1984) *Public Reactions to Nuclear Power: Are There Critical Masses?*

complexity and through extended schedules. Many of these requirements have not been shown to be justified in terms of reducing risks effectively. Due in large part to these changing requirements, however, the schedules for completing nuclear power projects now range between 12 and 14 years, rather than the seven to eight years that were achieved in the United States early last decade, and that are now being achieved in other countries (Crowley, 1981). The current lead time almost exceeds the bounds of rational planning, and it invites further inefficiencies and costs.

Even with all the constraints and problems created by an unwieldy regulatory system, nuclear power has maintained an economic edge over its companion electricity-generating producer, coal, and it stays well ahead of oil. In 1980, a kilowatt hour cost an average of 2.3 cents to produce by nuclear power, which accounted for 11% of our electricity. It cost 2.5 cents by coal, which accounted for 51% of our electricity, and 5.4 cents by oil, which accounted for 11% (Atomic Industrial Forum, 1981a).

Looking to the future, comparative economic assessments of total generation costs over the life of the plant for nuclear and coal-fired options still tend to favor nuclear power generation, with regional differences tipping the scale one way or the other (Mycoff, 1981). The continuing competition this creates is also important in itself, as an anchor for holding down electric power costs.

To turn again to the question of public perception, a more complicated issue has to do with the ways in which government decision makers take into account the perceptions of the public, and evaluate the underlying validity of these perceptions. These decision makers view the energy situation and related energy system risks from their vantage of reality. This vantage must include access to a broad spectrum of information and opinions. It seems almost axiomatic that elected and appointed government officials, who represent the public constituency, should do what they believe to be right under the law, based on the best and most reliable information made available to them.

Industry and government projections tend to agree that more energy will continue to be needed, even with major improvements in conservation and fuel efficiency (Esselman,

1981). One basic reason is that our labor force will be some 30% larger by the year 2000. Another is that our people are still motivated to increase their well-being, which means an increase in Gross National Product (GNP) per worker, and hence an increase in energy used per worker.

Our growing labor force alone would require an average growth in GNP of one percent per year for the rest of the century. Consistent with the growth needed to satisfy even minimal social expectations, a 2.5% minimum or low GNP growth rate can be averaged from a number of sources (Esselman, 1981; Walske, 1981). Corresponding to this minimum GNP growth is a minimum electrical capacity growth rate of about 3.3% to 3.5% per year (Esselman, 1981).

Even assuming all nuclear and coal power plants now in the pipeline are built, and taking into account reserve margins, another 200 to 300 power plants will be needed to meet this projection. Coal and nuclear power are the prime candidates for this additional capacity. And if serious efforts are made to substitute these for existing oil-fired plants, the number of needed power plants would increase significantly. We currently have over 100,000 megawatts of installed oil-fired electrical capacity. It should certainly be a national objective to replace a significant fraction of that capacity with nuclear energy or coal. But in the current financial and regulatory climate, it is unlikely that these projections and objectives will be met.

An inefficient regulatory process, in the industry's view, does not serve the public interest. The public interest is served by a regulatory process that ensures safety. The public interest is not served by a process that is cumbersome and inefficient, and that unnecessarily increases costs and keeps needed electricity from being made available. The next two sections of this chapter will discuss the changes that must be made if nuclear power is to be allowed to serve the public interest. I will turn first to two overall goals; next I will deal with several near-term actions that can be taken within the context of existing laws, and then with longer-term actions that may require new legislation. If these changes are made, the regulatory climate will be improved to the point where the process can be turned around: safe plants can come on line and serve the public, and new orders can again be feasible.

OVERVIEW

Since the accident at Three Mile Island (TMI), the nuclear power industry has passed through more than three years of turmoil and uncertainty. Despite its early and conscientious efforts to embrace the important lessons of the incident, the industry has experienced a slow road back to recovering some sense of normalcy.

New organizations, such as the Institute of Nuclear Power Operations, have raised the level of safety awareness within the industry. Many new requirements gleaned from the Three Mile Island experience have been established, and implemented, which will contribute to improved margins in plant safety. Other regulatory requirements and procedural changes, however, have added complications to a licensing process that had been convoluted and inefficient even before TMI. These have exacted a heavy toll in dollars and resources, with no appreciable benefit in safety.

With this distinction in mind, the industry has been looking forward to the growth of a regulatory climate that promotes safe plant design and operation, but that encourages efficient licensing practices at the same time--a regulatory climate that allows the establishment of a new equilibrium in safety requirements and licensing procedures. Recent management initiatives within the Nuclear Regulatory Commission (NRC), along with the thrust of the October 8, 1981, Presidential Statement on nuclear power (Reagan, 1981), give some reason for hope that this can happen. The industry wants this hope to become reality.

Stated in simplest terms, the industry is looking for regulatory reform measures that will really work. Two overall changes are necessary to achieve this for plants in the pipeline and for any hopes of new orders:

First, a regulatory commitment must be made to reaching a new equilibrium in licensing requirements in the post-TMI era. From the experience of those deeply involved in the process, the dominant lessons of TMI have been conscientiously embraced by the industry. The results are evident in the new institutions set up to improve safety, and more importantly, in the enhanced programs carried out by nuclear power plant owners and operators. The regulators, however, in their zeal to upgrade as many new requirements as possible, may have gone a little overboard. This is the clear conclusion of a July 1981 report by the NRC Office of Inspection and Enforcement; the report's primary recommendation is that the NRC should "take prompt action to bring the issuance of requirements 'under better control'" (U.S. Nuclear Regulatory Commission, 1981:9). The report goes on to say that, "Once NRC safety priorities have been established, the NRC should carefully consider, or reconsider, requirements in relationship to the time required for implementation. A greater degree of planning, flexibility, and stability in licensee organizations is needed."

The problem of ever-changing requirements during the last decade of licensing has been endemic; it is believed by many to be a major contributor to the cost and scheduling problems that continue to plague nuclear power plant projects. The post-TMI era added another layer to this problem. The key to any future licensing improvements will rest to a large extent on the capability of NRC management to get new requirements under control. The development and use of safety goals, which will be discussed later, could provide an effective decision-making tool to assist management in this endeavor.

Second, a more positive regulatory climate must be set in motion. The efforts of the reconstituted Nuclear Regulatory Commission, both in policy making and in the efficient processing of licenses in the pipeline, can form the foundation for a regulatory framework that is more conducive to future orders. The major issue to be addressed is the need to obtain stability in licensing requirements. The solution includes both the capability and the will at the top to produce an effective and controlled regulatory process. Related to this, and of equal importance, is the corresponding attitude of both the NRC technical staff and the hearing boards in the execution of their day-to-day functions.

While management attention to this problem would provide the context for improvements, some legislative initiatives may be necessary to form a statutory base for efficient licensing. Most notably, this would include the authority for one-stage licensing, which will be discussed later.

Near-Term Actions to Turn the Process Around

The context for future improvements is success in the near term in dealing with plants in operation and those in the pipeline. Several near-term actions will provide the bases for these needed improvements; all of them are possible within the constraints of existing legislation.

Disposition of Post-TMI and Other Licensing Requirements. The Commission and its staff are moving toward the development of a review system which discriminates among proposed requirements that are safety- and cost-effective and those that are not. Toward this end, the Commission has taken steps to improve NRC controls over requirements imposed on the industry through the creation of a new Deputy Executive Director who is assigned that specific responsibility. He is being assisted by a new Committee to Review Generic Requirements, which reviews and recommends approval or disapproval of requirements to be imposed by NRC staff.

Safety Goals and Cost-Benefit Criteria. The nuclear power industry is strongly encouraging the NRC to move forward on its initiatives to develop safety goals that include the use of cost-benefit criteria. The industry believes that the numerous plant-specific risk assessments which have been conducted to date can provide the NRC with a basis for evaluating current regulations on the basis of the level of safety they achieve. This can then become the starting point for assessing the relevance of specific requirements to real risk reduction. If the results of this review show that the body of existing requirements produce plants whose level of safety surpasses pre-set safety goals, then specific existing and proposed new requirements can be judged on the basis of their additional risk reduction as compared to the related costs. This, in essence, is the proposal of the Atomic Industrial Forum Committee on Reactor Licensing and Safety in its May 1981 statement, "A Proposed Approach to the Establishment and Use of Quantitative Safety Goals in the Nuclear Regulatory Process" (Atomic Industrial Forum, 1981b).

Establishment of an Enforceable and Consistent Backfitting Policy. Related to this previous discussion, the continual and unsystematic backfitting of new requirements onto existing licensed plants must be controlled. Most design changes required to be backfitted on existing plants have not been shown to be justified as providing significant improvements to safety. They have, however, resulted in extremely costly modifications. They have also diverted industry attention away from evaluating operational experiences, and have diverted NRC staff resources from the evaluation of new plants. The industry believes that current backfitting policy should be strengthened and enforced by NRC management, and integrated with a safety goal/cost-benefit approach.

Administrative Resolution of Problems with the Hearing Process. While significant progress has been made in loosening the bottleneck created by hearing processes, continuing diligence and management attention are needed to emphasize the current authority of the boards to control their proceedings. Even with this management attention, however, some fundamental changes are required; the process was designed some 25 years ago for an infant industry that has now matured. In support of this need, the Atomic Industrial Forum commissioned former NRC Chairman, Marcus Rowden, to look at this problem and suggest a solution. His report (Rowden, 1981) recommends changes in the aims, and consequent structure, of the licensing hearings. These changes can be implemented by the Nuclear Regulatory Commission within existing statutory authority, and they could benefit pending power reactor applications. (One such change, for example, would limit the role of hearings to the resolution of genuine disputes.) If Mr. Rowden's proposals were to be accepted even partially, we believe that significant improvements could result.

Longer-Term Actions for a Stable Regulatory Framework

Near-term actions can provide a basis for future improvements, but further action is also needed, particularly on the legislative front, if the prospects for future plants are to be improved significantly. The two most important changes are outlined below.

Development of a One-Stage Licensing Approach. The prospects for any additional reactor orders depend on a number of factors. These include needed improvements in general economic and financial conditions, government actions to implement an effective waste disposal program, and the previously mentioned initiatives by the Nuclear Regulatory Commission to make the licensing process and related decision making more rational and certain. Related to the last point, the utilities feel that they will be in a much better position to proceed with new construction projects if a one-stage licensing process is put in place--one which will give them assurance that the plants they design and construct will go into operation as planned. While some discussion remains on whether this one-stage process can be implemented within the current regulatory framework or only by legislation, most utilities report that they would prefer to have the assurance of new statutory language to give them the confidence they need to move forward with new orders.

In keeping with this need, the Atomic Industrial Forum Committee on Reactor Licensing and Safety, through its Subcommittee on Standardization, has developed a conceptual framework and proposed legislative language for one-stage licensing improvements. The proposed bill would amend the Atomic Energy Act to make it clear that one-stage licensing is allowed. In other words, while not removing the current two-stage process, the proposal would allow a utility applicant to submit sufficient information for a one-stage review, the outcome of which would be a construction and operation license. The plant that would subsequently be built could then go into operation without an additional review step. Audits would be conducted during the construction of the plant, however, to assure that the plant was being built as designed.

To facilitate this one-stage review process, the proposal also includes the concepts of early site review and preapproved standardized designs. This would allow a utility to have its site approved in advance. It would also allow architect-engineers and reactor manufacturers to have their designs approved in advance. A utility could then refer to these designs, and not be forced to have them reviewed again in its own licensing proceeding.

In essence, this approach would allow a utility to proceed with the assurance that it could expect a plant to be built and operated in a reasonable time frame, and without constant or unjustified changes in design requirements. This last assurance will be provided by the use of cost-benefit criteria in judging the necessity for any changes to accepted designs. The industry is hopeful that legislation along these lines will be considered by Congress in the near future.

Resolution of Long-Term Rulemakings. Long-term licensing trends will be particularly affected by the manner in which degraded core issues[1] and the development of safety goals proceed. The issue of revised siting population criteria is also of concern. In fact, these three issues are integrally related; the outcome of each can affect the others.

In October of 1980, the NRC published an *Advance Notice of Rulemaking* as the first step toward "long-term rulemaking to consider to what extent, if any, nuclear power plants should be designed to deal effectively with degraded core and core melt accidents" (U.S. Nuclear Regulatory Commission, 1980:1).

The nuclear industry believes that this rulemaking proceeding is of great importance, since the outcome may have a crucial impact on the viability of the nuclear option. As a result, the Atomic Industrial Forum proposed a collective, industry-funded effort--intended to prepare a concise, logical, and well-documented technical position for the impending degraded core rulemaking proceedings--which has been designated as the Industry Degraded Core Rulemaking Program.

Recent information indicates that this rulemaking will probably not converge to resolution prior to the end of 1983. The resolution of this issue is crucial to the industry, however, since uncertainty will remain on whether designs will have to be changed. The NRC and industry's progress on safety goals will add additional insights toward the resolution of this issue. The industry is hopeful that these efforts will result in convergence of opinion on the safety adequacy of current design bases, and on the use of rational design criteria in making any major changes to these bases.

Finally, the issue of siting population criteria is of relevance to this discussion. In an *Advance Notice of Rulemaking* published in July of 1980, the Nuclear Regulatory Commission solicited comments on proposed new siting criteria. These revised criteria would have set arbitrary limits on population density. The rulemaking proposed to separate siting and plant design considerations. The Committee on Reactor Licensing and Safety of the Atomic Industrial Forum provided extensive comments in September 1980. These comments indicated that plant safety is dependent on the proper integration of design, siting, and emergency planning, and that treating any in isolation might serve to increase public risk.

Recent information on the siting issue indicates that the NRC is awaiting the outcome of its efforts on safety goals and the source term[2] issue. In this regard, research activities underway at the NRC and the Electric Power Research Institute are aimed at investigating the source term issue. Many experts familiar with these activities believe that the amount of radioactivity available for release in the event of a serious accident has been greatly overestimated. When more of the results are assimilated during 1983-84, there could be substantial impacts on public perception of nuclear risks and on the NRC's approach to specific safety issues, such as siting, emergency planning and degraded core issues.

CONCLUSION

While the nuclear power industry has encountered problems in recent years, these problems have in part been due to excessive regulation. No one in the nuclear industry questions the need for safety; indeed, the industry's commitment to safety is shown by its record, which is one of the safest of all industrial records.

Closer examination reveals, however, that the regulatory process has been inefficient. Such inefficiencies--rather than serving the public--actually work to prevent the nuclear power industry *from* serving the public.

Fortunately, there are a number of actions and initiatives that could be taken to improve the regulatory situation, streamlining existing procedures without in any way compromising the protection of public safety. Such changes would provide needed relief to the beleaguered utilities now in the licensing pipeline. Success in near-term initiatives, in turn, would breed the climate for longer-term improvements in the process. This improved climate--coupled with one-stage licensing, the use of safety goals and cost-benefit criteria in decision making, and the increased attention of the Nuclear Regulatory Commission to project management--could help encourage utility decision makers in going forward with new nuclear power plant orders beyond the 1985 time frame.

Utility decisions will not of course be based solely on the regulatory climate; financial and institutional issues must still be solved satisfactorily. Even so, however, regulatory reforms will be significant, both in terms of dollars and in terms of reduced uncertainty. If the problems outlined in this chapter can be dealt with, the result should be a more stable and efficient regulatory process--one that will remove the most substantial and emotionally laden impediment which currently exists for the future success of nuclear power, and that will allow nuclear power to continue to serve the public during the decades ahead.

FOOTNOTES

[1]"Degraded core" issues have to do with the risk of potential accidents involving damage of the reactor core.

[2]The source term is the amount of radioactivity that is potentially available for release to the environment from a damaged reactor core.

REFERENCES

Atomic Industrial Forum

1981a "Nuclear Power Continues to Edge Coal in 1980 Costs, Performance." *INFO News Release* (December):1.

1981b *A Proposed Approach to the Establishment and Use of Quantitative Safety Goals in the Nuclear Regulatory Process*. Washington, D.C.: Committee on Reactor Licensing and Safety, Atomic Industrial Forum.

Crowley, John H.

1981 "Nuclear Energy--What's Next?" Pp. 63-69 in *Proceedings of a Workshop on the Electric Imperative, Monterey, California, June 1981*. Washington, D.C.: Atomic Industrial Forum.

Esselman, Walter H.

1981 "The Need for Nuclear Power." Paper presented at the Atomic Industrial Forum Workshop on

Reactor Construction and Operation: Revitalizing the Industry, Chicago, IL, October 19.

Freudenburg, William R. and Eugene A. Rosa (eds.)
1984 *Public Reactions to Nuclear Power: Are There Critical Masses?* Boulder, CO: Westview Press/American Association for the Advancement of Science.

Mycoff, Clark W.
1981 "U.S. Nuclear Generation Economics." *Nuclear Energy Digest* of Westinghouse Electric Corporation (September):9-15.

Reagan, Ronald
1981 "Domestic Nuclear Policy Statement." Washington, D.C.: Office of the White House Press Secretary, October 8.

Rowden, Marcus A.
1981 *Achieving a More Effective Licensing Process--Basic Reform Within Existing Law.* Washington, D.C.: Atomic Industrial Forum.

U.S. Nuclear Regulatory Commission
1980 *Advance Notice of Rulemaking.* Washington, D.C.: U.S. Nuclear Regulatory Commission.
1981 *Report on a Survey by Senior Management to Obtain Viewpoints on the Safety Impact of Regulatory Activities from Representative Utilities Operating and Constructing Nuclear Power Plants (July 1, 1981).* Washington, D.C.: Office of Inspection and Enforcement, U.S. Nuclear Regulatory Commission.

Walske, Carl
1981 "The Role of Nuclear Power in the U.S.A." Paper presented at the meetings of the Canadian Nuclear Society, Ottawa, Ontario, Canada, June 8.

Cora Bagley Marrett

13. Public Concerns About Nuclear Power and Science

INTRODUCTION

Various participants in the debate over nuclear power claim to speak for the public at large, yet they offer radically different interpretations of the public's views and interests. Consider, for example, the contrasting versions of the public interest that are evident in the preceding three chapters of this volume--Chapters 10-12, by Davis (1984), Commoner (1984) and Szalay (1984). Given such markedly different assessments, it is clear that there is a need for direct information on the perspectives of the populace.

Public opinion polling data offer that information. Survey and polling data have limitations as well as strengths, as noted by several other contributors to this volume, but at a minimum, the surveys give us far better insights into the views of the wider populace than do the published statements from participants in a given debate. Indeed, one could use the survey data as reported in this volume to gauge the response the public has made to the nuclear power controversy. The views of the public also have considerable relevance to the ongoing nuclear power debate. As noted by the President's Commission on the Accident at Three Mile Island, the ultimate resolution of the broad question of energy "involves the kind of economic, environmental, and policy considerations that can only be evaluated through the political process" (The

Pp. 307-328 in William R. Freudenburg and Eugene A. Rosa (eds., 1984) *Public Reactions to Nuclear Power: Are There Critical Masses?*

TABLE 1
TRENDS IN PUBLIC ATTITUDES TOWARD SCIENCE AND TECHNOLOGY

Item and Year	Percent favorable to science[a]
All things considered, would you say that the world is better off because of science?	
1957	88%
Do you feel that science and technology have changed life for the better or for the worse?	
1972	70%
1974	75%
1976	71%
All things considered, the benefits of science outweigh its harmful effects.	
1979	70%
In your opinion, over the next 20 years will the benefits to society resulting from continued technological and scientific innovation outweigh the related risks to society, or not?	
1980	58%

[a]The response categories varied in these studies. The 1957 survey gave five choices; the 1972, 1974, 1976, and 1979 surveys provided five slightly different ones; and the 1980 survey gave two.

Source: National Science Board, 1981.

President's Commission on the Accident at Three Mile Island, 1979:7).

In this context, the present chapter reviews the public's own views on the role that the broader public ought to play in the debate over civilian nuclear power. Special emphasis will be placed on the link between attitudes toward nuclear power and those held toward science and technology in general. Since surveys point toward waning support for science and technology, broadly conceived, as well as for nuclear power, some observers have suggested that the crisis of confidence in nuclear energy is merely part of an overall disenchantment with science and its applications (see the discussion of the issue in Mazur, 1981). The first major section of this chapter examines that contention. The second section analyzes public opinions about the appropriate roles of the citizenry, government officials, and scientists and engineers in resolving the nuclear power controversy. The final section discusses the policy implications of the public concerns.

ATTITUDES TOWARD SCIENCE AND TECHNOLOGY

Trends in Attitudes

Surveys conducted from the late 1950s to the early 1980s suggest an erosion in public confidence toward science and technology, although one must interpret trends cautiously given differences in the questions used. The earliest survey asked only about the positive benefits; contrastingly, later ones asked about risks as well as benefits, and about technological and scientific innovation, not "science" in general. The surveys varied, too, in the number of response categories used; some provided only two (agree/disagree) while others used more categories to assess the intensity of views. Overall, the data are useful, but less than ideal, for informing us about changes in public attitudes.

As can be seen from Table 1, in the late 1950s only about 10% of the populace felt negative or ambivalent about the contributions of science; nearly thirty years later that proportion had more than doubled, although as noted above, the questions were worded differently in the two surveys.

The 1957-58 survey (Withey, 1959) found that most people believed the world was "better off because of science." When a survey for the National Science Board asked a similar (but not identical) question in 1976, 71% answered that they thought "science and technology [had] changed the world for the better," not "for the worse." In a later survey for the Board, carried out in 1979, 70% agreed that "all things considered, the benefits of science outweigh its harmful effects."

There are no signs of an impending upturn in public approval of science. At best, the indicators suggest that the current situation will remain unchanged; at worst, they hint of still further erosion. For example, young people in the U.S. are taking fewer and fewer mathematics and science courses in high school. This could mean that interest in science continues to drop. Even if interest remains high, the number with no exposure to scientific inquiry is rising, and it is quite possible that non-exposure to science could result in considerable skepticism about its uses. If the next generation includes a higher proportion of persons who are uninterested in or skeptical about science, then the future of science might be precarious indeed.

The prognosis is not as dire, however, if we examine the actual attitudes of youth toward science. In one survey of three different age groups, 40% of the 13-year-olds, 36% of the 17-year-olds and 37% of those between the ages of 26 and 35 expressed wonder or excitement about science (Education Commission of the States, 1979). Few in any of the age groups (3% for each) felt any fear or alarm about science, but there were more in the 26-35 category than in either of the others who reported that they reacted to science with satisfaction and hope. Obviously, we should use caution with data drawn from young respondents, but it is helpful to remain alert to trends, and the survey in question hints that these individuals are neither far more nor far less supportive of science than are their elders.

Few surveys have distinguished attitudes toward science from those toward technology. One study that makes the distinction (LaPorte and Metlay, 1975) shows that the public is bothered more by the uses of science than by pure scientific research.[1] The group of Californians who were sampled saw technology as having a number of disturbing consequences. Over 70% either agreed with this statement--"people have become too dependent on machines"--or disagreed with this one--"people shouldn't worry about harmful effects of technology because new inventions will always come along to solve the problems." The authors call attention to the fact that only 5% expressed no "disenchanted" sentiments while 70% expressed at least two. Uncertainty about science and technology is not limited to the United States. A 1977 study by the European Economic Community (cited in Bickerstaffe and Pearce, 1980) found that 69% of the respondents, drawn from nine nations and varying backgrounds, thought that scientific discoveries can have very dangerous effects. This percentage excludes the responses that referred to military applications. The results showed widespread anxiety about applied science, although support for science accompanied that anxiety, with 69% feeling that "science is one of the most important factors in the improvement of daily life."

Sources of the Concern

Science and technology spawn some of the same anxieties that nuclear energy induces. Some who oppose nuclear energy do so because they see it as a development over which the individual has little influence. In the case of science and technology in general, sizable portions of the population think some controls should be exercised but know of no institutions that could manage the task effectively.

Overall, Americans believe that scientific research should be unfettered. But there is widespread opposition to research on certain subjects and growing support for establishing more control over the scientific enterprise. Most survey respondents object to studies that might lead to new forms of life; Europeans express the same view (see Table 2). The interest in controlling science and technology is not limited to genetic engineering, however. About 30% of the public believe that society's control over science and technology should be increased, and that figure has risen slightly over time.[2]

Some of the concern centers on assumed threats to moral codes and basic values. Concretely, the skeptics include an element that sees science as an increasing threat to social values and cultural stability. In 1957 about 44% of the population thought that "scientific discoveries make our lives change too fast;" by 1979 the figure had risen to 58%. The proportion feeling that science breaks down people's ideas of

TABLE 2
PROPORTION OF THE PUBLIC OPPOSING
GIVEN RESEARCH TOPICS

Item and Nation	Percent Agreeing With Statement
Scientists should not conduct studies for creating new forms of life.	
United States	65%
Experiments on the transmission of hereditary characteristics "carry unacceptable risk."[a]	
Denmark (1978)	61%
West Germany (1978)	45%
Netherlands (1978)	41%
France (1978)	37%
United Kingdom (1978)	36%
Scientists should not conduct studies for discovering intelligent beings in outer space.	
United States (1979)	36%

[a]The full item referred to: "experiments on the transmission of hereditary characteristics which could make it possible to improve the qualities of living species."

Source: National Science Board, 1981, appendix tables 6.8 and 6.9.

right and wrong rose from 23% to 37% over the same period. Overall, more people in the earlier survey than in the later one (87% vs. 66%) thought that the benefits of scientific research outweighed the harms (Survey Research Center, 1958; Miller et al., 1980).

Much of the public uneasiness has to do with the long-term rather than the immediate consequences of scientific and technological innovations. As Table 1 shows, about four out of ten people doubt that the innovations will produce greater benefits than risks over the next twenty years. The number of people who feel disquiet when they contemplate the future of scientific research is by no means insignificant.

Continued Confidence in Science

While science and technology have lost some of their backing over the past three decades they still garner substantial support. This is evident in the public's positive evaluations of scientific developments--with more people seeing them as beneficial than as harmful--and in the social standing of scientific institutions.

Positive Evaluations of Science as an Institution. Surveys of public trust in institutions show that the public continues to have greater confidence in the scientific community than it has in many other institutions in our society; science fares considerably better than government, for example. Between 1974 and 1980 the proportion of the public that expressed high confidence in science declined from 45% to 41%; by comparison, high confidence in Congress dropped from 40% to 28% over that same time (see Table 3). The LaPorte and Metlay study also reports greater favorability toward science and scientists than toward government officials. The researchers presented respondents with six topics--energy consumption, mass public transportation, genetic engineering, data banks and civilian and military uses of outer space--and asked them to identify the most likely as well as the most credible decision makers for each topic. The list included congressmen, executive branch officials, the courts, consumer groups, business leaders, technical experts and the public in general. Technical experts usually were chosen as the most legitimate decision makers; in contrast, government officials

TABLE 3
TRENDS IN PUBLIC CONFIDENCE IN INSTITUTIONS

	Percent expressing high confidence in institution[a]			
	Year			
Institution	1974	1976	1978	1980
Scientific community	45%	43%	36%	41%
Education	49	37	28	30
Organized religion	44	30	31	35
Congress	40	39	29	28
Executive Branch	14	14	12	12

[a]Respondents were asked, "As far as the people running these institutions are concerned, would you say you have a great deal of confidence, only some confidence, or hardly any confidence at all?" Figures represent those who chose the first option.

Source: Surveys by the National Opinion Research Center.

drew relatively little support. Significantly, the respondents expected the public to have some influence in the process.

Public disenchantment with government is widespread, as is evident by the fact that 60% in a recent poll agreed that "the people in Washington are out of touch with the rest of the county," and 80% felt that "special interests get more from government than the people do" (Harris, 1980). Associated with and perhaps indicative of the disenchantment is a tendency for the public to blame officials rather than scientists and engineers for science-related problems. Consider the results of a survey that asked: "When science and technology cause problems, who is most at fault?" Far more respondents (60%) chose government decision makers than any other category; business decision makers were a distant second (14%) and scientists and technologists next with 12% (Opinion Research Corporation, 1976).

The poll results on science and other institutions suggest two conclusions. The first is that some of the displeasure with government perhaps spills over onto science. It might be that many citizens feel uneasy because they see the government as being ineffective in controlling far-reaching and socially significant ventures, some of which originate in scientific research and application. Unable to exert indirect controls over these ventures through the political process, members of the public might be directing their disquiet at the scientists who are involved in the ventures. But the second conclusion suggested by the data is that science continues to be held in considerable respect. Public uneasiness about scientific institutions has risen, but not nearly at the rate or to the level found for other major institutions.

The Prestige of Science and Engineering. Data on the prestige or social standing of occupations tend to corroborate the second conclusion. Although several other occupations are accorded greater prestige than are science and engineering, many more fall below them in the eyes of the broader public. For example, the position of congressman once lagged behind that of scientist by only a few points; a wide gap now separates the two (see Table 4). Engineers also attract broader backing than do political leaders.

Recent information from the Gallup organization illustrates the fact that engineering is held in high esteem in this

TABLE 4
THE PRESTIGE OF SELECTED OCCUPATIONS

Occupation	Percent seeing this as an excellent or good occupation		
	1972	1974	1976
Physician	92%	91%	86%
Scientist	86	89	81
Engineer	83	86	77
Minister	80	80	75
Architect	82	85	74
U.S. representative in Congress	73	65	52

Source: Opinion Research Corporation, 1976

TABLE 5
ASSESSMENTS OF THE HONESTY OF ENGINEERS

	Percent regarding engineers on honesty and ethical standards	
Year	High[a]	Low[b]
1976	49%	4%
1977	46	4
1981	48	5

[a]Includes responses, "very high" and "high."

[b]Includes responses, "low" and "very low."

Source: Gallup, 1981

society. The organization asked people to evaluate the honesty and ethical standards of various occupations. Sixty-three percent rated clergymen as "very high" or "high" on the criteria, giving that occupation the highest standing. Engineers were fifth on the list--48% of the respondents described engineers as being quite honest and ethical. The rating placed engineers only slightly behind medical doctors, whom 50% of the sample thought to be highly honest and ethical. The evaluation of engineers was not very different from what it had been in the surveys taken in 1976 and in 1977 (see Table 5).

Nuclear Technology and Science

If the recent drop in public support for nuclear power is simply part of a declining support for science in general, this would have quite different policy implications than if the nuclear power issue is a distinct development with its own characteristics. If the anxiety about science is the

TABLE 6
INTEREST, LEVEL OF INFORMATION AND PERSONAL INVOLVEMENT IN SELECTED ISSUES, 1980

Issue Area	Percent of Attentives[a]	Percent of Total Public
Greatly interested in:[b]		
Space exploration	34	15
Chemical food additives	46	32
Nuclear power plants	57	33
Well informed about:[b]		
Space exploration	24	9
Chemical food additives	29	17
Nuclear power plants	39	17
Would definitely take part in debate on:		
Space exploration	12	7
Nuclear power plants	39	24

[a]"Attentives" were those who scored high on a measure of interest in science and technology, on knowledge about science and technology, and on regularity with which they availed themselves of information on science and technology.

[b]Limited to those who had heard of these controversies.

Source: Miller et al., 1980.

overriding problem, then by addressing the broader anxiety, policy makers would be responding to concerns about nuclear energy as well. If the public regards nuclear energy as a distinct issue, on the other hand, then policies for science in general will affect the nuclear power controversy only minimally.

There are several indications that the public sees nuclear power quite differently than it sees science in general. First, support for nuclear power trails that for science: seven out of ten people have a positive view about science, but as noted by Rankin and his colleagues (1984) in Chapter 2 of this volume, only five out of ten hold positive views toward nuclear power. As Farhar-Pilgrim and Freudenburg (1984) note in Chapter 7, the difference is even greater when people are asked about nuclear power facilities near their own homes. Second, opposition to nuclear power has spread more quickly than has skepticism about science. Third, for both science and nuclear power, people report that there are harmful effects, but when asked for specifics the public gives more certain and more consistent responses on nuclear power than it does on science.

It is probably inappropriate, however, to compare nuclear power and science in general, given the varied reactions the public makes to different areas of science and technology. Science in the abstract receives wide support, but that is not true for every application of science. Thus to understand whether nuclear power raises unique policy issues, we should compare it with other troublesome technical developments.

Other Controversial Technologies. Several areas of science and technology draw public opposition; these include weather modification, genetic engineering, space exploration, and chemical food additives. Of these topics, the last one seems most reasonable to compare with nuclear power, for a number of reasons. First, the level of public interest in both is high. While many people do not know that space exploration is controversial, almost everyone realizes that food additives and nuclear power are disputed. Of those who are aware of the scientific debates, more express great interest in the issues of food additives and nuclear power than in some of the other topics (see Table 6). Forty percent of those who have heard about the controversy think that space exploration produces some harm, whereas about 80% believe

TABLE 7
GROUPS THOUGHT APPROPRIATE FOR DECIDING CONTROVERSIES, 1979

	Percent Selecting This Group as Most Qualified[a]	
Group	On Food Additives	On Nuclear Power Plants
Scientists/engineers	82%	59%
Federal agency	44	32
Citizens	27	45
President/Congress	4	5
Local government	4	16
Governor/State legislature	3	9

[a]Includes first and second choices.

Source: Miller et al., 1980.

that chemical food additives and nuclear power plants have harmful effects.[3] Second, the level of interest is nearly identical for the two issues. Few people feel that they are well informed about nuclear power, and that is the case, too, for food additives.

Despite the similar levels of public knowledge about and interest in the controversies, nuclear power and chemical food additives are not interchangeable issues. For one thing, the public is more interested in being involved in decisions about the former than the latter. Larger proportions would delegate decisions about food additives to scientists and engineers than would allow those specialists to decide about nuclear power (see Table 7). For another, people feel that the local government is more qualified to make decisions about nuclear power than about food additives. Contrastingly, the federal government gets higher marks on food additives than on nuclear power.

All of these trends reveal that the populace sees the nuclear issue as one with its own script in which the public at large must play starring roles. Even more importantly, they clash with the view that the downturn in public support for nuclear energy is simply part of a growing disaffection in the United States with science and technology more generally. The data do not support the conclusion that, from the standpoint of the public, any given scientific controversy differs minimally if at all from any other one. Policy makers, then, must understand the special ways in which the public perceives and strives to influence the debate about civilian nuclear power.

POLICY MAKING AND NUCLEAR POWER

Surveys inform us not only about public views on nuclear technology, but also about the roles the public would assign to various actors in the nuclear debate. As noted earlier, the public regards its own part as a central one. Importantly, it also expects scientists and engineers to be pivotal. Nearly 60% of the population thinks that specialists are the persons most qualified to resolve nuclear problems. Only 2% identify scientists and engineers as the ones least qualified on the issue (Miller et al., 1980). Yet the broader public does not want to relinquish all control over nuclear power decisions.

For several reasons--the continuing trust in science and scientists noted above, along with the belief that the public at large knows little about the subject, and the belief that many scientists are opposed to nuclear power--citizens see scientists and engineers as appropriate participants in the controversy. Simultaneously, although for other reasons--increased wariness about science and scientists, dissatisfaction with governmental officials, and belief that the problems surrounding nuclear energy are not entirely technical--citizens want a direct involvement of their own. In short, policy makers should understand that the public seeks not to displace but to share the stage with scientists and engineers.

The Issue of Knowledge. The selection of scientists and engineers as appropriate actors could stem from the belief that the public lacks the necessary expertise for acting alone. Surveys do indeed illustrate widespread misperceptions about and unfamiliarity with civilian nuclear energy, and interest in the nuclear controversy outdistances participation in it. The reason people most frequently give for their non-participation is "lack of knowledge."[4] Whether or not it is the primary explanation for non-involvement, perceived lack of knowledge about nuclear power is rather common in the populace. Even among people who pay attention to scientific and technical matters, there are few who regard themselves as well-informed on nuclear power.

Studies indicate that the perception is accurate: knowledge is indeed limited. For example, Murray (1981) reports that only a fraction of the Wisconsin residents in a statewide survey he conducted knew that nuclear power supplied a substantial amount of the electricity in the state, and fewer still had any idea how radioactive waste from plants is currently handled. Some thought that there was no waste, while others believed that the Federal government stores it underground. Murray concludes from the Wisconsin survey and other analyses that "Despite the national attention to energy problems over the past decade, Americans have a poor understanding of basic energy facts" (Murray, 1981:1). Chapters 5-7 in this volume, by Slovic et al. (1984), Mitchell (1984), and Farhar-Pilgrim and Freudenburg (1984), reach similar conclusions on the basis of national data. Generally the public is not well-informed on technical aspects of nuclear energy, including those aspects having to do with radiation. Given the absence of expertise in the wider population, the public relies on scientists and engineers. In fact, this is the only group on whose qualifications most individuals agree.

The Perceived Concerns of Scientists. It may also be that the public accords leading roles to scientists and engineers on the assumption that these specialists are likely to question nuclear technology themselves. Most people believe that opposition to nuclear energy prevails among the scientists who are energy experts (Rothman and Lichter, 1982). Rothman and Lichter show the belief to be unfounded and speculate that it grows out of the kind of press coverage given to the controversy. The researchers examined the views of three groups of scientists: (1) those in energy-related disciplines, such as atmospheric chemistry, solar energy and ecology; (2) those in fields closely related to nuclear energy, such as nuclear engineering, radiological health and radiation genetics; and (3) those in other scientific disciplines. All three groups supported the continued development of nuclear energy, although more in the third group than in the first two favored the "proceed slowly" option. Nearly all of the nuclear experts (99%) regarded the risks associated with nuclear energy as acceptable, as did seven out of ten energy specialists and six out of ten scientists in other fields.

The researchers found far more opposition to nuclear energy among journalists than among scientists. Science reporters, especially those associated with major newspapers, gave less support than the random sample of scientists, but more than television reporters and producers. The authors of the study conjecture that the media might give greater weight to antinuclear scientists than to pronuclear ones and hence leave the public with the impression that scientists oppose the technology.

Whether or not the public perception of scientists is accurate, the existence of that perception might shape views on the role of scientists in the nuclear debate. If growing segments of the public feel uneasy about nuclear energy, they might be willing to include scientists in the decision-making process on the assumption that scientists share the unease.

The Role of the Public

The public wants scientists and engineers to participate in the debate, for the reasons just reviewed, but not to dominate it. As noted in Table 7, almost half of the general public names "citizens" as being particularly qualified for deciding controversies over nuclear power plants, although a sizable minority of 16% consider citizens to be a poorly qualified group (Miller et al., 1980). The desire of the populace to remain involved stems from several sources. First, it may indeed have some roots in the apprehension the public expresses about science. Science holds a relatively high position in this society, but it attracts doubt and discontent as well. The doubters are not inclined to leave scientific matters completely in the hands of scientists. Second, the public also has misgivings about elected officials, as noted above. Citizens who favor controls over science fear that their officials cannot exert such controls effectively. Third, the urge to affect policy on nuclear energy perhaps emerges from the wider movement for public involvement in decision making more generally. A recent Gallup poll illustrates the strength of this feeling: In April 1981, Gallup asked a national sample the following question: "The U.S. Senate will consider a proposal that would require a national vote--that is, a referendum--on an issue when 3% of all voters who voted in the most recent Presidential election sign petitions asking for such a nationwide vote. How do you feel about this plan--do you favor or oppose such a plan?" An overwhelming majority--more than 2 to 1--favored it (Gallup Organization, 1981).

The fourth source may be the most important, however. The public bids for involvement because it recognizes that the nuclear debate concerns more than just engineering problems. It involves such matters as the level of risk that is and should be acceptable in a society. Many of these problems cannot be solved by careful experimentation and detailed statistical analyses. Rather, they must be recognized as questions of values and ideals, and be dealt with in the political theater instead of the scientific laboratory. When the public seeks involvement in the debate on nuclear power, its aim is not to fashion control rooms or weigh the relative merits of one reactor design over another; it is to have the experts and elected officials recognize that complex technologies raise social as well as technical problems in which citizens clearly have an interest.

PUBLIC VIEWS: POLICY IMPLICATIONS

Not all members of the public endorse public involvement in scientific and technical controversies, but because the endorsers include a large fraction of the population, public policy makers can ill afford to ignore the call for participation. At the moment, that demand is not raised in the case of every scientific and technical development; the public somewhat willingly leaves non-controversial issues to the experts. But it is not easy to distinguish "controversial" from "non-controversial" ones. Moreover, if support for science and engineering continues to ebb, then more and more issues will be candidates for controversy.

Relative to other pursuits, science does well; but this fact should not make policy makers complacent. Doubts about science have spread in the general population; unless those doubts are acknowledged and unless efforts are made to attend to the concerns on which they rest, respect for the experts as well as for public officials will undoubtedly plummet. As of now, attitudes toward nuclear power do not fully converge with or follow from attitudes toward science and engineering in general. If, however, policy makers fail to establish mechanisms that will take account of public concerns surrounding nuclear power, the result may be a convergence characterized by greater and greater challenges to science and the scientific community.

In conclusion, let me again quote from the President's Commission on the Accident at Three Mile Island:

> We are convinced that, unless portions of the industry and of its regulatory agency undergo fundamental changes, they will over time totally destroy public confidence and, hence, *they* will be responsible for the elimination of nuclear power as a viable source of energy. (President's Commission on the Accident at Three Mile Island, 1979:25.)

FOOTNOTES

[1]The public appears to have little interest in basic research, however. It supports "useful" science but worries about some of the likely uses.

[2]The Opinion Research Corporation asked if control over science should be increased, decreased, or remain unchanged. In 1972 28% answered "increased," and 7% said "decreased." In 1976 the responses were 31% and 10%, respectively (Opinion Research Corporation, 1976).

[3]People were asked of each issue area whether it was only beneficial, both beneficial and harmful, neither beneficial nor harmful, or only harmful. Of those who had heard of the space exploration controversy, 13% chose the fourth option; on chemical additives, 30% made that choice, and on nuclear power, 32% did so (Miller et al., 1980).

[4]In a 1979 survey, 59% who wanted no active part in the nuclear controversy gave as their reason, "I don't know enough about the issue." The next most frequent response (32%) was, "It wouldn't do any good." See Tanfer et al., 1980.

REFERENCES

Bickerstaffe, Julia and David Pearce
1980 "Can There be a Consensus on Nuclear Power?" *Social Studies of Science* 10:309-344.

Commoner, Barry
1984 "The Public Interest in Nuclear Power." Pp. 267-294 in William R. Freudenburg and Eugene A. Rosa (eds.), *Public Reactions to Nuclear Power: Are There Critical Masses?* Boulder, CO: Westview Press/American Association for the Advancement of Science.

Davis, W. Kenneth
1984 "Nuclear Power Under the Reagan Administration." Pp. 257-265 in William R. Freudenburg and Eugene A. Rosa (eds.), *Public Reactions to Nuclear Power: Are There Critical Masses?* Boulder, CO: Westview Press/American Association for the Advancement of Science.

Education Commission of the States
1979 *Attitudes Toward Science.* Denver, CO: National Assessment of Educational Progress.

Farhar-Pilgrim, Barbara and William R. Freudenburg
1984 "Nuclear Energy in Perspective: A Comparative Assessment of the Public View." Pp. 183-203 in William R. Freudenburg and Eugene A. Rosa (eds.), *Public Reactions to Nuclear Power: Are There Critical Masses?* Boulder, CO: Westview

Press/American Association for the Advancement of Science.

Freudenburg, William R. and Eugene A. Rosa (eds.)
1984 *Public Reactions to Nuclear Power: Are There Critical Masses?* Boulder, CO: Westview Press/American Association for the Advancement of Science.

Gallup Organization
1981 *The Gallup Report.* Princeton, NJ: The Gallup Poll.

Harris, Louis and Associates
1980 *The ABC-Harris Survey.* New York: The Harris Survey.

LaPorte, Todd and Daniel Metlay
1975 "Technology Observed: Attitudes of a Wary Public." *Science* 188 (April):121-127.

Mazur, Allan
1981 *The Dynamics of Technical Controversy.* Washington, D.C.: Communication Press.

Miller, Jon D., Kenneth Prewitt and Robert Pearson
1980 *The Attitudes of the U.S. Public Toward Science and Technology.* Chicago, IL: National Opinion Research Center.

Mitchell, Robert C.
1984 "Rationality and Irrationality in the Public's Perception of Nuclear Power." Pp. 137-179 in William R. Freudenburg and Eugene A. Rosa (eds.), *Public Reactions to Nuclear Power: Are There Critical Masses?* Boulder, CO: Westview Press/American Association for the Advancement of Science.

Murray, Thomas
1981 "Energy Literacy." Unpublished manuscript. Madison, WI: Engineering Research Center.

National Science Board
1981 *Science Indicators 1980.* Washington, D.C.: National Science Foundation.

Opinion Research Corporation
1976 *Attitudes of the U.S. Public Toward Science and Technology: Study III.* Princeton, NJ: Opinion Research Corporation.

President's Commission on the Accident at Three Mile Island
1979 *The Need for Change: The Legacy of TMI.* Washington, D.C.: U.S. Government Printing Office.

Rankin, William L., Stanley M. Nealey and Barbara D. Melber
1984 "Overview of National Attitudes Toward Nuclear Energy: A Longitudinal Analysis." Pp. 41-67 in William R. Freudenburg and Eugene A. Rosa (eds.), *Public Reactions to Nuclear Power: Are*

There Critical Masses? Boulder, CO: Westview Press/American Association for the Advancement of Science.

Rothman, Stanley and S. Robert Lichter
1982 "The Nuclear Energy Debate: Scientists, the Media, and the Public." *Public Opinion* 5 (August/September):47-52.

Slovic, Paul, Baruch Fischhoff and Sarah Lichtenstein
1984 "Perception and Acceptability of Risk from Energy Systems." Pp. 115-135 in William R. Freudenburg and Eugene A. Rosa (eds.), *Nuclear Power and the Public: Are There Critical Masses?* Boulder, CO: Westview Press/American Association for the Advancement of Science.

Survey Research Center
1958 *The Public Impact of Science in the Mass Media.* Ann Arbor, MI: Survey Research Center, University of Michigan.

Szalay, Robert A.
1984 "A Nuclear Industry View of the Regulatory Climate." Pp. 295-306 in William R. Freudenburg and Eugene A. Rosa (eds.), *Public Reactions to Nuclear Power: Are There Critical Masses?* Boulder, CO: Westview Press/American Association for the Advancement of Science.

Tanfer, Koray, Eugene Ericksen and Lee Robeson
1980 *National Survey of the Attitudes of the U.S. Public Toward Science and Technology.* Philadelphia, PA: Institute for Survey Research, Temple University.

Withey, Stephen
1959 "Public Opinion About Science and Scientists." *Public Opinion Quarterly* 38:382-388.

Conclusion

William R. Freudenburg, Eugene A. Rosa

14. Are the Masses Critical?

Three decades have passed since the nation expressed its initial commitment to civilian nuclear power. It was a commitment of great expectations. But nuclear energy, once thought to be a solution to the nation's energy predicament, has generated complex problems all its own. The technology has not followed a straight path to its expected success, traversing instead through a thicket of controversy. Now at the beginning of its fourth decade, nuclear power has arrived at a crossroads, and there is little doubt that public acceptance will influence the course to be taken in the future.

Assessing the level of public acceptance has been the primary aim of this volume, and the chapters have examined various facets of the topic. In this concluding chapter, we take stock of the evidence presented, highlighting the main themes, and discussing the implications that emerge from the accumulated body of evidence.

When we ask if the masses are critical, we can be asking either of two questions. One has to do with public attitudes toward nuclear energy: How critically or favorably does the public view this technology? The other, an outgrowth of the first, asks about influence upon outcomes: How critical, in fact, is public acceptance to a nuclear future?

Pp. 331-348 in William R. Freudenburg and Eugene A. Rosa (eds., 1984)
Public Reactions to Nuclear Power: Are There Critical Masses?

CRITICISM TOWARD: WHERE DOES THE PUBLIC STAND?

As social scientists, the authors of the first three sections of this volume have attempted to divorce themselves from the heat and rhetoric of the nuclear debate, and to treat the first question--the actual viewpoint of the masses--as a cluster of issues that are amenable to empirical investigation. They have gathered available evidence or collected original data on the actual levels of public acceptance, and have attempted to illuminate the factors leading to acceptance or rejection of nuclear power. For the most part, the chapters speak for themselves; the discussion that follows is not intended to provide a detailed recapitulation of the findings. Our aim is more modest--to take note of ten empirical generalizations that seem to deserve re-emphasis here.

(1) During most of the decade of the 1970s, a clear majority of the public favored nuclear power, but after the accident at Three Mile Island (TMI), this support declined considerably.

(2) Since the TMI accident, support for nuclear power has fluctuated somewhat, but has not reached pre-TMI levels. By 1981, there was no clear majority of support or opposition on the general idea of nuclear power; the public was evenly divided on the issue.

(3) Citizens are generally opposed to the idea of having a nuclear power plant built near their own communities. There was a fairly consistent trend of increasing opposition to local reactors over the decade of the 1970s, beginning well before TMI, so that by 1978 a majority of the public was in opposition. This contrasts sharply with majority support for local siting in the early 1970s.

(4) The public is hesitant to proceed with the further development of nuclear power, holding a "go slow" position on this issue. Although a majority does not favor the closing of nuclear plants currently in operation, further construction is also opposed. A sizable minority is sufficiently opposed to nuclear energy to opt for a closing down of existing plants.

(5) The public consistently mentions plant safety and nuclear waste disposal as the most serious concerns about nuclear energy technology.

(6) Patterns of support and opposition are not confined to any specific segment of the population. Men are generally more favorable than are women, and whites tend to favor nuclear power more than do non-whites. But support and opposition can be found across all social and demographic groups.

(7) Except for imported oil, nuclear power consistently ranks at the bottom of the list when the public is asked about a range of energy options. Similarly, if the public is asked to name the least-preferred energy source, nuclear power is mentioned most often.

(8) Contrary to the belief of many observers, public opposition to nuclear power does not appear to stem from a fundamental conflict between energy supply expansion versus demand reduction strategies. Sizable segments of the public favor both nuclear power and conservation, and sizable segments oppose both.

(9) There is also little evidence to indicate that opposition to nuclear power is a reflection of a fundamental shift of public confidence in science; the public's faith in science remains much stronger than does its support for nuclear power.

(10) Most citizens have little knowledge about the technical details of fission technology. Even so, the evidence does not support the assertion that opposition to nuclear power reveals an "irrationality" among the general public, nor among identifiable segments of the public. Instead the opposition may reflect not so much the technical details as a set of broader concerns that have often been overlooked in the nuclear debate; some of these concerns have to do with the accountability and credibility of the technical experts themselves.

The broad outlines of the opinion picture are reasonably clear. On the one hand, Americans are evidently not prepared to take to the streets *en masse* to oppose further expansion of nuclear power. That level of criticism does not now exist, nor has it ever. On the other hand, it is similarly difficult to find widespread or enthusiastic support for the nuclear option. The public, in its global assessment, stands between these two polar extremes.

This picture is quite different from the one that prevailed during the decade of the 1970s. Through most of that decade, as through most of the history of nuclear power development, proponents could expect clear majority support for the technology. That expectation is no longer realistic. Several events have intervened, with a key one being the accident at Three Mile Island in 1979, the most serious mishap in the history of U.S. nuclear power development. The opinion fallout from the accident was unmistakable: In the year immediately following the accident, the level of support declined markedly, and on several occasions, opposition exceeded support for the first time since the collection of national data began. After that time, support for nuclear energy recovered some, but not all, of its lost ground. By 1981, neither supporters nor opponents could claim to dominate the public viewpoint toward nuclear fission, with both sides drawing roughly equal numbers.[2]

When other issues are considered, the picture becomes still less favorable for further nuclear power development. If people are asked to choose among various energy supply sources, nuclear power is singled out repeatedly as one of the least popular. It may be *the* least popular technology, particularly if we are speaking of facilities that are planned for someone's own neighborhood. Opponents have clearly outnumbered supporters for the last several years in all known representative national samples when respondents were asked about nuclear facilities near their own homes. Even at the more general or abstract level of facilities "someplace else," moreover, nuclear power appears to be the focus of more public opposition than any other approach to meeting U.S. energy needs, with the already-noted exception of importing more oil. The masses are not openly hostile, in short, but they are scarcely friendly.

As discouraging as this picture may be for the continued development of nuclear power, it is partly counterbalanced by the evidence in Chapter 3, by Rosa and his colleagues (1984). While reinforcing the conclusion that nuclear power is clearly the least preferred of energy options, that chapter also finds potentially good news for nuclear power supporters. The public does not seem to be irrevocably polarized over broad energy policy strategy. Opposition to nuclear power is evidently not a result of the public's firm commitment to conservation; a sizable fraction of the population is willing to pursue both options. Nonetheless, the most important common denominator is the widespread support for energy conservation. Even the strongest supporters of nuclear power also believe in the importance of energy conservation, and many of them report practicing it themselves.

Taken together, the evidence reveals a deep ambivalence in the public mood. Americans, it appears, are now quite uneasy about the nuclear option. Surveys reveal lingering concerns over reactor safety and the disposal of radioactive wastes, and suggest concerns as well about a number of broader questions. The public is hesitant to go forward rapidly, and has a real skepticism over whether the benefits of nuclear power demonstrably outweigh the risks. Across broad segments of the population, citizens appear to be calling for additional time to evaluate the risks and benefits of the nuclear option.

While the ambivalence does seem to be based in part upon fears of potential hazards, it is worth re-emphasizing that opponents' perceptions of these hazards seem neither more nor less realistic than those of the proponents. The chapters by Mitchell (1984) and by Slovic and his colleagues (1984) both come to this conclusion. Slovic and his colleagues find evidence of a kind of folk rationality, and Mitchell--despite extensive analyses--finds no evidence that the opponents of nuclear power are any less "rational" than are the supporters of the technology. Quantitative analysis, in short, provides no credible basis for dismissing opposition to nuclear power as being inconsequential or inappropriate. The analysis shows instead that the opponents of nuclear power view the world in a way which is no more nor less valid than is the worldview of nuclear power supporters. It is simply--if deeply--different.

There is also little evidence that the upswing in opposition to nuclear power is somehow a reflection of inadequate information or inaccurate news coverage. Instead, Mazur's chapter indicates that the mere fact of increased media coverage--specifically including "even-handed" as well as unfavorable coverage--has been associated with increases in opposition. It goes virtually without saying that the implications of this finding for the possibility of lessening opposition through a "public education campaign" are not good. In fact, as Mazur's chapter emphasizes, the nature of the technology is such that additional public relations campaigns might actually serve to deepen opposition, bringing new potential dangers to the consciousness of many, while failing to change the minds of opponents who have sincere and fundamental concerns about the technology.

On the basis of the best available evidence, in sum, it is clear that public support for nuclear power has declined, and it does not appear that the decline can be "explained away" as an inconsequential phenomenon. Some of the major factors in the decline appear instead to reflect the characteristics of the nuclear power industry itself--including its technical and sociopolitical complexity, the economic problems it has encountered, and the ways in which public questions about nuclear risks have been handled or overlooked by the industry in the past. Other major factors include a set of broader questions for which no technological answers are available--questions having to do with issues such as equity, scientific accountability, and the types of societal arrangements that may be necessary to keep wastes properly stored for thousands of years into the future. Such questions, while often "non-technical" in nature, may ultimately prove more difficult to answer than the technical questions that have received the lion's share of attention to date.

Public concerns run deep. They are not matters of simple misinformation, as promoters of nuclear power have often insisted. They are not likely to go away if they are simply ignored, and public information or public relations campaigns are not likely to make them disappear. The restoration of public confidence is likely to be dependent not upon clever marketing and advertising, but upon genuine progress toward the resolution of key issues.

CRITICAL TO: THE ROLE OF THE PUBLIC VIEWPOINT

The goal of this book has been to summarize what is known about public attitudes toward nuclear power. This book, in other words, is not the place to present a detailed examination of the linkage between public opinion and public policy. Yet the issue is important enough in the nuclear debate to deserve at least brief treatment here.

It is convenient to consider the issue as involving two questions. The first question, an empirical one, involves the extent to which the public viewpoint actually shapes policy decisions. The second and more complex question has to do with the proper role of citizen input on technological decision making. We will discuss both matters briefly, but separately.

Does the Public Viewpoint Matter?

The influence of public sentiment upon policy decisions remains an open question. Although the subject has been the focus of a vast literature, political scholars are far from reaching consensus on the topic; interested readers can find a carefully developed review in Alford and Friedland (1975). But while the precise connections between public viewpoints and public policies have yet to be established, the broad outlines are clear.

At the very least, there is little question that the public climate establishes the general boundaries within which decision makers must operate. It becomes a formidable task to implement policies that seriously violate those boundaries--with the public's recent rejection of the Susan B. Anthony dollar providing a case in point. In a sufficiently hostile environment, implementation of public policy can become an impossible task.

Second, partisans in policy debates often look to the broader public as a basis of legitimacy and support. Partisans can more easily attract sympathizers, if not active supporters, when the social mood is ripe. In addition, the partisans often find that their efforts to influence public policy are facilitated or obstructed, as the case may be, by the levels of support or opposition that they encounter. As in the case of broader policies, partisan positions seriously out of step with the public mood are far less likely to win acceptance, while congruence with that mood is often an important feature of effective policy action.

Third, the embodiment of the public will in policy decisions is often subtle, indirect, or difficult to see. Even so, it would be erroneous to conclude that it is inconsequential. We need look no further than the nuclear waste issue for an illustration. Chapter 9 of this volume, by Zinberg (1984), notes the degree to which public concerns have been overlooked in earlier nuclear policy decisions, and discusses some of the long-term consequences that appear to have resulted from the oversight.

Finally, it is worth noting that questions about the relationships between public preference and political performance do continue to be matters of considerable and continuing concern--a fact which, if it does nothing else, should give us some indication of the importance of this topic in our democratic system. While people in our society often differ greatly in the outcomes they desire, there is a relatively high level of agreement on the rules of the game; in a democracy, it is widely believed, policy outcomes ought to reflect to some degree "the will of the governed." Scientific survey data on public opinions, in effect, allow us to gauge the degree of congruence that exists.

Surveys and public opinion polls provide means for reporting the public will. When the data are collected according to statistically valid sampling procedures, the results may be thought of as a non-binding, but reliable and up-to-date, form of a plebiscite. Looked at in this way, the evidence contained in this volume tells what the public has had to say about nuclear power. Even so, it does not tell us how the will of the people will affect decision making. What, in fact, are the channels for translating public expression into public policy? Although the chapters in this volume have not addressed this question directly, they have naturally led up to it--and given growing citizen demands for involvement in technological decision making, the question looms large in the nuclear debate.

How Can the Public Influence Technological Policy? In a participatory democracy, it is a right of citizens to determine the policies by which they are governed. This, of course, is a fundamental tenet of democratic governance. Unfortunately, the principle of citizens' participatory rights opens, rather than settles, the issue of incorporating the public viewpoint into nuclear decision making.

The problem arises because political processes in modern democracies must take place in the context of a difficult paradox. On the one hand, citizens have a basic right to take part in government, either directly or through elected representatives. On the other, many governmental decisions require the knowledge of experts.

This dilemma of balancing public participation with expert judgment is exacerbated in decisions over technology. While there are some issues, such as safe driving speeds, where everyone feels the right to claim a certain degree of expertise, many public decisions over technology are complex, requiring specialized knowledge that is beyond the ken of most citizens. With modern societies becoming more and more dominated by decisions over technology, technical experts have assumed an ever-greater role in the determination of public policy. Often the mass public is not technically qualified to make informed judgments on the issues or is simply willing to accept decisions made by the technical and policy establishment. But other decisions over technology, as in the case of nuclear power, attract serious public concern. In the process, they draw attention to the fundamental paradox involved in the allocation of political power between experts and the public.

Nelkin and Fallows (1978:297) recently summarized the problem:

> As a concept, participation is necessary for legitimate government, but as a procedure, participation may burden the decision-making process. While participation gives government the right to rule, it also may limit its ability to rule efficiently. The politics of participation in energy policy manifests the persistent tension between the ideal of participation as a basis of democracy and its pragmatic reality in contemporary democratic societies.

The paradox has attracted the serious attention of government officials and key decision makers; as a result, a number of proposals have been advanced for more direct citizen involvement in energy policy generally, and in nuclear policy in particular. Some of the most painstaking efforts have taken place in European democracies. These nations have been even more dependent upon foreign oil than is the United States, and in the aftermath of the 1973-74 oil embargo, several of them planned for major increases in their nuclear energy programs. Efforts to implement the programs encountered public agitation in the form of active opposition and mass protest, drawing the issue of the legitimacy of public decision making into sharp focus; the protest movements stimulated several national governments to broaden public participation in energy policy. Sweden, Austria, and the Netherlands, for example, experimented with elaborate schemes for involving citizens directly in choices over nuclear power (Nelkin and Pollak, 1977).

Proposals in the United States have been far less extreme. Recent energy and environmental legislation has strengthened the legal basis for citizen involvement in energy decision making through existing agencies. Procedures were established for improving public understanding of the issues, for public involvement in policy review, for facilitating dialogue between the public and decision-making agencies, and for negotiating points of controversy. But the efforts have proved to be less than optimal. In effect, they have placed public agencies in the delicate position of attempting to increase citizen participation, while at the same time attempting to implement policies efficiently (Nelkin and Fallows, 1978; Howell and Olsen, 1980).

The problem is complicated by another feature of the nuclear debate. The complex technical questions often involve honest disagreement among experts over questions of scientific fact. Complicating matters further is a persistent feature of the nuclear as well as other technical controversies: Questions of scientific fact become enmeshed--inadvertently or even indiscriminately--with questions of value preferences. It is a common practice for committed partisans to combine factual with rhetorical statements in an effort to present a convincing case for their position (Mazur, 1981).

This intermingling of fact and preference has created a split-level dialogue in the nuclear debate, with experts and other active participants often talking past one another, and with the public being left in the difficult position of trying to make informed judgments in the midst of conflicting technical information. Thus while scientific and technical information is essential to an understanding of the issues, when it is presented in the context of rhetoric it is often counterproductive--adding not clarity to the debate, but greater confusion.

The problem of confounding technical and policy issues is now widely recognized to be a serious impediment to the resolution of technological controversies--and it is a key difficulty in the nuclear debate. While several procedures have been proposed for separating questions of scientific fact from questions of policy preference, moreover, these proposals have not escaped criticism. Some analysts believe a full separation to be impossible, arguing that scientific procedures themselves--including those that determine the acceptability and interpretation of factual evidence--are too deeply embedded in our culture's values to permit such a separation (see, e.g., Douglas and Wildavsky, 1982). Even if a complete separation of fact from value is not possible, however, it would seem that progress toward such a goal could produce a significant advance over the current state of affairs--a technology mired in imbroglio. At a minimum, systematic procedures could conceivably lay the groundwork for distinguishing issues requiring technical expertise from those requiring the expression of public preference.

The most elaborate proposal for accomplishing this would involve the convening of a "science court," comprised of scientific and technical experts having no direct stake in a given technological controversy. The court would consider partisan positions on both sides of the controversy, and would be charged with separating factual questions from policy issues. At the very least the court would identify those points of scientific fact having expert consensus, those over which serious disagreement persists, and those where additional research might need to be undertaken. Once the court had discharged its obligations in identifying the relevant factual issues, normal political procedures would be followed to establish public policy. Direct public involvement, if it were to occur, would take place as part of the normal channels of political participation (Task Force of the Presidential Advisory Group on Anticipated Advances in Science and Technology, 1976).

But as several of the preceding chapters have emphasized, many of the key issues in the nuclear debate are not just technical ones. Thus even if some mechanism such as the proposed science court could successfully separate facts from values, the basic question would remain: as the technical facts and the public values are taken into consideration in the development of public policies, how can citizens influence the actual results? For nuclear power, the relevant question might be: given the established scientific facts--over the risk of reactor core meltdown, for example--how can the public's willingness or reluctance to accept that risk be embodied in nuclear policies?

The question attracts conflicting conclusions. According to one viewpoint, once the scientific facts are established, technical controversies can be treated as part of the normal flow of political activity. Though current mechanisms for political participation may be cumbersome and inefficient, they do tend to sharpen issues, drawing attention to genuine concerns that might otherwise have remained hidden, and eventually fixing on concerns where there is legitimate disagreement. This, after all, is the process by which public decisions are made on other national issues, such as economic and military policy. From this viewpoint, decisions over technology need not be treated any differently (Mazur, 1981).

A second and far more radical viewpoint sees normal democratic process as being painfully inadequate for the governance of technology. American society, in this second view, lacks effective mechanisms for mediating among the general public, the scientific and technical elite, and the political representatives and officials charged with developing and implementing policy. This position may have been summarized most forcefully by John Kemeny in reflecting upon the work of the Presidential Commission on the Accident at Three Mile Island, which he chaired:

> I am very much afraid it is no longer possible to muddle through . . . . Our democracy must grow up . . . . Our nation must recognize that the present system does not work . . . . I believe that Jeffersonian democracy cannot work in the 1980s--the world has become too complex (Kemeny, 1981:9).

In this extreme view, the impasse over the nuclear option stems not from the character of the technology itself, but from a serious flaw in democratic processes--a flaw that has become increasingly clear during the past several decades because of the growing frequency and prominence of controversies over science and technology.

Other viewpoints have been expressed as well. It is not necessary to decide here which of them has the greatest validity; in all likelihood there is some truth to each of them. The point is instead that the enduring difficulty of balancing public knowledge against expert participation has been brought to the surface by the nuclear debate--one of the most profound and prolonged of an increasing number of technological controversies. The paradox remains a serious problem for modern democracies, and no easy resolution is in sight.

Should the Public Viewpoint Matter?

Another point also deserves to be noted here, however. While questions about the connections between public preferences and policy outcomes are quite complex, they are often complicated further by an additional factor. In all too many discussions, debates over the question at hand--"How much difference do public opinions make?"--will actually turn out to be thinly disguised arguments about a very different question, namely, the question of how much difference public opinions *should* make.

The "should" question simply cannot be answered on the basis of social scientific research, or any other form of science; the question is inherently prescriptive and political, not scientific. We have not even attempted to answer it in this volume. Nor have we attempted to reach the more moderate but still ambitious goal of representing all possible viewpoints on the question. Rather we have chosen to include one major representative for each of what we perceive to be the three major points of view in the present case--the nuclear power industry (as represented by Szalay), critics of the nuclear power industry (as represented by Commoner), and the federal government (as represented by Davis). Persons with these three points of view often disagree even on technical questions where a "right" answer is presumably available--e.g., on the cost of nuclear power plants, where Davis and Commoner clearly disagree, with each citing studies to support his own point of view. Thus it should come as little surprise to most readers of this volume that they also disagree on the "less answerable" question--but arguably, the more fundamental one--the proper role of the broader public in major policy decisions on nuclear power.

Since the question cannot be answered on the basis of scientific evidence, then despite its importance, the matter is not one that this volume should attempt to settle. Such an effort would quickly come to be far more philosophical and conjectural than is appropriate here. The larger points are that ours is a democratic system, that it rarely reflects the will of the electorate perfectly, and yet that it would be particularly unwise for a technology as controversial as nuclear power to be thrust forward without consideration of the role to be played by the broader public.

This, however, may be just what has often happened in the past. A strong case could be made that, throughout the past history of nuclear power development in the United States, public concerns have tended to be brought in as an afterthought, if at all. An equally strong case could be made that this approach in the past may have contributed to many of the problems faced by the nuclear power industry in the present--and that alternative approaches might be more fruitful in the future. The issue of past behavior is by no means a simple one; it is conceivable that greater government and industry openness would have led to an even higher level of public concern than currently exists. It also needs to be noted that (despite the lack of openness) the nuclear industry has generally shown greater caution in handling its hazardous materials, at least in our estimation, than have most other industries that produce hazardous materials of their own. It is far too late, however, to change the early history of nuclear power; the fact is that public concerns have generally been handled with much less caution and analysis than have the physical materials, and that nuclear power is now playing to a distinctly skeptical audience. The real question now is what will happen in the future.

Social and political concerns may prove to be as important to the future of nuclear power as are technical considerations; this has become conventional wisdom in the energy policy establishment (see, e.g., National Academy of Sciences, 1980; Ford Foundation Study Group, 1979; Schurr et al., 1979; Stobaugh and Yergin, 1979; President's Commission on the Accident at Three Mile Island, 1979). It is less simple to find consensus on the precise role to be played by social and political concerns; the public's specific degree of influence upon policy outcomes, in the area of nuclear power development as elsewhere, is unclear. What is clear is that the broader public is indeed likely to have an effect upon outcomes, whether its concerns are considered in advance or not.

Existing participatory channels provide citizens with "veto rights," permitting them to intervene in licensing and regulatory proceedings through legislative influence, judicial actions, or--where these are seen to be inadequate--through extra-legal means. In the past, these interventions have often been disruptive to the nuclear power industry, causing delays in program implementation, leading to the imposition of burgeoning safety and environmental regulations and adding significantly to the skyrocketing costs of the nuclear industry. By some estimates, the resultant safety and environmental regulations have amounted to as much as two-thirds of the costs of new nuclear plants finished in recent years (Faltmayer, 1979). The question remaining for the nation is whether this is the most efficient way of trying to resolve the nuclear debate, or whether it would be preferable to deal with public concerns more directly and systematically, and on an ongoing basis.

Our own judgment is that the public is still willing to give nuclear power a fair chance, but is no longer willing to have the technology run by experts alone. If the public concerns are heeded rather than ignored, if a sustained safety record demonstrates the acceptability of nuclear risks, and if experience shows that nuclear power has an indispensable role to play in supplying the nation's future energy needs, it is still conceivable that the public will come to support the nuclear option with genuine enthusiasm.

The trust that once existed, however, is no longer in evidence; it will first have to be regained. That is not likely to be a simple task; the goal of energy policy consensus has now eluded four successive national administrations. The nation may even find it necessary to develop new procedures for channeling public choice into nuclear decision making.

If the trust can be regained, the nation may find it possible to move forward with an energy policy consensus, and nuclear power might even be able to regain its starring role. If not, the masses could come to be more critical in both senses of the word--an outcome that might not only prolong the nuclear stalemate, but that could eventually bring down the final curtain on nuclear power development in the United States.

FOOTNOTES

[1]As this book was going to press in mid-1983, the division of public opinion had become much less even. In conjunction with a national advertising campaign to improve the public image of nuclear power, the Committee for Energy Awareness and the Edison Electric Institute commissioned Cambridge Reports, Inc.--one of the two major national firms drawn upon by Rankin and his colleagues (1984) in Chapter 2--to conduct additional surveys. These surveys have shown clear evidence of increased opposition to nuclear power since 1981. In a presentation to the 1983 Nuclear Power Assembly, the president of Cambridge Reports noted that the organization's most recent national sample at that time had found only 33% of the public in favor of nuclear power, while a clear majority of 55% opposed it. This, he noted, marked "the lowest level of support nuclear power has ever had" in the United States, surpassing even the low levels reached immediately after Three Mile Island, when opponents barely outnumbered supporters (Graham, 1983:4).

[2]As noted above in Footnote 1, the recovery of lost ground may have been a temporary phenomenon. Public support for nuclear power continued to decline after 1981, dropping well below the levels that were reached immediately after Three Mile Island. By mid-1983, nuclear power opponents outnumbered supporters by a persistently wide margin--something that had not previously occurred in the U.S. at any point in the history of commercial nuclear power development.

REFERENCES

Alford, Robert R. and Roger Friedland
1975 "Political Participation and Public Policy." *Annual Review of Sociology* 1:429-479.

Douglas, Mary and Aaron Wildavsky
1982 *Risk and Culture.* Berkeley, CA: University of California Press.

Faltmayer, Edmond
1979 "Nuclear Power After Three Mile Island." *Fortune Magazine* (May 7):114-122.

Ford Foundation Study Group
1979 *Energy: The Next Twenty Years.* Cambridge, MA: Ballinger.

Freudenburg, William R. and Eugene A. Rosa
1984 *Public Reactions to Nuclear Power: Are There Critical Masses?* Boulder, CO: Westview Press/

American Association for the Advancement of Science.

Graham, John
1983 "A Majority of Americans are now Believed to be Opposed to Nuclear Power." *Nuclear Report* 6 (#4, May 5):4.

Howell, Robert E. and Darryll Olsen
1980 *Citizen Participation in the Socio-Economic Analysis of Nuclear Waste Repository Siting.* Corvallis, OR: Western Rural Development Center, USDA-DOE Report No. DE-IA-97 80 ET 46623.

Kemeny, John G.
1981 "Political Fallout." *Society* 18:4-9.

Mazur, Allan
1981 *The Dynamics of Technical Controversy.* Washington, D.C.: Communications Press.
1984 "Media Influence on Public Attitudes Toward Nuclear Power." Pp. 97-114 in William R. Freudenburg and Eugene A. Rosa (eds.), *Public Reactions to Nuclear Power: Are There Critical Masses?* Boulder, CO: Westview Press/American Association for the Advancement of Science.

Mitchell, Robert C.
1984 "Rationality and Irrationality in the Public's Perception of Nuclear Power." Pp. 137-179 in William R. Freudenburg and Eugene A. Rosa (eds.), *Public Reactions to Nuclear Power: Are There Critical Masses?* Boulder, CO: Westview Press/American Association for the Advancement of Science.

National Academy of Sciences
1980 *Energy in Transition: 1985-2010.* Final Report of the Committee on Nuclear and Alternative Energy Systems. San Francisco, CA: W. H. Freeman and Co.

Nelkin, Dorothy and Michael Pollak
1977 "The Politics of Participation and the Nuclear Debate in Sweden, The Netherlands, and Austria." *Public Policy* 25:333-357.

Nelkin, Dorothy and Susan Fallows
1978 "The Evolution of the Nuclear Debate: The Role of Public Participation." *Annual Review of Energy* 3:275-312.

President's Commission on the Accident at Three Mile Island
1979 *The Need for Change: The Legacy of TMI.* Washington, D.C.: U.S. Government Printing Office.

Rankin, William, Stanley M. Nealey and Barbara D. Melber
1984 "Overview of National Attitudes Toward Nuclear Energy: A Longitudinal Analysis." Pp. 41-67

in William R. Freudenburg and Eugene A. Rosa (eds.), *Public Reactions to Nuclear Power: Are There Critical Masses?* Boulder, CO: Westview Press/American Association for the Advancement of Science.

Rosa, Eugene A., Marvin E. Olsen and Don A. Dillman
1984 "Public Views Toward National Energy Policy Strategies: Polarization or Compromise?" Pp. 69-93 in William R. Freudenburg and Eugene A. Rosa (eds.), *Public Reactions to Nuclear Power: Are There Critical Masses?* Boulder, CO: Westview Press/American Association for the Advancement of Science.

Schurr, Sam H., Joel Darmstadter, Harry Perry, William Ramsay and Milton Russell
1979 *Energy in America's Future: The Choices Before Us: A Study of the RFF National Energy Strategies Staff.* Baltimore: Johns Hopkins University Press.

Slovic, Paul, Baruch Fischhoff and Sarah Lichtenstein
1984 "Perception and Acceptability of Risk From Energy Systems." Pp. 115-135 in William R. Freudenburg and Eugene A. Rosa (eds.), *Public Reactions to Nuclear Power: Are There Critical Masses?* Boulder, CO: Westview Press/American Association for the Advancement of Science.

Stobaugh, Robert and Daniel Yergin (eds.)
1979 *Energy Future: Report of the Energy Project at the Harvard Business School.* New York: Random House.

Task Force of the Presidential Advisory Group on Anticipated Advances in Science and Technology
1976 "The Science Court Experiment: An Interim Report." *Science* 193:653-656.

Zinberg, Dorothy S.
1984 "The Public and Nuclear Waste Management Policy: A Struggle for Participation." Pp. 233-253 in William R. Freudenburg and Eugene A. Rosa (eds.), *Public Reactions to Nuclear Power: Are There Critical Masses?* Boulder, CO: Westview Press/American Association for the Advancement of Science.

Index